Beef or Salmon

LEAP OF FAITH

Beef or Salmon

LEAP OF FAITH

DONAL KEENAN

ISP

Published by Irish Sports Publishing (ISP)
Unit 11, Tandy's Lane
Lucan, Co Dublin
Ireland
www.irishsportspublishing.com

First published, 2012

Copyright © Donal Keenan, 2012

The moral right of the author has been asserted.

All rights reserved.

Without limiting the rights under copyright reserved above, no part of this publication may be reproduced, stored in or introduced into a retrieval system, or transmitted in any form or by any means (electronic, mechanical, photocopying, recording or otherwise) without the prior written permission of the publisher of this book.

A CIP record for this book is available from the British Library

ISBN 978-0-9573954-2-8

Printed in Ireland with Print Procedure Ltd
Cover Design and Typesetting: Anú Design www.anu-design.ie
Cover Photograph: Inpho Sports Agency
Inside Photographs: Inpho Sports Agency

To Abbie, Dara and Aoife

Contents

Prologue :	A Death in the Family	1
Chapter 1:	It's Like Selling Your Children	10
Chapter 2:	Don't Sell that Horse	21
Chapter 3:	Good Racehorses Recognise Each Other	32
Chapter 4:	The Winner is No World Beater	43
Chapter 5:	Plan B	54
Chapter 6:	Big Arse, Ratty Little Head, and a Tail that Never Grew	63
Chapter 7:	Not for Sale at Any Price	72
Chapter 8:	This Game Would Tame Lions	83
Chapter 9:	Christ, What's Wrong with the Horse?	92
Chapter 10:	Happy People, Happy Horses	101
Chapter 11:	The Long Road Back	114
Chapter 12:	End of an Era?	122
Chapter 13:	Thank God We Still Have You	129
Chapter 14:	Cheltenham's Not Everything	138
Chapter 15:	You're One Lucky Sod, Hourigan	149
Chapter 16:	War, Listener and Kauto Star on the Rise	165
Chapter 17:	Salmon's Never Beaten. He'll Never Stop Trying	171
Chapter 18:	Just Bring Him Home	179
Chapter 19:	The Secret of Horse-racing? You Dream	188
Race Record		197

About the Author

Donal Keenan has been writing about major national and international sports events for Ireland's leading daily and Sunday newspapers for the last three decades.

He was GAA Correspondent for the *Irish Independent* and *The Sunday Times* between 1985 and 1996, travelling extensively throughout Ireland and to Australia and the United States to cover Irish teams.

He was a senior writer with the Sunday sports newspaper, *The Title*, which later became *Ireland on Sunday* and *The Irish Mail on Sunday*, where he was appointed Chief Sports Writer. In a career covering many sports, he has reported first-hand on World Cups, the Ryder Cup and many other major sporting events.

A native of Roscommon, and long-time resident of Dublin, he is a member of a well-known sporting family. His father, Dr Donal, was a member of the Roscommon football team that won the county's only All-Ireland senior football titles in 1943 and 1944. He later successfully trained many teams and was elected President of the Gaelic Athletic Association in 1973.

The family has a strong connection with horse-racing. Donal's grandfather, John, founded Keenan's Bookmakers which, at one time, was one of Ireland's largest chains, on and off course. The on-course tradition is maintained to this day by his brother, Brian.

Married to Abbie, the couple has two children, Dara and Aoife. Donal has written a number of books on Gaelic Games and lives in hope that he will, one day, see Roscommon win another All-Ireland senior football title.

Acknowledgments

Embarking on the research and writing of this book was a new adventure for me because horse-racing is one of the few sports that I have not covered in my career. I am indebted to Michael and Kay Hourigan for the time and courtesy shown to me as I probed their memories and expertise.

Beef or Salmon's breeder, John Murphy, and his wife, Marianne, welcomed me into their lovely home in Wexford and shared their experiences while also entrusting me with their memorabilia. It is my intention to have those treasures returned by the time the book is published!

Anna and Tom Barry selflessly gave up their valuable time to trace some of the early information that allowed me to uncover parts of the Beef or Salmon story that have not appeared in print before. A sincere thank you to both.

There were many others who provided material, information, encouragement and/or time – Brian Keenan Senior and Junior, Michael Fortune, my nephew John Ferguson, Martin Breheny and Niamh Flynn of Tattersalls.

Amongst the publications consulted were 'Horsetrader' by Patrick and Nick Robinson, Timmy Murphy's autobiography, 'Riding the Storm', Paul Carberry's 'One Hell Of A Ride', and the superb websites run by *The Racing Post* and At The Races.

Irish Sports Publishing were willing to take a risk and that was the greatest encouragement of all. They are displaying the fighting spirit Ireland so badly needs and the type of leadership that is so shockingly absent elsewhere. Thanks to Liam and Kevin and the team behind ISP.

The project could not have been undertaken without the support of Abbie. It would not appear as it is without the reading, correcting and critique of Dara. It would not have been as much fun without the patience and encouragement of Aoife. They are my family of winners.

To everyone involved with Beef or Salmon, the owners, the extended Hourigan family, stable staff and jockeys, a simple but heartfelt thank you for giving us, his fans, so much entertainment and excitement over the years.

PROLOGUE

A Death in the Family

The breeze carried the familiar early morning sounds of an awakening stableyard across the short distance to his home where Michael Hourigan allowed himself a rare moment of solitude.

On a mild October morning he dallied on the front porch and looked out over the expanse of fields, paddocks and yards that make up Lisaleen Stables. His stables. A little empire in a corner of County Limerick that had taken Hourigan, his wife Ann and young family less than twenty years but a lot of hard work, blood, sweat and tears of sadness and joy to create.

Alone with his thoughts he felt content. This was a special place, a place where lots of good racehorses, and some great ones, were cared for, nurtured and trained to compete. He wouldn't say so loudly in case others might hear but he told himself it was a triumph. Hourigan didn't generally care for such fanciful musings but from time to time it was important to acknowledge and appreciate what had been achieved.

His brief reverie was interrupted by a familiar sound: a whinny that carried all the resonance of chastisement. 'The bloody auld fella again,' he thought before looking across the fields to his left. The complaints continued; the complainant shaking his beautiful head, the mane waving silkily, the white blaze on the face almost fluorescent in the morning haze. His eyes never left the man who was the most familiar thing to him in the world. The man, Hourigan, felt a pang of guilt.

Doran's Pride was suffering like many retirees after an active life. He was restless and bored. After a nine-year career that began back in 1993, he had been consigned to the fields at the beginning of the summer of 2002 for what was supposed to have been a happy retirement. But, even at the age of 13, it was obvious he hankered for more than just gambolling around the paddock all day watching younger horses do the work. A horse generally with a good temperament, he was now displaying some irritation.

Jesus, Mike, let me out of here and back to doing what I do best, Hourigan imagined the horse saying.

The horse had made a handsome contribution to what Hourigan, the family and a loyal staff had made here. For the best part of a decade Doran's Pride had placed the Hourigans and Lisaleen at the centre of the racing world.

In the living room of the house just behind Michael hung a painting from 1995 of Doran's Pride winning at the Cheltenham festival. It was an expensive purchase but the trainer believed such an extravagance was permissible given the level of achievement.

Doran's wasn't the only big race winner to come from the yard but he had won the biggest races and he was the pet. Hourigan had a reputation for occasional fierceness amongst the lads around the yard if standards were allowed slip but they knew the mood would soften when he reached Doran's Pride in stable No. 7.

A multiple winner of Group One races, the horse had come third in the Cheltenham Gold Cup on two occasions and had won the Stayers Hurdle at the great festival in 1995.

He didn't owe anyone anything, not Hourigan nor his London-based owner Tom Doran, a native of Mayo who was one of the stable's regular patrons. Retirement had first been mooted in late 2001 after a season that had seen the horse produce remarkably consistent displays without getting to the winner's enclosure. His one run that year of 2002 was in Sandown where he was fifth in a competitive chase. Hourigan and Doran chatted briefly that evening. The decision was made. Doran's Pride's career as a racehorse was over.

His absence from the regular work routines was noticed only for a short time. Hourigan and his team were otherwise occupied. They had 90 other horses to look after that year. Some were experienced, some were still novices and others had only just arrived at Lisaleen and were being broken; the first step in finding out if they might have a future in the racing game.

Amongst them was a six-year-old Hourigan had purchased two years before. He was in the early stages of his career and they were still learning about him but Hourigan had a good feeling in his gut. His hunches weren't always right but the trainer sensed there was something different about this one.

Time would tell. He was not a striking horse in looks but there was movement about him that caught the attention of those who knew the business well. Assigned to stable 9, beside Doran's Pride, the youngster immediately took a liking to his older colleague and, out in the field, the two horses struck up a rapport that surprised everyone in the yard.

Doran's Pride was laidback; this youngster was inclined to be a bit bossy, wanting things his own way. But they munched together, rolled together and galloped together. Eight horses might be sharing a field but Doran's Pride and the youngster were always found together, away from the others.

Doran's was content when the young horse was around. In his retirement, however, they were separated at times of the day when they might previously have expected to be together.

The youngster was still learning his new trade and early in the morning headed off with the rest of the horses for work. Doran's Pride seemed to be looking on enviously. He wasn't happy in retirement anyway but seeing this frisky new friend of his doing what Doran's Pride had done for all of his life made the old horse even more irritable.

That morning as Hourigan went about the hectic routines of running such a sizeable yard, his mind kept returning to the sight of the older horse and what he sensed were pleas for release.

The trainer was unusually troubled. Surely at the age of 14 it was better to leave the horse out in the field? He had done his service and done it very well. But was he happy? The answer was a definite no.

And the youngster, officially known as Beef or Salmon but shortened to just Salmon in the yard, had clearly lifted the spirits of his new companion. But the trainer thought practically as well. 'He's eating plenty of the oats and grass and he might as well earn them,' he mused. A quick phone call to Tom Doran in London secured the decision. The retirement was over.

Kay Hourigan, Michael's eldest daughter, was 26 years old then and greeted the news enthusiastically. She had been too young to look after Doran's Pride in his prime but she loved the horse. She loved all the horses, of course, but this one was a bit different. Doran's was easy to love because he was so well mannered, so good-humoured, and so easy. And she would be looking after him now. Doran's Pride would not occupy all her time. There were others horses to be cared for, duties shared with the other staff. But he would be her primary focus.

His comeback would normally have caused a flurry of activity in the media but two factors conspired to keep attention on his return to a minimum. The first was that Hourigan planned the comeback on the point-to-point circuit where knowledgeable people would pass refined judgement but where the rest of world remained in almost complete ignorance. The second factor overshadowing his return was the fact that Beef or Salmon was very quickly becoming the star of the show, not just in this stable but throughout Ireland.

Hourigan had surprised even those who knew him best when he switched the novice from hurdling to tackling the bigger and more formidable fences of steeplechasing.

The consensus amongst the chattering classes was that Salmon was a little clumsy in his jumping. Hourigan, and his son, Paul, who had ridden the horse for most of his early hurdling adventures and on the gallops at Lisaleen, both felt Salmon's action would be better suited to the bigger fences.

They were right. Over the winter of 2002 and new year of 2003 Beef or Salmon became a chasing sensation, winning three major races and earning a quote as second favourite for the Cheltenham Gold Cup, an almost unheard of position for a mere novice.

Meanwhile the old star was trudging successfully through the farmlands of Kilfeacle and Nenagh in County Tipperary and Carrigtwohill in Cork winning three point-to-point races on three successive Sundays. He was a happy horse again and that contributed to the excited buzz around Lisaleen that had begun with Beef or Salmon's meteoric rise to prominence. The Cheltenham Gold Cup was, of course, a daunting target for a novice but Hourigan and the owners, Joe Craig and Dan McLarnon, realised it was a race that was becoming almost impossible to avoid.

The two equine pals travelled together to a racecourse, Leopardstown on the south side of Dublin, for the first time on February 3, 2003. Beef or Salmon was seeking his third Group One success in the prestigious Hennessy Cognac Gold Cup. Doran's Pride was running in the Hunter's Chase being named in memory of the late journalist Raymond Smith who had eulogised the horse in many colourful articles from various courses throughout Ireland and Britain.

Beef or Salmon won; Doran's Pride ran a very respectful second. The Cheltenham agenda for the Hourigan team began to expand and the yard was back in the spotlight: the TV cameras returned to Lisaleen.

There had been a time during the 1990s when the cameras had seemed a constant presence. Doran's Pride loved it – when a camera appeared his head appeared. He was a celebrity and he knew it. Salmon seemed to sneer at both the publicity and his older friend's love of the media spotlight. When the camera lights were turned on the younger horse he turned away. The pair galloped together for the assembled TV crews, photographers and journalists, Kay riding Doran's and Michael Junior riding Salmon. But when it came to posing for photographs, Kay was able to sit quietly, almost choking on her chuckles as Michael grappled with a horse that was clearly disinterested in the finer points of public relations.

At 4am on the morning of March 10, 2003, Michael Hourigan Junior, the eldest of the five children and a decent jockey in his own right, drove the horse box through the gates of Lisaleen on the long twelve hour journey by road and sea that would bring them to Cheltenham.

Eight years had passed since Doran's Pride had given the Hourigan's their greatest triumph by winning the Stayers' Hurdle at the festival.

Memories of the festival over the last decade were pleasant and the Hourigan family were looking forward to another good week.

Two other horses travelling from the yard for the big festival were Hi Cloy, owned by Derry businessman Seamus McCloy, who had introduced the owners of Beef or Salmon to Hourigan, as well as Clonmel's Minella, owned by the hotelier John Nallen.

These two ran on Wednesday, March 12. Hi Cloy, a year younger than Beef or Salmon, fell at the fifth fence in the Royal and Sun Alliance Novices Hurdle, giving jockey Timmy Murphy his first bruises of the week. Clonmel's Minella was tenth of 24 runners in the amateur riders' race. His jockey Richie Harding enjoyed the spin as good preparation for the ride on Doran's Pride the following day, Thursday, March 13.

Kay Hourigan slept well on Wednesday night and woke early on Thursday morning. She felt some nerves. She had been too young to go to Cheltenham when Doran's won and now she felt a tingle of excitement about his prospects in the popular Christie's Foxhunters Chase.

The horse was in good spirits, eating well and happy to have his young friend close by. The presence of the old champion and the young pretender had caused quite a stir around the yard at the back of the racecourse. Kay and Eoin Lynch, who was looking after Beef or Salmon, were busy trying to ensure that their charges were not distracted by all the interest while all the time preparing them for the races.

When Beef or Salmon took his place in the field for the Gold Cup, Kay stayed in the yard. The novice was second favourite, behind Best Mate, in a field of real quality. Kay glanced at the television placed in a corner of the yard for the start of the race and then returned to care for Doran's Pride who would race just 45 minutes later. Early in the race she heard the commentator's voice raise an octave: "Beef or Salmon's a faller at that one," he called at the third fence. Kay didn't see the fall but quickly turned again to the television as the commentator added, 'horse and jockey (Timmy Murphy again) both fine'. The addendum was something she would remember ruefully in the future.

As Eoin led Salmon back towards the stables, he met Kay leaving the pre-parade ring with Doran's Pride saddled and ready to go.

"How is he?" she asked quickly.

"He's sore Kay," answered Eoin, "but I think he's fine. Good luck."

The perimeter of the famous parade ring behind the stands was packed with spectators. They crushed together in discomfort, anxious to get a look at the horses and humans they considered lucky to be inside.

Doran's Pride got a special cheer from the thousands of Irish racegoers who remembered him in his prime. His return was an emotional experience for more than just the owners and the trainer and his family. The old boy was clearly content. He loved the attention. He was on his toes doing what he loved to do.

Having led Doran's Pride onto the course, Kay wished jockey Harding well and then ran back to the parade ring, now empty save for a few people closely connected with the runners. Every vantage point on the course was packed, so, many owners, trainers and stable staff chose to watch the race on the big screen above the parade ring or on one of the televisions at the Tote booths nearby.

Kay chose a spot in the parade ring and watched intently for about a minute.

Following instructions, jockey Harding had Doran's Pride in a prominent position from the start. They cleared the first well and Harding felt comfortable.

Doran's was moving well and finding a good stride.

They were racing right in front of the stands, heading for the second fence. Harding felt nothing awry. They took off at the second. Doran's Pride's spring this time did not get him high enough. His body brushed the top of the fence. He was thrust forward and the pressure on his front legs caused him to somersault. His near hind leg could not take the pressure caused by the tumble. It snapped below the hock and he went down.

Michael Hourigan ran to the gate in front of the stand that gives access to the course. By the time he reached the scene the course attendants had erected green screens around the horse. The vets arrived swiftly. Jockey Harding was uninjured but distraught.

When Hourigan saw his star his heart tightened. He heard an anguished cry behind him. It was Kay. "Go back," he shouted firmly.

"No," his daughter pleaded. "I can fix it, I want to bring him home. Please."

"Kay," replied Michael, gently but firmly, "go back and let me handle this."

The vets consulted and then spoke to Hourigan. He couldn't fully hear the words but grasped the meaning. He had been around horses all his life and he knew what this injury meant. He had heard Kay's cries, they echoed his own silent ones, and in his heart and mind he briefly searched for hope.

But he knew instantly there was none. He stood at Doran's Pride's head as the vet administered the injection that put the grand old champion into a sleep from which he would not awake. Michael helped cover his Doran's Pride with sheets and turned away as close to despair as he had ever been.

He walked back to the stables in a daze. People spoke to him, shook his hand, but he was numb.

Jesus, Hourigan, snap out of it, he chastised himself silently. *There are horses to be looked after.*

His wife Ann was waiting at the stables, eyes red. The strain was etched clearly on her face but she was strong. Kay was inconsolable.

Michael checked on Beef or Salmon. Eoin Lynch was silent, knowing that words were inappropriate. His horse knew there was something wrong. He was looking around for his old mate, not understanding the absence. Michael Junior quenched the pain by being busy as he prepared the transport for the long and lonely journey home.

Michael Senior, Ann and Kay headed for Birmingham airport. In the packed departures lounge scores of racegoers offered their sympathies. Kay's tears flowed ever stronger. Michael tried to bring some levity to the scene.

"Christ, ye won't cry half as much for me when I'm gone," he chided but inside he was in turmoil. When a friend from home rang him, Michael simply replied: "This is the worst day in my life as a trainer. I have lost one of the greatest horses I ever had and I almost lost another. People are so good and they mean well but every pat on the back I get is like a spear going through me."

He didn't want to show any emotion. Ann and Kay where shedding enough tears anyway. He had to be strong, keep his head up and be professional.

"But it is bloody hard," he admitted on the phone.

Back home it took time to recover.

What if? Hourigan kept wondering. Was he to blame, should he have left Doran's Pride in the field?

But he remembered how the horse had looked at him that morning just five months before. And he remembered how happy Doran's Pride was to be back racing.

The letters started to arrive.

They were abusive, accusing him of cruelty, admonishing him for pushing the old horse too hard.

It was nasty but he tried to hide the letters from the family. Their suffering had been difficult enough and they didn't need to endure further pain. It was important to get on with life.

"Losing Doran's Pride was like a death in the family. But like any death you have to move on," he told one friend.

It was weeks before he could bear to look at the newspaper coverage of what had happened at that fateful Cheltenham. The pain, which had marginally subsided, regained its intensity as he read the reports. He checked to see what horse had won the race which had claimed the life of his stable star. Kingscliff. He knew the horse, of course, but the horse's name stirred another memory in him, that he couldn't quite place his finger on.

It was only much later that he solved the riddle. Kingscliff had been lot number 165 that was withdrawn from the Land Rover Sales at Goffs on June 8, 2000, unable to attract a bidder. That was the same day that Michael had purchased an unwanted four-year-old who had caught his attention outside the sales ring. He bought him for a bargain price and named him Beef or Salmon.

Hourigan left the house by the back door and decided to walk to the stables rather than take the jeep. He strolled past the three schooling fences that had been erected at considerable expense to ensure his horses had the best possible preparation for the racecourse.

He reached the yard, quiet in the mid-afternoon with just a couple of staff tending to regular chores. Stable 7 was still empty, though that would have to change soon. At stable 9 Michael stopped. Beef or Salmon came to meet him, looking for a pat. "You look fine, boy," Hourigan said quietly. "I just wonder how you are really."

He questioned himself again. Should he have subjected a novice to the challenge of the greatest and most demanding steeplechase in the world?

The critics had already passed judgement and had been scathing in their verdict. He didn't care to dwell on their opinions but he was not immune to their sniping.

"I know how good you are," he told Salmon. "And I know you know how good you are. Let's show them."

With a final pat to the head, the trainer walked the few yards to the stable office. He perused the racing calendar and began to plan a new campaign.

Less than four months ago Beef or Salmon was just another promising racehorse. Today he was one of the most talked about horses in Ireland and Britain.

Whatever lay ahead, one thing was for sure – the horse's future would be interesting.

"I wonder how interesting," he said aloud, as a broad smile creased across his face.

CHAPTER I

It's Like Selling Your Children

The snowploughs had already cleared the Versailles Road as dawn arrived on January 9, 1988, and had moved further along Interstate 60 out of Lexington, Kentucky.

At the Bluegrass Airport the runways were fully operational. Snowfalls had been constant but light over the previous twenty-four hours and the depth of snow was not sufficient to threaten closure. It was the wind that caused the greatest discomfort for the passengers arriving. Reaching 8.4 knots at times that morning, it was especially rough on the small but influential group of men who were using private transport in preference to commercial aircraft; mainly eight-seater jets arriving from New York, Washington, the west coast of the United States and other destinations.

The winds buffeted the smaller craft mercilessly. Air traffic controllers spoke calmly to pilots. Memories were still fresh of a crash at the airport just weeks before in December, 1987, which cost the lives of the pilot and co-pilot of a Hawker Siddeley HS.125 business jet similar to those landing that morning.

On the far side of the four-lane Versailles Road the yards, boxes and sales ring of the Keeneland bloodstock centre were bustling with activity.

The racecourse itself had a covering of snow but, elsewhere, the ground staff were clearing up the driveways and parking lots in preparation for the arrival of wealthy clients for the annual January Bloodstock Sales. The end of the greatest decade in the history of Keeneland, when astronomical figures were paid for the most spectacularly bred thoroughbred racehorses, was coming to a close and there was a sense of certainty amongst everyone in the business that more difficult times lay ahead. This sale was the first indicator of the impending new reality.

The Keeneland population for the day was almost doubled with the arrival of the stable staff from the various holdings around the area that made up the Bluegrass Farm. Estimates varied over the decades as to the exact size of the farm but the lowest was 3,000 acres. What was not in dispute was that the Bluegrass Farm, and the stud industry within, had produced some of the finest champions in American and European racing. In its time, it had been the largest thoroughbred operation in the world, only overtaken in the 1980s by the oil-rich sheikhs from the Arabian Gulf and a variety of consortiums led by Pools millionaire, the suave Englishman, Robert Sangster, and the brilliant Irish racehorse trainer Vincent O'Brien.

It was those gentlemen, or their representatives, who had landed in Kentucky that morning. Sangster himself had flown from London to New York the previous day and taken a private jet from La Guardia Airport to Lexington.

Colonel Dick Warden, a hero from the Second World War who had once ridden in the Aintree Grand National, represented the interests of Sheikh Mohammed bin Rashid al Maktoum of Dubai.

Also present was the American aviation entrepreneur, Allen Paulson, as well as the legendary trainer and investor, Darrell (D) Wayne Lucas, who had flown in from California. Henryk de Kwiatkowski, a native of Poland, who had emigrated to Canada and then the US and made his fortune leasing and selling aircraft, had cut short a winter holiday in the Bahamas to be present.

They were the best known, but not the only, buyers who arrived in Keeneland early that day. They were there to do business, and had millions of dollars to spend. The stories of their spending were legendary, even if very recent.

Sangster and Sheikh Mohammed had engaged in some extraordinary bidding wars in the 1980s. Their rivalry began in 1981, when Sangster and his circle of friends and business associates – including O'Brien, the Greek tycoon, Stavros Niarchos, and American businessman, Danny Schwarz – had outbid Sheikh Mohammed and Colonel Warden for a colt. It cost them US$3.5million. A year later they were at war again when Sangster was successful with a US$4.25million bid for another colt.

In the most celebrated sale of the period in July, 1983, Sheikh Mohammed instructed Colonel Warden to spend whatever it took to buy a colt by the hugely successful and popular sire, Northern Dancer.

Despite a seemingly endless supply of dollars pumping from the oilrigs of his emirate, the Sheikh was regarded as practical with his money. Still, his desire to keep this colt out of the hands of the Sangster people permitted bidding of an almost uncontrollable nature.

Keeneland had never witnessed anything like it. The electronic sales board could not cope as the figures rose to eight digits. When Colonel Warden bid an incredible US$10.2 million for the colt the sales board could only show 0200,000. They got their horse. He was named Snaafi Dancer and never set foot on a racecourse. Worse, when he went to stud it was discovered he was infertile.

Despite his seemingly inexhaustible resources, the Sheikh was not involved in Keeneland's next major bidding war of July, 1985.

This time Sangster and his people slugged it out on the floor of the sales ring with a powerful American consortium led by Wayne Lucas. Sangster approved a bid of US$13.1million for a son of Nijinsky and grandson of Northern Dancer.

The horse – Seattle Dancer – was trained by Vincent O'Brien and won five times in Europe, including the Derrinstown Stud Derby Trial and the Gallinule Stakes in Ireland, earning less than £200,000 in prizemoney, though he was more successful at stud. He stood initially in Kentucky, was then brought to Coolmore in Ireland before being transferred to Japan and finally to Germany. His stud fee was US$20,000 in Kentucky and his progeny won over US$30million in prizemoney.

But the gathering of old combatants on a cold January morning in 1988 was held on a more cordial basis. These giants of the thoroughbred industry met in temperatures they had never before experienced in Kentucky. The July-sales set usually enjoyed brilliant sunshine and clear skies. But the dark and gloomy skies this morning reflected the mood of the Bluegrass Farm staff. A fog was lifting but temperatures were rising slowly from a low of minus 7 degrees Celsius (about 20 Fahrenheit) to a high around midday of 3 Celsius (38 Fahrenheit).

Sangster, Warden, Paulson and Lucas donned heavy overcoats that held bulging wallets. They would spend lots but it would not all be about money. There was some sentiment, too.

This was the dispersal sale of the entire bloodstock empire built up over three decades by their competitor, and sometime friend, a Texan named Nelson Bunker Hunt, who, at various times through his life, was recorded as the wealthiest individual in the world. He was a man accustomed to success but was now facing the greatest battle of his life. His business was in ruins – he faced bankruptcy as well as federal charges under trading rules. His farm staff had known this day was coming for some months but many were openly crying as the cortege of limousines, Cadillacs and other vehicles began to discharge their passengers.

Keeneland's best-known auctioneer, Tom Caldwell, and the man who ran the sales ring, announcer Tom Hammond, greeted some of the visitors. Caldwell's expertise with the gavel, and Hammond's slick patter, had helped break sales records over the previous decade. These were hardened businessmen but they, too, were feeling emotional that day.

"Any sign of Bunker?" asked Sangster as he shook hands with Hammond.

"I think, sir, he has remained in Dallas. He could not face this, of all sales."

• • • • •

Nelson Bunker Hunt was indeed in Dallas. At 8am that morning (7am in Kentucky) he had stepped out of the elevator on the 24th floor of Thanksgiving Tower at 1601 Elm Street in the centre of the Texas capital. Bunker, as he liked to be known, and his family had built the tower six years previously, just like they had built a lot of the changing landscape of Dallas. At the time, it was the second-largest building in the city with 50 storeys rising to just under 650 feet and it was a source of pride to the three Hunt brothers – Bunker, Lamar and William Herbert – who ran the multi-faceted empire that ranged in interests from oil, to silver, breeding, sports franchises in American football, soccer, tennis, ice hockey and golf, as well as a myriad other activities.

The 24th floor had become the epicentre of that business empire and, despite the early hour, the offices were already busy. Bunker would generally have a hearty greeting for all the staff and then meet with his closest personal aides to discuss overnight developments and copper-fasten the programme for the day. This morning he strode briskly across the floor and entered his own office, muttering a few courtesies along the way and leaving no one in any doubt that he wanted to be left alone.

He was not the sort of man to show emotion, other than laughing heartily in company at family gatherings, or on racetracks around the world, when one of the great racehorses he owned and loved won one of the biggest races.

For over three years he had been fighting to save his business and his billions and rarely had even those closest to him seen any sign of serious pressure or despair. From time to time there were flashes of anger. These were directed mostly at banks or federal institutions.

But Bunker never displayed any sign of weakness. Tears were a sign of weakness and, on that morning in Dallas, Bunker Hunt was as close to tears as at any time since his childhood. The threat of emotion explained his aloofness and his instruction that he was not to be disturbed.

Bunker stood at the large window looking over the Dallas skyline towards the Allied Bank Tower, unique in its green glass colour.

This morning the centre of Dallas was shrouded in a heavy, grey mist and Bunker could see little. He turned to his desk where bundles of correspondence awaited his attention. They would remain untended for some time.

Until now nothing had distracted Bunker from his daily routine. His fortune, and that of his family, was disappearing at an alarming rate; the banks were queuing up to bring him to court; he was facing allegations of conspiring to manipulate the silver market in the United States; the Internal Revenue Service was investigating his finances.

He dealt with it all stoutly. Only when faced with the decision to sell his beloved racehorses did Nelson Bunker Hunt fail to keep his emotions in check. Publicly, he made all the right noises but, deep down, he was in pain.

Tears welled in his eyes as he thought of the sales beginning shortly across the continent in Keeneland. He reminisced on his life of extraordinary privilege.

He would have given it all up – the billions, the buzz of the deal, bartering with the world's power brokers from Persian and Saudi royalty to the most powerful men in America, if he could have saved Bluegrass and his thoroughbreds.

Born on February 22, 1926, Nelson Bunker Hunt was the son of Haroldson Lafayette (HL) Hunt, an oil millionaire who led a domestic life of great eccentricity.

HL had fifteen children with three different women. Bunker, William

Herbert and Lamar were sons of HL's first wife, Lynda, and they inherited their conservative genes from her.

Unlike their father, the three boys were not in any way ostentatious. They owned large mansions but didn't display any other trappings of their enormous wealth away from business. They didn't drive flashy cars and famously refused to fly first-class. From time to time Bunker would use private aircraft but always claimed it was a necessary business expenditure and nothing to do with personal vanity.

Bunker did like to gamble in the business world. Oil was in his blood and, at the end of the Second World War he had concentrated on drilling in places like Pakistan and Libya. It is reckoned he lost more than US$11million in Pakistan alone during the 1950s. Undeterred, he expanded his interests in Libya. Losses incurred in large-scale drilling led to a sale of 50 per cent of his leases to British Petroleum. The funds raised allowed him to continue drilling and eventually he got his reward. In 1961 the largest oilfield in Africa was discovered on a tract jointly owned by Bunker and BP. His stake was valued at US$7billion and, at the age of just 35 years old, Bunker was the wealthiest individual in the world, though he still had to borrow US$5million from his father to bring the oil to production because all of his cash had been committed to drilling. When the oil was brought to the surface Bunker's wealth went into the stratosphere.

A substantial proportion of that wealth was invested in bloodstock. He bought farms in Dallas and Kentucky and expanded his interests into France, Australia and New Zealand.

The Bluegrass Farm outside Lexington, which was essentially a collection of holdings in what is known as the bluegrass region of the State, became the epicentre of what would for a time become the world's largest breeding centre for thoroughbred racehorses.

Bunker studied breeding operations in Britain and France and became a widely respected expert on bloodlines. He met men like Sangster and O'Brien and absorbed their knowledge. He also enjoyed a slice of good fortune, the sort that seems to fall the way of those who can afford risk most.

Bunker was friendly with a Los Angeles-based plastic surgeon, Dr Robert Franklyn and his wife, Wilma. They shared a love of racehorses and Dr Franklyn was investing quietly in some young racehorses in Britain. He was made aware of the opportunity to buy a promising horse named Vaguely Noble, which had been bred by an English businessman, Major Lionel Holliday, at his Irish farm, Cleaboy Stud near Mullingar, County Westmeath.

Major Holliday's death in 1965 eventually forced his son, Brook, to release some of the family assets to pay death duties. Vaguely Noble had won the Doncaster Gold Cup at the end of 1967 and was sold to Dr Franklyn for US$350,000. Dr Franklyn immediately sold a half share to Bunker.

Originally based in Ireland with trainer Paddy Prendergast, Vaguely Noble was then sent to France where he won the great French classic, the Prix de l'Arc de Triomphe in September, 1968. A quarter share of the horse was then sold to John R Gaines, one of America's most successful breeders, and the racehorse was shipped to the United States to start a new career at stud.

Throughout the 1970s Bunker found himself traversing the world, combining his various dealings in oil and silver with his passion for horse racing.

He cut deals in Tehran with the Shah of Iran, then stopped off in Paris on his way back to the United States to spend some time in Chantilly, where the trainer Maurice Zilber was looking after some of Vaguely Noble's finest progeny.

Included amongst those was the beautiful mare, Dahlia, who won the hearts of racegoers all over the world between 1972 and 1976, winning races that included the Irish Oaks in 1973 at the Curragh and the King George VI and Queen Elizabeth Stakes at Ascot.

She didn't run solely against her own sex. She took on the boys and beat them soundly. Amongst her wins in France were the Prix Niel and the Grand Prix de Saint-Cloud. She won the Washington DC International in 1973 and travelled to Canada to win the Canadian International Stakes at Woodbine in Toronto. Hunt liked to run his horses in Europe because, he said, "the grass is softer, the pace is slower and they don't get so banged up".

Dahlia's breeding career produced many stakes winners including Dahar, Delegant, Wajd and Dahlia's Dreamer. When pressed to name his favourite horse, Bunker didn't have to deliberate long – Dahlia held a special place in his heart.

Vaguely Noble sired other champions for Bunker, including Empery, trained by Zilber to win the Epsom Derby in 1976 when ridden by Lester Piggott, and to come second in the Irish Derby the same year when beaten by another French-trained horse, Malacate.

Exceller was another son of Vaguely Noble that won major stakes on both sides of the world. He is best remembered for winning the Belmont Park Jockey Gold Cup in 1978, coming from the last of 22 runners to catch both Seattle Slew and Affirmed on the line.

Less heralded, but no less significant, in the legacy left behind by Vaguely Noble, Bunker and his breeding operation, was the mare, Jet Ski Lady, which won the Epsom Oaks in 1991 for Irish trainer Jim Bolger and owner Sheikh Mohammed.

These champions proved a welcome distraction for Bunker as the 1970s unfolded and his business difficulties began to mount. Those difficulties had started in Libya when Muammar Gaddafi seized control in a coup, in 1969.

Bunker hired John Connally, the former Governor of Texas who was known worldwide as one of the occupants of the car in which President John F. Kennedy was assassinated in Dallas, in 1963, to negotiate with Gaddafi about the future of the oil fields.

Connally's charm and diplomacy failed. Gaddafi nationalised the fields in 1973 and worked out deals with some of the big oil companies that allowed them to continue to drill while handing over vast proportions of their profits to the Libyan leader.

Bunker was frozen out and turned to a different trade. Along with his brother, Herbert, Bunker began to buy up as much of the world's silver as they possibly could. At one stage it was estimated they owned 10 per cent of the world's supply of silver.

In 1974 they chartered three Boeing 707s to fly 40 million ounces of silver to Switzerland for storage in banks there because it saved on taxes. Their fortune continued to increase: Placid Oil was drilling in the North Sea and was generating about US$200million a year. They invested in other commodities, including soybeans.

But though the brothers were making money – lots of it – they also borrowed heavily from a number of banks to sustain their business activities.

New restrictions were placed on the amount of silver that could be owned by a single entity in the United States, but Bunker and Herbert kept buying with borrowed money. When the price of silver began to drop dramatically in March 1980, the Hunts were in trouble.

When their assets were set against their borrowings the Hunts were down around US$1.5billion.

A rescue plan was agreed but it became inevitable that Bunker would have to file for bankruptcy. The first steps in that procedure were taken in November, 1987, when it was announced to the bloodstock industry worldwide that the entire holdings of Bunker at Bluegrass Farm, including his beloved Dahlia, would be sold in Keeneland on January 9 and 10, 1988.

• • • • •

The catalogue of 580 lots (referred to as Hip in the US because the category number of the horse for sale is pasted to the hip of the horse) was distributed to the large contingent of potential buyers by well-groomed young men and women around the sales ring in Keeneland and in the reception areas attached. Amongst the 580 were 281 broodmares, including Dahlia, 186 yearlings, 113 two-year-olds, as well as a number of other older horses.

Allen Paulson chatted with Wayne Lucas.

"Bunker is worried about what's going to happen with Dahlia," said Lucas. "The man is really fretting."

"You bidding?" asked Paulson.

"Nope. I hear the Arabs are interested."

"Damn," replied Paulson. "I want to keep her here in Kentucky. She may be 18 but she still looks good. It wouldn't be right to let her go."

He was right, Dahlia did look good. Led into the parade ring by a stablehand she held her head high, looking proud and dignified. "She's looking better than some of the fillies," sighed one admirer.

Up to her arrival the bidding had been brisk. Brood mares and the older horses were quickly snatched for prices averaging just under US$100,000, but that was about to change.

As Dahlia paraded, the auctioneer called for bids and six figures were reached very quickly. The bids were large. Paulson waited patiently. He had been in situations more fraught than this in Keeneland. The only difference this time is that there was a touch of sentimentality about what he was going to do.

A hush settled over the ring as the price rose to one million dollars. The electronic board now catered for the biggest prices. Paulson, who would normally have someone bidding for him took on the role himself on this occasion, nodded at US$1.1million. The gavel came down and the attendance erupted into loud and sustained cheering and applause. Paulson was surrounded by well-wishers, his back and shoulders quickly aching with the intensity of the congratulations. It had been an expensive favour but Paulson was, for those moments, the most popular man in Kentucky. The bidding became intense thereafter. The race mare Sangue, in foal to the outstanding stallion Alydar, was purchased for US$2.5million by Heronwood Farm. Narvick International, bidding for Henryk de Kwiatkowski, bought a number of brood mares, including one for which they paid US$525,000. Bloodstock agent, Robert Bricken, was also busy, paying a top price of US$700,000 on behalf of a South African businessman.

When a daughter of Dahlia, a filly foaled in 1987 by Northern Dancer, was brought into the ring, the Arab representatives became active. Under the Darley Stud banner, Sheikh Mohammed paid US$1.3million for the filly. She was sent to France to be trained by Andre Fabre. Named Wajd, she enjoyed modest success on the racecourse but was more productive at stud. Wasnah, a February 1987 filly by the great Nijinsky, fetched US$850,000 dollars on behalf of Hamdan Al Maktoum and was sent to England for a short racing career with John Dunlop. She, too, was more successful as a dam and recouped some of the purchase price for Shadwell Estate.

In his Dallas office that Friday, Bunker checked his watch. It was early afternoon and outside it was almost dark. He could not contain himself any longer. What had happened Dahlia? he wondered.

The telephone number for the sales office at Keeneland lay on his desk. He dialled.

A secretary answered. "Could I ask who bought Hip 125?" asked a voice that was familiar to her.

"One moment, sir," she replied, pretending she didn't recognise his voice.

She wasn't permitted to give out such information on the phone but, turning to one of the auctioneers who had stepped into the office, she explained: "It's Mr Hunt. He is asking about Dahlia. What can I tell him?"

"He has been through enough, tell him," said her more senior colleague.

"Sir, that mare was sold to Mr Allen Paulson."

She heard a muffled 'thank you' that sounded like relief.

Back in the sales ring the major players were beginning to depart. There was still business to be done but they had got what they came for. A number of agents, with pockets far less deep than the high rollers from the private jets, became alert when Hip number 257 was led into the ring.

He was a good-looking February 1986 bay colt by Run The Gauntlet, America's champion turf horse of 1971, out of the dam, Intensive. This colt was one of the last sired by Run The Gauntlet, who had died the day after the foal had been born. Though Run The Gauntlet's progeny had been successful they no longer commanded the bigger prices.

A number of young horses had already been sold for transfer to France. There was room in the consignment for one more. Bidding for Hip 257 reached US$42,000 dollars when 'sold' was called.

Nelson Bunker Hunt was unaware of this particular sale. When totted up, the dispersal sale of his entire stock of thoroughbreds had reduced his mammoth debts by US$46,912,500. It was the largest public auction of thoroughbred stock in history, a record that would stand until November, 2011, when the dispersal of stock owned by breeder, the late Ned Evans, raised US$47,211,500, also at Keeneland.

Bunker could not have imagined when examining the figures, nor even understood at the time that, of the millions of dollars spent that weekend, the US$42,000 paid for Hip number 257 would have such far-reaching consequences on the far side of the Atlantic and make dreams come true.

"I've always enjoyed horse sales," Hunt told the *Los Angeles Times* in an interview a few days later, "but I wouldn't have enjoyed this one. I didn't think I'd ever have to do this, but it's something I have to do, and there's nothing I can do about it.

"It's like selling your children."

• • • • •

Child number 257 was sent to his new home in France, now the property of a wealthy Swiss businessman, Leo Schwyter.

The colt was named Cajetano.

CHAPTER 2

Don't Sell that Horse

John and Marianne Murphy are accustomed to early mornings. They are both farmers' children and, after their marriage in 1982, they devoted their lives to family traditions and to raising a family.

John moved to Marianne's home place in the townland of Ballybeg, near the village of Screen, in County Wexford, halfway between the major towns of Gorey and Wexford and less than twenty minutes from Enniscorthy.

Located a short distance from what was once the main road from Dublin to the south-east coast of Ireland, long before planners even dreamed of motorways and bypasses, their home is a place of serenity and tranquillity. Oulart Hill, scene of an historic battle during the Irish rebellion of 1798 is just a few miles away. Curracloe beach, where the fictional account of another famous battle, the D-Day landing in Normandy, was filmed for the film 'Saving Private Ryan', lies a similar distance to the east.

The land is level and fertile; good for raising cattle and growing crops. The weather tends to be kind, too, or so the locals, including the Murphys, will insist. It is called the Sunny South East and, while the tourist authorities like to trade on that name, John and Marianne know better than any couple that Wexford gets its share of inclement island weather, sometimes bitterly cold mornings when the rain would hit your face like a glove of needles.

It was an enduring mystery to John why suckler cows often chose mornings like those to produce their calves. They didn't have cameras in the sheds in those days to allow them watch over the cows from the comfort of the kitchen and, during calving times, John made regular trips from the house to the yard to check on progress and to be on hand if required when the calves began to arrive. They kept up to 50 cows on the farm at all times, so the calving season was a busy time.

Marianne spent those mornings in the mid-1990s getting their eldest children, Aidan and Ciara, ready for school. At just three years old Brian was the youngest and, like his mum and dad that morning of April 30, 1996, he was awake around 6am. He had heard his father moving around the house and rose to investigate. There was a chill in the air so he didn't follow John out to the yard. Marianne would have intercepted him anyway as she prepared the early breakfast.

John had not slept well, though he felt fresh. The mare he kept was in foal and coming near term. In the four years since he had bought the mare, the first he had ever owned, she had produced three foals. All the births had been routine but John remained excited and alert. The mare had been skittish the night before, though that wasn't terribly unusual because she could be a rogue at the best of times. But John knew by her agitation that the birth could not be far away. He had checked her earlier and moved her into the small shed, which he had prepared some days beforehand. At the time he didn't have a stable in the yard. The shed had been thoroughly hosed and he put down fresh straw. When he looked in at 6am the mare, which had a brief racing career under the name, Farinella, was circling the shed in quick steps entering the last stages of labour. Her bad temper was not improving and Murphy was wary that his own movements would not be a distraction for her.

He watched carefully as the birth began. He saw the front hooves of a new foal begin to emerge, a little streak of white on the left, and the mare lay down.

Before daylight had completely broken through, the foal, a male, had been born. It was a straightforward birth that allowed John watch from a distance, Farinella barely aware of his presence. Happy that both mare and foal had come through the process well, John left them to the natural bonding process. He knew the mare would soon stand and break the umbilical cord and then lick the foal clean. John would let the family know about the new arrival and return hopefully in time to see the foal make its first attempt to get to its feet.

His mood was light as he made the short walk to the back door. The kids were at an age now that they could visit the foal immediately. They would have a story to tell their schoolmates this morning. The birth of a foal was always a topic for happy discussion. John Murphy's lifelong dream of keeping a brood mare was living up to all his expectations.

Born and raised just four miles from where he farmed, John Murphy always had a love of horses. His father kept a workhorse to assist on their farm but they had never kept a brood mare or considered getting involved in the industry. Cattle were the priority and kept them sufficiently busy.

As a child, however, the animals fascinated him. Walking through fields, or on the roads around his home, he would never pass a horse without walking over to have a look and give him a pat if the horse proved friendly enough.

The land surrounding the pretty villages of Ballyedmond, Ballycanew and Screen was home to many horses. The tradition of breeding, showing and racing horses was centuries old in virtually every part of county Wexford.

Though the Murphys were not involved with horses they, like everyone else in the area, felt part of that tradition. Apart from agriculture and business, the local people's passion was for horses and hurling. John Murphy worked, traded and socialised with these people. They discussed the good horses, admired the great ones and attended race meetings together – the trips only serving to grow his own ambition to own a brood mare.

At a wedding in 1992, John met a neighbour, Paddy Bolger, and they started chatting. Paddy was a brother of Jim, the hugely successful trainer of classic winners on the Flat in Ireland, Britain and France, who was also developing a stud farm that Paddy managed for him in their native village of Oylegate. Inevitably, horses came up for discussion and John, prompted by Marianne, finally revealed his lifelong ambition to keep a brood mare. An invitation to Redmondstown Stud, just a few miles from Murphy's home, was immediately issued.

Paddy told John of a yearling filly they had at the stud that would never race because of injury. John immediately liked the look of the filly when he visited a few days later, but he also caught his first sight of Farinella. She was a good-looking chestnut with a bad reputation. She was regarded as difficult to handle. Now in foal to the successful sire, Project Manager, which stood at Redmondstown, Bolger told him that she was also for sale.

Farinella had been purchased as a yearling by Jim Bolger. There was thoroughbred royalty in her blood. Her grandsire had been Northern Dancer, the Canadian-bred winner of the Kentucky Derby and regarded as the most successful stallion of the 20th Century, and her sire was Salmon Leap, who had a successful racing career in Ireland in the 1980s when trained by Vincent O'Brien.

That she was bred by Joe Crowley caught Bolger's attention. Crowley, from Piltown in Kilkenny, was regarded the world over as one of the shrewdest men in the thoroughbred industry but, at Bolger's stables in Coolcullen, it became apparent very quickly that Farinella would be difficult to handle. "Very highly strung and not easy to train," was how Bolger later described her.

She worked alongside the stars of the Bolger yard in 1991. Jet Ski Lady, a daughter of Vaguely Noble, who had been born just weeks after the dispersal of Bunker Hunt's collection of thoroughbreds, won the Epsom Oaks that summer; Star of Gdansk, owned by Henryk de Kwiatkowski, was third in both the Epsom Derby and the Irish Derby. But, though she shared the elegant facilities of Coolcullen with these champions, Farinella failed to pick up any of their good habits.

Working alongside Bolger in Coolcullen at the time was a 21-year-old amateur jockey and aspiring trainer named Aidan O'Brien, who would soon wed Joe Crowley's daughter, Anne Marie.

As Bolger's assistant, O'Brien looked after the apprentices who were only a few years younger than himself. But O'Brien's seniority was obvious – his obvious knowledge and his quiet demeanour ensured that their similarity in age counted for nought.

The apprentices were a talented group of riders. Amongst them were a youngster from the north of Ireland named AP McCoy, who rode alongside Seamus Heffernan, Willie Supple and Paul Carberry.

These future champions rode whatever horses O'Brien or Bolger assigned to them as they learned their trade.

O'Brien, himself, took on the task of riding out Farinella and teaching her how to be a racehorse. He loved her looks and believed Farinella had the potential to win big races, but only if he could convince her to do what he wanted and not what she wanted.

For her part, Farinella didn't want to know. No matter what O'Brien tried – various techniques that worked on other difficult horses and helped create some of the greatest racehorses in the world in the future – he could not control her natural instinct to do her own thing.

"She wanted to do more than was necessary," he later said of the filly.

They got her to the track once, on April 4, 1991, in Tipperary (then known as Limerick Junction) where she ran sixth in a fifteen-runner race, ridden by Derby-winning jockey Christy Roche. It became obvious, painfully for those handling her daily, that Farinella would be better suited to stud duties rather than taking up space in a yard devoted to racing.

John Murphy was made aware of her history but, still, he liked the look of the filly and was more than content with her breeding.

If she was good enough for a man like Joe Crowley she would certainly be good enough for this first-time breeder, so he paid IR£700 and brought her home to Ballybeg.

His first brood mare was in foal and his dreams were about to be realised. A filly that would be named Ballyvelig Lady was born. She raced five times without making any impression. Murphy agreed with the Bolgers that Farinella would make two further visits to Project Manager but the first-born of the mating remained the most successful. The new breeder was not discouraged. He knew it would take time, and he had plenty of that. He bought two more brood mares which was an indication of how serious he was about breeding.

• • • • •

Though he was still finding his feet in the breeding world, John Murphy was enjoying himself. The suckler cows were still his main priority. His children were growing up, and caring for them meant that horse breeding remained a hobby, something to take his mind off the day-to-day demands of running a farm.

Having a few brood mares around provided a new topic of conversation for various friends who called almost every evening. These were men who were fascinated by horses and horse-racing. They discussed bloodlines and wondered where the next great racehorse would come from. They were surrounded by great trainers, mingled with the people who worked in studs and training stables and they loved to swap stories, some of which were exaggerated but all were the result of a shared passion.

But, despite all those evenings in John Murphy's home, and their love of horses and racing, none of them had an inkling that they were about to be witnesses to one of the most extraordinary stories of all.

Frank Cashin, a near neighbour, was one such visitor. One evening early in 1995, Frank mentioned that a stallion was standing at the Ballycanew stud owned and run by James Maguire. The stallion had been purchased by Maguire a few years earlier in France and had a good pedigree but hadn't attracted much interest from Irish owners of brood mares. The Maguires were keen to have mares sent to the stallion and Cashin reckoned the service fee might not be that high and that Murphy should have at least have a chat with Maguire.

Maguire was a well-known and highly-respected figure in the breeding world, involved as much with sport horses (show jumpers and dressage) as with racehorses.

He had been a race-rider himself in his youth but it was as a breeder at his Ballyteigue Stud, just outside the village of Ballycanew, that Maguire had gained fame. Like Joe Crowley, he had an eye for a good horse and an ability to mix bloodlines to produce quality progeny. He had developed contacts all over the world and some of his foals were sold in Australia, the US, the Middle East and Europe.

At the outset of the 1990s Maguire kept a number of mares at his farm and was looking to acquire a new stallion. He found nothing of interest locally but a chance encounter one afternoon with Enniscorthy trainer, PM 'Padge' Berry, piqued his interest. Berry had an eclectic mix of owners involved in his yard, including a wealthy Swiss businessman named Leo Schwyter, who had horses stabled in his home country as well as in France and Britain.

Maguire had met Schwyter and liked him and now Berry was telling him that Schwyter was retiring a well-bred racehorse based in Paris and might sell him for stud duties. The horse was called Cajetano.

Having arrived in France from Keeneland in January of 1988, Cajetano was sent to the yard of trainer Jack Barbe at Maisons-Laffitte in the plush north-western suburbs of Paris.

His racing career under Schwyter was hardly distinguished, although he did win the prestigious Group One Swiss Jockey Club Grand Prix in 1990, as well as two other races in that country. Back in France, he won two races over hurdles but his flat record was disappointing.

Ridden by Maurice Philipperon, he was fourth in the Group Two Prix Kergorlay in Deauville in August of 1990 and was last of eight in Longchamp two months later. By the end of the 1992 season, it was decided by Schwyter and Barbe that it would be more economical to sell the horse, probably for stud duties. A phone call was made to Ireland and the news relayed to Maguire.

When James heard the pedigree – the sire Run The Gauntlet caught his attention immediately – he decided it warranted further investigation.

He immediately flew to Paris to see the horse and was impressed. He felt it had a, "lovely gait," and was, "so quiet to handle".

Maguire had been in the business long enough, however, to know that any purchase would depend on further investigation. He needed a stallion to produce sport horses. Maguire agreed to bring the horse back to Ireland on condition that purchase would only be completed if the horse passed a Stallion Inspection Assessment. These were official inspections run by the Department of Agriculture in Ireland to maintain the highest quality in breeding. That was accepted and Cajetano was transported to Wexford at a cost to Maguire of just over IR£320.

Cajetano had been trained to jump hurdles, but Maguire would have a lot of work to do with the horse before presenting him for assessment.

In Ballycanew, over a number of months, he taught Cajetano how to stand and trot for inspection and how to jump fences before entering him in the Stallion Assessment Championships in 1993, which were held in Millstreet, Co Cork.

The judges were well known – international show jumper Robert Splaine, the legendary Colonel Ned Campion, who had ridden in the Olympic Games in 1968 and was the Commanding Officer of the Army Equitation School, and Michael Leonard, a highly respected owner and breeder from Newcastlewest in Limerick.

Cajetano was one of 25 horses selected for performance testing at Splaine's stud and farm in Belgooly, near Kinsale in Cork.

In January, 1994, the 25 horses arrived for judging in Millstreet. Marks were awarded under the headings of confirmation, movement, temperament, jumping aptitude and ease of riding. Cajetano was led around the ring and a report noted he was, "an attractive sort with a very nice head and neck who rode calmly with his ears pricked and a relaxed attitude on his approach to fences."

The judges awarded Cajetano 80 marks out of 100, the highest score achieved by any of the finalists. It was an extraordinary achievement for a racehorse that, just two years earlier, had been running flat races in Europe.

James Maguire's judgement had been vindicated, and he brought Cajetano back to Ballycanew for what Maguire expected would be a successful and lucrative career at stud.

But it was not to be. Cajetano was one of the rare occasions in his career as a horseman that Maguire's instinct let him down. Cajetano's breeding, and his brilliant results from Millstreet, were insufficient to convince the horse-breeding fraternity in Ireland that this new stallion might measure up to their requirements, and Maguire's phone remained depressingly quiet.

So, while covering his own mares, Maguire continued to advertise the presence of the stallion at his stud by printing 400 leaflets, which he posted to other stud farms around Ireland.

The sound of silence shocked him – there was virtually no response. In the four years that Cajetano stood at Ballyheigue Stud a total of four mares were sent for covering. Three foals were born to those four mares and Cajetano sired just seven in total in that time. That fuelled a belief that Cajetano was not very fertile.

Maguire bred Dark Crusader and Mr Maguire and, while the latter horse ran in just three point-to-point races in Northern Ireland without success, Dark Crusader enjoyed a satisfactory racing career in England, winning a couple of races for trainer Mark Pittman before being sold to trainer Lucinda Russell for Stg£11,000 in 2001. He ran ten more races but was never placed.

Meanwhile, Blue Flu, foaled in 1994, was purchased by Michael Hourigan and raced seven times between August 1998 and December 1999, his best placing being sixth in a hurdle race in Tralee in June of 1999. Lady Pep went to the racecourse five times without success and Idontcare was pulled up on his only run in Roscommon. Another 1994 foal, named Seat Belt, ran in three point-to-point races but never made it to the racecourse proper.

By May 1995, a dejected James Maguire was considering the future for Cajetano. He remained convinced that the stallion had promise but felt the world of racing was showing a distinct bias against a small stud. He later recalled, "I suppose it's a prestige thing really. If you have a mare and bring her to the National Stud then it's a big talking point, but, if you bring her to a farm like this in the middle of nowhere, then nobody's interested."

So, when John Murphy phoned, Maguire was happy to take the call from a man who lived less than ten miles away. They were not previously acquainted but Maguire was struck by Murphy's enthusiasm and told him to bring Farinella over.

For his part, Murphy was impressed on seeing Cajetano for the first time. "He's a grand horse," he said in admiration.

"That he is and I hope you will get a nice foal," said James Maguire. The service fee was a mere IR£200 and, on payment, Maguire handed IR£20 back to Murphy.

"For luck," he said as the two men shook hands.

Farinella turned out to be the last mare covered by Cajetano in Ballycanew. James Maguire transferred the stallion to the care of his brother-in-law, John Hughes, who ran Williamstown Stud in Co Meath.

There the stallion covered a number of sport horses and sired the likes of Kiltoom, later to become a very successful showjumper in partnership with Captain David O'Brien.

It was to Williamstown Stud that the former world showjumping champion and Olympian, Tommy Brennan, called with an unusual offer one afternoon in 1996. A stud farm in Sardinia was looking for a stallion and the owners were interested in buying Cajetano.

Eleven months and a few days after John Murphy and James Maguire had shaken hands for the last time, and Cajetano and Farinella had concluded their relationship, John opened the gate of the shed where the new foal, the seventh sired at Ballycanew, had been born a day earlier.

The son of Cajetano took his first steps around the small yard, carefully monitored by his mother, Farinella, who was in comparatively good humour. Within a day or two John and little Ciara were able to lead the foal up the lane beside the house. The foal was easy to handle, eager to please.

"He doesn't buck or leap like the others," said Ciara in wonder. At one year old, Murphy gelded the horse and thought about the day he would bring him to the sales. He was a strong yearling and was thriving on the farm. He had never given any trouble, was good with the children and was generally good to have around.

The dam, Farinella, was moving on. She was being sold and John was looking out for other mares to bring to the farm.

All the time, his neighbours continued to call and they enjoyed watching the young horse out in the field. He was growing stronger all the time and when in full flight was a lovely spectacle. One neighbour and friend, Seamus Doyle, crossed the fields one evening from his own farm, to stand with Murphy and watch. Seamus was unusually quiet.

"What's up?" asked John.

"I've been thinking, John, that you shouldn't sell that horse," said Doyle.

It was something Seamus Doyle repeated a number of times over the following months. John and some of the others who gathered at Ballybeg would joke with him.

"You'd swear you had horses all your life the way you're talking. Sure, what would you know about it?" they would laugh.

"I know, lads, I know," Seamus would respond, chuckling to himself. "But there's something about him, I'm telling you. Don't sell him, John."

"And what do you want me to do with him?" asked John. "I'll have to sell him. I can't keep him hanging around here."

Murphy had enjoyed his short career as a breeder but he had neither the knowledge nor the time to consider training a racehorse. He was breeding racehorses to sell them on – it was an economic practicality. If the racehorse was to be successful then someone else would manage that success. If the horse wasn't much good on a racecourse, that too would be the responsibility of another.

So, early in 1999, John Murphy contacted the Tattersalls Bloodstock Sales office at the Fairyhouse complex in Ratoath, County Meath, to enquire about entering his horse in the annual Derby sale at the end of June.

The Derby sale is regarded as one of the top sales events in the world for three- and four-year-old potential National Hunt horses and the list of owners wishing to enter horses is greater than the capacity of the sale.

Tattersalls sent a representative to the Murphy farm to inspect the horse and decide whether he was a suitable candidate for presentation at the sales.

"I'm afraid he won't qualify for the Derby sale," Tattersalls' assessor told Murphy. "You can enter him for the August sale."

The Cajetano name still didn't impress anyone in the world of horses.

Finally, on August 12, 1999, lot number 526, an unbroken three-year-old gelding, the property of Mr John Murphy, was sold for 5,400 guineas to a cash buyer. John had placed a IR£5,000 reserve on his horse and was naturally very pleased with the return on his investment.

But despite his generally calm demeanour, the young gelding's new owners discovered their purchase possessed some of the characteristics of his oft-times troublesome dam and the three-year-old proved difficult to break.

So, they decided to move him on within a year and, on June 8, 2000, the still-unbroken but now four-year-old son of Cajetano was up for sale again – this time at Goffs near Dublin.

It was there that Michael Hourigan first set eyes on lot number 206, the horse that would consume his life for the next eight years.

CHAPTER 3

Good Racehorses Recognise Each Other

The car park at the Goffs sales complex in Kill, County Kildare was filling rapidly as Michael Hourigan arrived early on Thursday morning, June 8, 2000. It contained a variety of vehicles from the most modern horse transportation to battered trailers, from Jeeps to Mercs and Mondeos.

The Junes Sales, known as The Land Rover Sale, attract buyers and sellers from all over Ireland, as well as some of the best known trainers and bloodstock agents from England.

Hourigan recognised some of the cars: Andrew McNamara from Croom was there, as was his namesake Eric McNamara from Rathkeale, Hourigan's original home in Limerick. Noel Glynn had come from the fabled Spancil Hill in County Clare and there were Northern Ireland registrations which he guessed belonged to Ian Ferguson who would have travelled from his base near the historic village of Cullybackey in Antrim; maybe William Patton had come from Carrickfergus. They were regular attendees at these sales, good judges of horses.

Apart from the serious business of buying and selling horses, the sales were also social occasions. Hourigan could meet trainers like Pat Flynn, Frank Codd, Padge Berry or Francis Ennis at race meetings any day of the week in Ireland, but lads like Noel Chance and Ferdy Murphy were based in England and they might only meet once a year or once every couple of years.

Chance was one of the first he met that morning. Chance had originally trained nearby on the Curragh but had moved to England in 1995 and the two men had not spoken since Chance had trained Looks Like Trouble to win the Cheltenham Gold Cup in March of 2000.

Hourigan's great horse Doran's Pride had finished in sixth place in that race. It was Chance's second Gold Cup success, he'd also trained Mr Mullligan to win in 1997, the year when Doran's Pride finished third.

Also back in Ireland that morning was Ferdy Murphy, a man who had enjoyed three decades of success both as a jockey and a trainer in England and Ireland.

Murphy was one of the great success stories of National Hunt racing. At one stage he'd quit the sport to work as a builder's labourer in London explaining at the time: "There was more money to be made."

But Paddy Mullins, the patriach of the great racing family from Goresbridge in Kilkenny, held Ferdy in high regard as a jockey and coaxed him back into the sport.

Amongst many great achievements in a colourful career, Murphy holds the unique distinction of training a horse, the great Anaglog's Daughter, to win the Arkle Trophy at Cheltenham in 1980 and to ride the horse to victory less than two weeks later at Chepstow, when regular jockey, Tommy Carberry, and potential replacement, Jonjo O'Neill, were both injured before the race.

Other visitors included the bloodstock agent Aiden Murphy, a man who had some well-heeled buyers waiting back at his base in Warwickshire. Alan Swinbank, a breeder and trainer, had also travelled and had money to spend.

Hourigan greeted other familiar faces, including David Wachman who had worked as travelling head lad at Hourigan's Lisaleen Stables for a period during the mid-1990s but had recently begun his own career as a trainer. Frances Crowley from the famous racing family who had been Irish amateur champion jockey twice in recent years and was now training, was also there.

An impish grin broke on his face when he noticed Noel Meade approaching in the distance. Meade was a fanatical follower of the Meath Gaelic football team and had been braying with delight when they won the All-Ireland championship the previous September. Since then, the football banter had been unrelenting, but, four days ago, Meath had surrendered their crown in the opening round of the competition in one of the biggest upsets of the year when they lost to Offaly.

Meade expected a reaction, especially from Hourigan.

"Noel, tell me this, there's more people here at these sales today than live in Offaly so how come your great football team couldn't win last Sunday?" he ribbed Meade.

The Meath native had enjoyed great success as a trainer and was a man on a mission at the sales in Ireland in 2000. A year earlier he had lost the very promising young horse, Cardinal's Hill, winner of the Punchestown Champion Novice Hurdle, to colic.

Although Sausalito Bay had brought him his first Cheltenham success in 2000, Meade was still building up the stock at his Tu Va stables in Meath.

There were many others with whom Michael Hourigan would exchange pleasantries that morning.

Liam Cashman had arrived from Cork where he ran the Rathbarry Stud, founded by his father, and the Glenview Stud he himself had established less than ten years before. Both stud farms were world renowned for producing champions on both the flat and over jumps.

Kevin O'Brien, who had ridden many winners for Hourigan and had carved out a career as a trainer in the picturesque area known as The Swan in County Laois, had made the relatively short trip. Harry Rogers was developing his stables in Ardee in County Louth and was at Goffs looking for potential occupiers of his boxes.

Michael Cunningham, who had trained winners of classics on the flat at the Curragh and Newmarket and Cheltenham Festival winners over jumps from his Gormanston Stables in Meath, was another interested attendee. Hourigan met Dessie Hughes, based locally as a trainer and forever remembered as the rider of Monksfield, one of the most popular horses in the history of jump racing.

The Goffs Bloodstock Sales, like its only rival in Ireland, Tattersalls, which is based at the Fairyhouse racing complex in Meath, has a long and rich history. Named after Robert J. Goff, the first official auctioneer appointed by the Irish Turf Club in the mid-nineteenth century, Goffs operated from the Royal Dublin Society premises in Dublin's Ballsbridge until it moved to a new site on the Dublin to Naas road, near Kill in County Kildare, in 1975.

Many of the greatest racehorses in history were sold at the Goffs Sales over during that century. Arkle, perhaps the greatest of them all, was bought for 1,150 guineas by Anne, Duchess of Westminster. Red Rum was sold as a yearling in 1966 for just 406 guineas and went on to win the Aintree Grand National three times.

On this bright June morning Michael Hourigan had arrived early, as usual. He'd perused the sales catalogue at home the previous evening but nothing stood out.

That was the way with these sales of three- and four-year-old horses that were unraced. You could spend hours studying pedigrees but it was only when you got a good look at the horse, how he or she stands and walks, their general deportment, that you could decide whether or not to take a risk on making a purchase.

He liked to look at the horses in their boxes before they were sent to the parade ring or sales ring. If one caught his eye he'd ask the stablehand in charge to take the horse out of the box for a brisk walk or trot to see how it moved. The horse would later be led around a parade ring where Hourigan would take another look and make a final decision on whether or not to bid, and also assess how much he was willing to spend.

Hourigan's philosophy at the sales was straightforward.

"I like a bit of value," he'd say. "If I have IR£25,000 in my pocket to spend I don't want to spend it all on one horse. I would prefer to buy five horses."

He wasn't afraid to spend more, and often did, with varying degrees of success, but the more horses he bought the better chance he would have of finding a good one, or a few good ones.

Hours had passed that day in Goffs and Hourigan was still searching for something to buy. He had looked at four or five horses but nothing had convinced him to open his wallet.

Occasionally, he entered the sales ring to see what was happening. He enjoyed the cut and thrust of the sales. It was part of the ritual, part of the addiction to the sport. It was always special to train a winning racehorse, especially a winner of a big race. But equally satisfying was the challenge of identifying potential in a sales ring, winning the purchase of that potential with a shrewd bid and then seeing that potential fulfilled on the racecourse.

From experience Hourigan knew that with all the skill in the world, all the knowledge possible of horses, there was still an element of luck in producing a great champion.

Events on that day would provide a telling insight into the world of sales and racing. The stallion, Phardante, seemed popular with buyers in the morning when the first batch of the 250 horses available were presented for sale. A bid of IR£10,500 secured a four-year-old son of Phardante who would be named Americain Paddy but who would have a short and undistinguished career, racing twice without success.

Luckier bidders were Abbeyleix Stud who paid IR£27,000 for a three-year-old gelding from the same stallion, out of the mare, Stepfaster. He was named Pharviva and, when trained by Mick Halford on the Curragh, won six times in a 32-race career and won over IR£50,000 for his owners, a racing syndicate based in the village of Rathcoffey.

Prices of IR£20,000 and IR£31,000 were paid for a son and daughter of the stallion Be My Native. The son, Native Talker, ran twice and disappointed on both occasions while the daughter, Lorna's Lady, ran twelve times and won once, earning a mere IR£7,000 in prizemoney.

When Eddie Hales paid IR£10,000 for a three-year-old colt it went virtually unnoticed but it was the second best bit of business carried out in Goffs that day. Hales named the horse Pizarro and trained him to win a race at Fairyhouse before selling him on. Pizarro won the Champion Bumper in Cheltenham in 2003, trained by Eddie O'Grady, and enjoyed a highly successful career amassing over IR£200,000 in prizemoney.

The most expensive purchase of the day was made by Noel Chance. He paid IR£70,000 for a four-year-old son of Toulon, a winner of the English St Leger in 1991 who was also fourth in the Prix de l'Arc de Triomphe. Named First Day Cover when he reached the racecourse a year later, he won once in Plumpton in December 2001. He ran five more races, twice in Folkestone, once in Kempton and finally at Fontwell on St Patrick's Day, 2003, without achieving further success, and earned a total of Stg£1,558 in prize money.

If he'd had an endless supply of money Hourigan would have spent more time studying pedigree. But he didn't have that kind of largesse and horses with the right pedigree, bred from champions, cost too much money.

He relied on his own judgement and, so far, he hadn't done too badly. His approach was as colourful as it was simple: "You look at a horse the way you would look at a woman. The good-looking woman that makes my head turn might not make your head turn. Beauty is in the eye of the beholder. So, when I am at the sales I might see a horse that I think is stunning but you won't."

During the day he'd looked at a lot of horses. There were a lot of nice horses available but nothing turned his head until he was considering his return home. Then, as he ambled towards the sales ring for one last time, a horse caught his eye. It was the strong athletic type he liked.

Thinking the horse had already been sold and was being led away, he cursed himself: "How did I miss him?"

As the lad leading the horse passed by, Hourigan asked, "What did he fetch?"

"He hasn't been in yet, I'm just giving him a walk," replied the youngster.

Hourigan took a closer look. It was the power in the animal's walk that had caught his attention moments earlier and, as he watched the horse and handler move away, Hourigan could see where the power came from. The horse was big behind, naturally well-muscled. He strode out well, a splash of white visible on his left front and hind feet, rolling along almost lazily, easily carrying a frame that looked to be sixteen hands high.

As they walked back towards him, Hourigan noticed the star on his forehead. He wasn't a handsome horse in the conventional sense – if there had been a beauty contest on the day he wouldn't have been selected for the final round.

But there was a ruggedness about his face that piqued Hourigan's interest. He had the look of a strong character, a horse that wouldn't be afraid of work. Hourigan knew he couldn't be certain of that in any horse until he was broken, but he had seen enough of them over the years to risk making such an assessment.

This fella looked like he didn't have a care in the world. He was almost inconspicuous. Even Hourigan, fast becoming an admirer, had failed to notice him before now.

The trainer checked the catalogue: Lot 206, a four-year-old chestnut by the stallion, Cajetano. He knew the sire's name and had already trained another of his sons, named Blue Flu. Hourigan had had fun naming him during a controversy when members of the Gardai, who are prohibited from taking industrial action, failed to turn up for work in early 1998 claiming illness. This became known as an outbreak of 'blue flu'. The horse had run a few times the previous year but had achieved little success, Hourigan recalled. His best placing being sixth in a thirteen-runner hurdle race in Tralee.

Giving further study to the pedigree of this chestnut he noted the line back to Run The Gauntlet, Cajetano's sire. There was a jumping connection there that he remembered from past examination. Run The Gauntlet was also the sire of the good flat horse, Ardross, that had been bred by Paddy Prendergast. Ardross himself had produced champions when he went to stud, though they were mainly jumpers, including Alderbrook which had won the Champion Hurdle at Cheltenham in 1995.

Hourigan was getting interested.

Next he checked at the sales ring for particulars about Farinella. There wasn't a huge amount to encourage him there. Her own racing career had been brief and her other progeny had not made any impression. The one positive that he did note was that Joe Crowley had bred her and that had to be a plus in her favour.

Lot 206 was being presented for sale for a second time but it was obvious that he was not attracting much interest. One or two other potential buyers were watching Hourigan and listening to his questions but they grew less enthusiastic as information was provided.

What little attention was being paid to the ring when the horse was being shown was primarily from Hourigan. The sale was winding down, some buyers had already spent their money and had headed for home. Others simply decided not to spend today. There would be other days.

"Any word on why this one is being sold so quickly again?" Hourigan asked in reference to the note that the horse had originally been sold less than a year before.

"Word is he's hard to break," came the reply and though Hourigan pressed the point, no one could confirm that claim.

That didn't unduly concern him anyway even though the horse was now four years old. Over the years he had broken many difficult horses. And there was something about this one. He just moved well. He was a Hourigan-type horse. Athletic. That word constantly popped into his mind. He had a feeling about this horse, it was just an instinct but instinct was important. There was no certainty in such situations but men like Hourigan gambled on their judgement. Every time they went to the sales they hoped to find a champion. It was the driving force; that dream meant they kept going back, again and again.

Some buyers spent very large sums and never bought success. In other cases, like Red Rum, very small sums were paid and dreams came true.

He made his decision and offered IR£6,500. The auctioneer was not inundated with counter offers and quickly brought the gavel down. Sold.

The sale would turn out to be easily the best business done that day in Goffs though it would be some time before anyone other than Michael Hourigan would realise it.

Back home at Lisaleen the horse, nicknamed Salmon (his grand dam being Salmon Leap), settled in quickly. The yard was busy and he seemed to thrive in the company of other horses.

The process of breaking the horse began immediately. Hourigan was conscious of the belief that the horse might have been hard to break so he took extra care. It wasn't actually necessary as Salmon learned quickly and without any problem.

Once broken, Hourigan and the team began to prepare Salmon for a career in racing. Almost immediately, Michael and his family, along with the staff, began to suspect there was something a little bit special about the horse.

Chatting at home each evening about the events of the day, the conversation would inevitably return to the new recruit. His sons, Michael Junior and Paul, shared their father's enthusiasm about the horse.

"What is it about him?" their mother Ann would ask.

"He's a real jumper," they would answer in unison.

They were right. Salmon's jumping action came naturally, he didn't need teaching. The horse was still developing physically but he had a big stride and stayed in the air longer than any other horse in the yard.

They had also noticed something else.

When the horses were released to the fields the new occupant of box No. 7 and their champion, Doran's Pride, became a pair.

Doran's was nearly seven years older than the young horse but they were always together. They seemed to look out for each other when taken from the stables to go to the field. Eight horses might be brought out together but once they got to the field Doran's Pride and Salmon stood apart, happily eating grass together, playing together.

"They say good racehorses recognise each other," Kay Hourigan, the eldest daughter, commented one day. "I hope that's true because if it is we could have good times ahead."

There were other matters to attend to with a new horse in the yard. He had to be named and registered with the racing authorities before he would be allowed to race.

And an owner had to be found.

It costs a lot of money to keep a racehorse in a yard and the trainer did not want to have to bear that cost. Michael had been lucky with owners over the years and the success of Doran's Pride had attracted others who were interested in investing some spare cash in bloodstock.

The yard was constantly expanding and some owners had been with Lisaleen for more than ten years. The number of new owners was also growing every year.

Hourigan's reputation for recognising talent and honing it had grown over the years. He was also regarded as a shrewd businessman, worth dealing with. He liked deals, was good at them. That's what buyers wanted.

However, this time, for some reason, he began to think his luck had run out when he started looking for someone to pay the fees for Salmon.

He couldn't understand why. There was no shortage of buyers for other horses and he wasn't providing as positive a recommendation for those as he was for Salmon. Was it the pedigree? It might put off some people, but a lot of investors trusted the judgement of the trainer. Good pedigrees also meant bigger prices.

According to some, Salmon wasn't the prettiest horse in the yard but he was physically impressive. And on the gallops he cut an impressive figure when in full stride.

But, still, Hourigan couldn't find a buyer.

Lisaleen held an Open Day on October 1 that year, and invited the racing community and the general public to meet the horses.

A representative of a syndicate based around Athlone and Moate in County Westmeath took an interest in Salmon. The horse was led around the yard and a price of IR£12,000 was agreed. The woman said she would speak to the members of the syndicate and confirm the purchase the following day. But when she got home that night and relayed the news, her fellow syndicate members were not as impressed and the deal fell through.

Representatives of the main bloodstock agencies visited Lisaleen but they were not impressed by Salmon.

Later, in October, Michael felt sure he had the horse sold when another offer of IR£15,000 was tabled by a long-standing client. But, again, the deal was frustrated after the prospective buyer was unable to put a syndicate together when one member refused to get involved. When a third offer fell through a week later, Hourigan despaired that he would ever sell the horse.

To compound the problem, the horse developed ringworm in December. A skin infection caused by a fungus, ringworm appears as a series of spots and the horse loses hair in that area.

Salmon suffered a bad dose. "He's an awful looking sight," Michael reported home one evening. "The ringworm is all over his body and down his legs. He has some spots as big as a half crown. You couldn't give him away looking like that."

Salmon was kept away from the other horses to try to stop the infection spreading around the yard. There were various forms of treatment but very often it was best to leave the horse's metabolism to treat itself. Salmon did, in fact, heal himself in a couple of weeks.

He still had to be properly named, officially registered and a campaign planned. He would start on the local point-to-point circuits, the traditional training ground used by many trainers with young horses before moving on to National Hunt races. There Salmon would learn the routine of a day at the races – travelling with other horses, getting used to horse boxes, crowds and competition with horses other than those he was familiar with around the yard.

Michael and Ann were attending the usual round of dinners and receptions that take place in the build up to Christmas of 2000. It was a hectic time for the racing community with lots of meetings taking place, including some of the biggest festivals of the year.

They didn't always feel like socialising. The days were long, the weather was generally unpleasant and when darkness came it was tempting just to sit by the fireside and relax. Ann Hourigan ensured that her husband would participate in these social events to get a break from the heavy work schedule he undertook every day.

One evening as he got ready for just such a social event after a long day's work in the yard, Hourigan thought about the night ahead. In some ways it wouldn't be different from any other night. The menu would be the same anyway.

"I suppose we can expect either Beef or Salmon again tonight," he remarked to Ann in reference to the choice of food available. Instantly they both knew. Without an owner the new horse was registered in Ann Hourigan's name and was called Beef or Salmon.

The man who bred him, John Murphy, received official notification of the registration. He was pleased to see his foal was in the hands of one of the country's most established trainers.

"We'll have to keep an eye on this lad," he told his wife, Marianne, and the children.

His original investment of IR£180 had already been handsomely rewarded. There was a lot more to come.

CHAPTER 4

The Winner is No World Beater

Even in his most optimistic moments, back when it all started in 1973 and the vigour of youth provided the impetus to scale the most imposing obstacles, Michael Hourigan never allowed himself the luxury of fantasising.

That didn't mean he was without ambition. The work ethic he and Ann employed immediately after he took out his first training licence convinced family and friends around them that this adventure was one to follow.

As they settled into the new year of 2001, Hourigan had ninety boxes occupied in his stables. Salmon, one of the newest recruits, was in box 7 while the superstar, Doran's Pride, was in box 9.

Hi Cloy, an unraced four-year-old Michael had paid 14,000 guineas for at the Tattersalls Sales towards the end of 1998, and of whom there were high expectations, was a couple of doors away.

Over the course of almost three decades, Lisaleen Stables had grown into one of the largest collections of thoroughbred racehorses in the south of Ireland and Hourigan was now one of the country's most recognised and respected trainers.

It was a far cry from the days when he kept a few horses behind the family pub in Rathkeale. Having originally left home at the age of 14 to pursue his dream of working with horses, he'd served his apprenticeship with the trainer,

Charlie Weld, at Rosewell House on the Curragh and rode nine winners during his time there.

More years were spent in Scotland before Michael reached a decision that he'd never make it at the highest level as a jockey and should return to Rathkeale. So, in 1973, he returned to his native town to help in the family pub. His young wife, Ann, was a constant support during the early years.

Hourigan bought and sold cattle and sheep, as well as horses. He drove a lorry, not always in the best of condition, to transport whatever animals needed to be transported around Munster. All the time he dreamed of training a winner, just one, and there were times when he wondered if it would ever happen. There were even times when he thought about giving it all up and concentrating on farming.

The couple waited six years for their first winner. Then, on St Patrick's Day, 1979, at Limerick racecourse, a horse named Ramrajah won the 2.10.

"Are you still quitting?" Ann chided him jokingly back in Rathkeale that evening. She had listened to his talk of quitting in silence because she knew he wouldn't let go, his passion was too intense. "I'll stick at it for another while, if that's okay with you," he answered sheepishly. It was, of course, okay with Ann.

The flow of winners picked up at a slow but increasing pace. He had five winners in 1979, twelve in 1980.

The number of horses was growing in the small yard. He needed a proper premises; fields and paddocks, stables. He wanted space but the search took him five years until he took a left turn off the main road on the outskirts of Adare, where the manor lands begin, and drove the short distance to a farm that was for sale.

As soon as he laid his eyes on the gently sloping grassland he knew it was perfect. Lisaleen Stables was purchased and Michael and Ann Hourigan moved their few horses, fewer possessions, and a young and growing family into the sparse accommodation.

Money was scarce. Everything was re-invested in the stables and much-needed improvements to the family accommodation were set aside in the early years.

"If one of the kids needed a new pair of shoes we had to think about it," is how Hourigan describes the early, lean years of Lisaleen. Buying horses cheaply, training them for the racecourse and selling them on funded the development of the stables. Most of the racing in those days was done on the point-to-point circuit. Hourigan would groom his horses there and then sell them on, at a profit, to other trainers in Ireland and England.

In 1990, Lisaleen Prince, a five-year-old bay, won point-to-point races at the rural venues of Lisgoold and Kilworth in Cork. Hourigan sold the gelding to the prominent English trainer Nicky Henderson and put the profits towards the construction of a swimming pool for his horses. He built schooling fences, developed gallops, created paddocks and built an indoor schooling arena.

All the time the number of horses in the care of the Hourigans began to grow. A significant arrival in 1990 was a chestnut gelding bred in Wexford by Jim Mernagh at his Coolamurry Stud, between the towns of Clonroche and Enniscorthy.

Mernagh retained ownership of the horse, named him Deep Bramble, and sent him to the care of Hourigan. He provided both owner and trainer with many great days but none better than at the Leopardstown Christmas meeting in 1993, when Deep Bramble won the Grade 1 Ericsson Chase, beating Flashing Steel owned by Charles J. Haughey. Deep Bramble was sold to England in 1994 and was subsequently trained by Paul Nicholls.

As one horse left the yard another arrived.

Tropical Lake moved into Lisaleen in 1993. Bred for flat racing she was sent to Hourigan to go hurdling. A year later in April 1994, piloted by Kevin O'Brien, she won the prestigious Glenlivet Hurdle at the Aintree Grand National meeting. Just under twelve months later, in 1995, she won the Irish Lincolnshire over the flat at the Curragh, where Hourigan's career in racing had begun 33 years earlier.

Doran's Pride had arrived at the same time as Tropical Lake and made Lisaleen one of the best-known stables in Ireland and Britain.

Doran's was their first superstar. His victory in the 1995 Stayers' Hurdle at Cheltenham, where he was ridden by Shane Broderick, confirmed Hourigan's status as one of the foremost National Hunt trainers on the islands of Ireland and Britain.

Doran's was the first horse from the yard to capture the attention of the media. For the first time, the Hourigan family experienced the demands of that media, the presence of cameras and the price of fame. It was a price they were happy to pay for the good of the stables though, at times, their patience was tested.

By now Michael and Ann's children were already heavily involved in racing and in the stable. Michael Junior had been crowned champion amateur jockey in Britain in 1992 at the age of just 17. He divided his time between the two countries, just as his younger brother, Paul, would after he became champion conditional jockey in Ireland in the 1997–1998 season. Paul rode all of the best horses at work and many of them on the racecourse.

Eldest daughter, Kay, was quickly becoming Michael's most trusted lieutenant. She rode out, mucked out and, at an early age, showed enough managerial expertise to suggest she had the potential to become the yard administrator. Laura was also showing great promise as a rider. The youngest, Mark, was just starting out at school.

There were some interesting characters working at the yard, young jockeys riding at point-to-point meetings and in races all over the country. Enda Bolger didn't do any mucking out anymore, having reached a different status as a jockey at that stage of his career. He had ridden many winners for Hourigan and was preparing to wind down his riding career. But, though he was already training himself, he remained a big influence on the youngsters around the yard.

Kevin O'Brien, David Casey, Shane Broderick, John Cullen, Peter Henley and Timmy Murphy were some of those learning their trade from Hourigan.

Michael had a reputation for being a tough boss but that didn't deter young men from working at the yard if the opportunity arose. They knew they would learn and dreamed of following in the footsteps of Adrian Maguire, Hourigan's first protégé, who had left Lisaleen to pursue a career in England in 1991 and was becoming one of the most successful Irish jockeys of all time.

The big race winners kept coming.

The mare, Anusha, ridden by Broderick, won the Ladbroke Hurdle in Leopardstown in January of 1995; in 1999 Deejaydee won the National Hunt Chase in Cheltenham and Inis Cara rounded off a good year by scooping the valuable Paddy Power Handicap Chase at Leopardstown.

It was a measure of Hourigan's growing status that he would spend IR£14,000 on a yearling at the sales in 1998. His judgement was vindicated when the horse graduated to racing a few years later under the name, Hi Cloy.

There was other significance in that purchase, too. Michael sold the gelding to a businessman from Bellaghy in County Derry named Seamus McCloy. The pair shared interests other than racing. McCloy was a passionate follower of

Gaelic games and they enjoyed talking about the sports and the rise, in Gaelic football, of McCloy's native Derry during the 1990s.

So, Hourigan immediately recognised McCloy's voice when he answered his mobile phone early one afternoon at the beginning of January 2001.

Though he had extensive business interests across the north of Ireland, from Donegal through Derry and into Antrim, McCloy loved to make time to travel to Adare a few times a year to see the horses and spend some time chatting with the trainer.

"When does it suit you for me to come down?" asked McCloy.

"How does Saturday suit?" replied Hourigan.

"Grand. Oh, by the way, Joe and Dan might come along, if that's alright?"

"I'd be delighted," confirmed the trainer.

Joe Craig and Dan McLarnon, were also successful Northern businessmen.

Joe Craig had built up the Moyola Mattress Company, based in Castledawson, into a thriving family business. Dan McLarnon was an hotelier who owned the Adair Arms in Ballymena. They were both heading for retirement and shared two passions, horse racing and golf. The two men had been captains of the Moyola Park Golf Club and had become firm friends over the years.

Dan had been heavily involved in breeding for most of his life, while Joe had a horse named All For Luck – trained by Martin Pipe at his stables, Pond House, in Somerset – which had won in Aintree at the Grand National meeting, in 1994. Both Craig and McCloy had, at one time or another, owned a horse called Tell The Nipper. It had been stabled with Pipe for a short period and, later, with Hourigan for a longer term. Joe Craig already had a horse at Lisaleen, a six-year-old named Annaghmore Gale who had failed to set the racing scene alight in two years and which the trainer was preparing to switch from hurdling to chasing later that year.

By the time the Northerners arrived the morning chores had been completed at Lisaleen. After refreshments at the house they toured the yard, examining the horses and taking a particular interest in looking at the star that was Doran's Pride.

They chatted with Ann, Kay and the other staff around the stables but as they strode towards the office, where Michael and McCloy had some formal business to complete, the party stopped outside box No. 7.

Salmon, who would often show a complete lack of interest in the activities of humans when he was resting in the comfort of his stable, stuck his head over the door. He was right on cue.

"Michael," said McCloy, "we didn't say anything before, but these two boys are not leaving here without investing in one of these horses."

Without hesitation, Hourigan replied; "Well, if that's the case, then they should buy this fella behind me. He's running in a point-to-point tomorrow week and he'll win, that I guarantee you."

As the two men looked at the horse with interest, Hourigan turned to Kay: "Will you take him out and let these good men have a look at him?"

"Jesus Christ. That lad could stick his head into the halter and lead himself up and down the yard he's done it so bloody often," Kay muttered loud enough for everyone to hear.

But she played her part and Salmon played his. He was well behaved, walked and trotted well and the three visitors were impressed. Craig and McLarnon conversed briefly, McCloy offering encouragement.

"We'll buy him."

Over lunch in the nearby Woodlands Hotel the deal was worked out. With various incremental payments when the horse won his first point-to-point, his bumper, first hurdle race and his first chase, the price would eventually rise to over IR£30,000.

"By the way, what's his name?" they asked eventually. "Beef or Salmon," said Michael to the obvious amusement of the horse's new owners.

There wasn't sufficient time to register Dan and Joe as new owners when Beef or Salmon raced for the first time in a point-to-point race in Dungarvan eight days later, on January 28.

Hourigan was confident the horse would win. Fully recovered from the bout of ringworm and showing enthusiasm in schooling, Salmon was ridden by the talented amateur from Mallow in County Cork, Damien Murphy.

The ground was typically soft for the time of year but Beef or Salmon took to his first experience of competition with considerable relish.

Murphy was having a wonderful ride. His horse was jumping beautifully and running smoothly. They had almost completed the three miles and had successfully jumped fourteen fences before reaching the last.

Salmon was one of three horses in a line as they approached, alongside River Paradise and Euro Alert, with Beechbrook Gale on their tails. Inexperience on the part of the horses possibly played a part as there was a skirmish in the air.

Beef or Salmon was thrown sideways and, knocked off balance, fell on landing. River Paradise went on to win from Euro Alert.

A muddied but unhurt Murphy met his trainer at the side of the course. "He would definitely have won, his jumping was incredible," said the jockey who wouldn't normally be so effusive in his praise of a young horse.

But the fall was only a minor setback. Hourigan had been pleased with what he saw. It didn't confirm absolutely his belief in the horse but it was enough to ensure excitement about Salmon's future.

He had entered the horse in another point-to-point in Clonmel, on February 18, but couldn't find a jockey. Murphy was unavailable on that date and Hourigan couldn't find anyone else he wanted to put on the horse. With a few days to go, he heard that a promising amateur from Youghal, Davy Russell, was available. Russell, who went on to become one of the greatest jump jockeys to emerge from Ireland, was delighted to get the ride.

The race was held over a three-mile circuit on a track inside the regular racecourse at Clonmel. Again, the going was heavy but Beef or Salmon was comfortable. Russell rode him towards the front of the field of 16 runners and, with three of the 13 fences left, Beef or Salmon was one of four clear of the field. The other three – the quirkily named duo of Halla Halla and Doodle Addle, along with Bacardi Boy – fell at that fence.

Salmon was past the winning post before the two other horses remaining in the field, Karnico Bricanti and Ben's Luck, had jumped the second last fence. Six horses had been pulled up and seven had fallen.

Russell rode three other winners that day, including a horse named Much Birch which was also trained by Hourigan, but it was Salmon the jockey enthused about.

"He's easily the best jumper I've ridden so far," he reported to Hourigan.

Ironically, the freelance journalist reporting the event for the national media was not as impressed.

"The winner is no world beater," he penned.

Salmon's next outing would be his first official start under National Hunt rules. Horses purchased at the July 2000 sales at Goffs qualified for the Land Rover Bumper, a flat race run under National Hunt rules, at Fairyhouse on May 5. Salmon lined up against horses that had attracted a lot more interest and, in almost every case, more money than he had less than a year previously.

Hourigan had once again engaged Davy Russell to ride the horse. Run over two miles and good ground, it was not an ideal race but there was good prizemoney to be picked up.

Columba, which had cost IR£40,000 at Goffs the previous June, was sent off the 5/1 favourite ridden by Philip Fenton and trained by Dessie Hughes in the colours of Tom Winters. Other expensive purchases from Goffs in June 2000 that went to the starting post were Rupununi, sold for IR£30,000; Aughawillan which had cost IR£17,500 and Majella's Boy which had cost IR£17,000. Bar, trained by Tom Foley was a IR£16,500 purchase at Goffs. He would finish second in a race eventually won by Tuco, an IR£11,000 buy by Hourigan's former pupil David Wachman.

Russell nursed Salmon around the two miles and kept him well covered up in the big field of 30 runners. The pace was solid and it could have been an intimidating experience for these young horses. Salmon seemed comfortable and when Russell asked him to quicken he did so satisfactorily. They went for the line, together with Bar, and were just held off and collected IR£3,629.03 for third place.

The trainer was content. Over the years he had learned that patience was a special requirement when working with racehorses.

This one had promise but he needed to be nurtured. He was never going to be a summer horse, though Hourigan's son, Paul, felt that he could run on any ground. Salmon was released to the fields at the end of the month and spent his summer growing and gaining strength.

He'd be back in the autumn for a busy training schedule.

● ● ● ● ●

On November 25, Beef or Salmon ran in the Cahir Flat Race at Clonmel with Philip Fenton booked for the ride.

The confidence from the yard and the owners was reflected in the odds as he started at 6/4 favourite. Twelve horses ran and the instructions were clear – stay in touch and take control close to home.

Fenton and Beef or Salmon did just that. They took the lead around the final bend and ran away from the rest of the field. Cailin's Perk was second, fifteen lengths behind.

Salmon had shown impressive pace once Fenton asked him for an effort around the last bend.

He returned to action in Fairyhouse just a week later, on December 1, in another flat race. Philip Fenton had been booked to ride Kickham, a horse which had cost IR£35,000 at Tattersalls in 1999 and was running in the colours of JP McManus and trained by Eddie O'Grady, so Hourigan gave the ride to Richie Harding. They shared the favourite's tag with a horse from Noel Meade's yard, Woodys Deep Ocean.

In the end, though, it was Kickham and Beef or Salmon who fought out a captivating finish for the small Fairyhouse attendance. Kickham held on to win but only half a length separated them. It was a minor disappointment, the trainer reported to the owners: "We'll go jumping now."

Hourigan had been mulling over a St Stephen's Day competitive maiden hurdle in Limerick, the local track for Lisaleen. His form meant that Salmon would carry top weight of 12 stone but the trainer was happy that he could cope.

The horse, which would be ridden competitively for the first time by Paul Hourigan, would have familiar company in the race. The Hourigan-trained Court Clonagh would be ridden by Harding and the John Nallen bred and owned Minella Leisure would also run. But the expectation was that Beef or Salmon would win and he started as odds-on favourite at 8/11.

It seemed the gamble would pay off as Paul confidently brought Salmon through the field to lead after the third last hurdle. There were already cheers from the stand as he ran to the second last with the race at his mercy.

Suddenly, his front feet caught the top of the hurdle and he fell on landing. As the rest of the field raced by Salmon didn't move.

Regaining his feet, Paul rushed to the horse reaching him along with the racecourse attendants.

From their vantage point, Michael and Kay watched in horror as the protective screens were erected around the horse.

A groan rose from the crowd and time seemed to hang in the air as everyone waited for news of the horse.

Michael went onto the track but the longer he was gone, the longer the screens were up, the more the Lisaleen team and the crowd feared the worst.

Horses were getting ready for the next race, including two from Lisaleen, but staff were distracted by the uncertainty of what was happening on the track.

The stable had ten horses altogether racing in Limerick that day but the Lisaleen lads and lasses were unusually silent as they continued with their work, worry etched deep into their faces.

Suddenly, after an agonising wait, there was movement at the fence and Salmon was on his feet. He had only been winded.

The crowd roared and a huge wave of relief rolled all the way from Patrickswell to Adare.

Happy Christmas.

A very relieved Paul was uninjured and went on to provide the stable with a triumph later in the day by winning a chase on a horse named Joyful River, the 3/1 favourite.

Despite the fall confidence was now beginning to grow in the yard. It was clear from his work and from the racetrack that Salmon had potential.

Hourigan wanted to win another bumper with the horse so he entered him in Cork on January 5. This time, the only problem that the horse, his jockey (Philip Fenton again) and the trainer encountered was the thick fog which enveloped the course and made it impossible to see anything from the stand.

Salmon won by three lengths at odds of 8/11. Hourigan depended on the report from the jockey because he hadn't been able to see the race.

Not one to mince words, Fenton gave an upbeat synopsis: "He's very good."

At home Michael continued to school Salmon and he and Paul talked constantly about the horse's action. He was a natural jumper yet he seemed to run through hurdles rather than try to jump them.

"He's got such a big action he'll be much better over fences," Paul insisted.

But they wanted to win at least one hurdle race before they would tackle the bigger fences. The big Thyestes Chase meeting at Gowran at the end of January was the next target, a conditions hurdle at that meeting providing a good challenge.

Paul rode again. The horse mixed some competent hurdling with some clumsy jumping and attracted much scepticism.

"He's not fluent," observed some from the stands, before asking, "Will he get over fences?"

Still, he did enough that day to pass Boneyarrow, trained by Willie Mullins and ridden by Ruby Walsh, at the second last. The pair battled together over the last and gave the crowd in the stand a spectacle as they raced to the line, Salmon stretching to a three-length win at the post.

"He wasn't really enjoying the bad ground and didn't do a lot when we hit the front. He should be better on decent ground and should win again before the season ends," Paul told the assembled media.

Salmon's education continued at Leopardstown two weeks later in a Grade 2 hurdle at the big Hennessy meeting. This was a step up in class but Hourigan was convinced he hadn't seen the best of the horse as he trailed in in seventh place, well behind the winner, Like-A-Butterfly.

The next assignment was a novice hurdle in Limerick on St Patrick's Day where he led with three obstacles to be jumped but faded to finish fifth.

They went to the Curragh for the opening meeting of the flat season and Seamus Heffernan, a hugely respected figure in racing, rode the horse to a decent second behind Ned Kelly and ahead of Limestone Lad.

Heffernan provided an upbeat report and Hourigan decided to have an end of season run at the Punchestown Festival on April 27. David Casey was booked for the ride. Again, questions about his jumping were raised when the horse made a mistake at the third last. It broke all of his momentum and, while Casey gathered him together, there was little point on being hard on the horse now that his chance was gone.

He faded to finish with just one of the 22 runners behind him.

Beef or Salmon was not yet generating hot debate but he was a subject for discussion and judgement.

There was a consensus that there was a problem with his jumping. Hourigan and his son, Paul, were dismissive. They chatted with the owners and re-assured them.

"He'll be better over the bigger obstacles," they told them. Craig and McLarnon placed their faith with the trainer who told them: "I have a plan and it will surprise everyone."

Hourigan was ready to gamble. Despite repeated criticisms of Salmon's jumping, Hourigan had decided it was time for his novice hurdler to take on the challenge of the big steeplechase fences and he would do it in the company of some of Ireland's best, and most experienced, chasers.

CHAPTER 5

Plan B

Just a few of the more-experienced Irish racing journalists huddled together in the parade ring at Galway's Ballybrit Racecourse on a cold and wet October afternoon.

There was little glamour at this meeting, unlike the summer gathering when the entire course was packed to capacity and the skies above reverberated to the sounds of helicopters ferrying old and new money from nearby taverns to the centre of the action.

In the summer, the corporate tents would dispense as much alcohol as people could stomach – often more than some could stomach.

But this autumnal gathering was more business-like. There were few frills in terms of fairground attractions or best-dressed lady competitions. The dirty, grey clouds above failed to inspire the fair-weather journalists who prefer to pen wildly colourful articles about the rich and famous.

Today, there were no celebrities present. The conditions discouraged everyone, save those with a genuine interest in horses and racing, from making the trip to the track on the outskirts of the city.

Still, for those who did attend there were moments to savour. Even without the crowds and the aircraft, Ballybrit is a welcoming place for a day's racing.

Maybe because they race so rarely there – three festivals a year in August, September and October – the course retains a novelty factor.

The track, a sweeping right-hander with a dramatic dip before the finishing straight, and a demanding climb to the finish, is always a good test for a horse, whatever the age or Grade. It's also far easier for punters to get around, to mingle in the betting ring, on the perimeter of the parade ring or in the bars where staff are less hassled and have more time to serve satisfied customers.

Those journalists who had made the journey that October day were getting value for their efforts. Michael Hourigan was always available to have a word with the gentlemen, and sometimes ladies, of the media. He might be curt from time to time but he could also be colourful.

Today he was the centre of attention. As he walked into the parade ring following the completion of the 2.45pm flat race for amateur riders, the photographer, Pat Healy, joked: "You're bad for business today, no one wants a collection of photos of you."

Hourigan laughed: "It's alright, Pat, you can stick Laura in this one and I'll stay out of it. That will get printed."

Laura, his youngest daughter, had just ridden Beef or Salmon to a comprehensive win on his first run of the new season.

She had ridden a patient, mature race for someone so young, took the lead with a furlong to run and had eleven lengths to spare over a horse named Buffalo Bill, trained by Aidan O'Brien.

It was the third victory in a row on the card for Lisaleen, and Laura's ninth career win. Barry Geraghty had ridden Jolly Moonbeam and Old Kilminchy to win the previous two races, so it wasn't just the enjoyment of seeing Laura ride so well on Salmon that brought the broad smile to Hourigan's face.

He also knew that he would surprise the journalists today. He recognised some of the regulars: Pat Keane from the *Irish Examiner*; Damien McElroy from the *Irish Independent*; Peter O'Hehir and Dessie Scahill.

Keane and McElroy led the questioning. What were his plans now for Beef or Salmon?

"Lads, ye're going to think I've lost my marbles," he told them. "Ye're going to write headlines that Hourigan is gone stone mad. That horse is going chasing. He's entered for the Morris Oil."

They stared at him. This was madness alright. The Morris Oil Chase was a Grade 2 event for experienced chasers staged in Clonmel that had attracted some of the best horses in Ireland over the previous decade. Hourigan had won the race four times with Doran's Pride. Other outstanding winners included Moscow Express the year before and the Gold Cup winner, Imperial Call.

Now, here was Michael Hourigan entering a novice who had never tackled fences before and whose hurdling had been unconvincing on a number of occasions in his short career.

"Are you joking?" one journalist bravely asked.

"There's no joke about this fella," said the trainer, giving Salmon a pat before the horse was led away.

"He'll have a run at Leopardstown in a couple of weeks on the flat and I think he'll win that, too. Then it's all systems go for Clonmel."

It was a gamble, and Hourigan knew it. But it was a gamble he had been planning meticulously for some time. Since that first day he had watched the horse jump the fences beside his home under his son, Paul's, careful guidance, Hourigan believed he was looking at something special.

With a good stride he could stay in the air longer than any other horse in the yard, his nostrils flaring as he filled his lungs, ready to run strongly when he landed.

Of course he was young and totally inexperienced. There was an element of risk involved and Hourigan had taken that into account.

One of the reasons he chose the race at Clonmel was that it attracted good horses who knew how to jump, so it was unlikely they'd run into unforeseen problems.

Furthermore, it was a race that generally attracted no more than eight runners, so his novice would not be distracted by numbers or face any rough and tumble that might put him off.

As a novice competing against more experienced horses, Salmon would also run off the lightest weight, gaining as much as a stone over the more highly-rated horses. Every advantage had to be exploited.

News of his plans spread rapidly around Ballybrit.

The trainer was walking towards the weigh-room when he met the jockey, Paul Carberry.

"You've certainly got everybody talking now," said Carberry. "Are you really going for the Morris Oil?"

"I am. I'm just wondering if you're coming with me?" Hourigan queried in return.

"I can't commit yet but don't do anything until you've been in touch," advised Carberry.

"Well, you know better than anyone what he's capable of," concluded Hourigan. "I'm telling you, Paul. This is one not to miss out on."

Carberry departed deep in thought. Hourigan was right, the jockey did know what Beef or Salmon was capable of. Carberry had ridden a number of horses for Hourigan during the Listowel Racing festival in September and had agreed to make the short trip to Adare on a couple of mornings to ride out Salmon and another horse.

Like most top jockeys, Carberry was well used to tales of novices that owners and trainers were sure would be the next superstars of the jumping scene. It was the same in every sport; the world was full of the next George Best in soccer, the new Jack O'Shea in Gaelic football or DJ Carey in hurling.

More often than not, the potential was never realised – perhaps had never been there in the first place.

But Hourigan was not one to get carried away too easily and that had caught Carberry's attention when they spoke in Listowel.

The trainer had not been effusive; he merely suggested that the horse had promise and he would value Carberry's input. When Carberry first got up on the horse in Lisaleen he didn't notice anything special. But once he galloped, Carberry could feel the power. And, when he jumped! *Yes*, the jockey noted to himself, *this horse could be good*.

But there were other horses around that could be good, too, and Noel Meade, Carberry's boss, housed some of them.

Other trainers also sought the services of Carberry when he was free from commitments to Meade, so the jockey had a lot to think about. He spoke to his agent, Chris O'Toole, and they decided to monitor the situation.

Hourigan said he would be in touch and he was a man of his word. They would wait and watch.

Beef or Salmon travelled to Leopardstown in early November, 2002, for the valuable November Handicap. Hourigan didn't travel but the owners had made the journey south.

There was the usual large field for this race, 17 runners in all. It was the final day of the flat season in Ireland and most of the attention centred on the battle for the jockey's championship between Michael Kinane and Johnny Murtagh.

Hourigan would have been happy to have either of them available to ride Salmon but their services had already been retained. But he learned that the

English jockey, Franny Norton, had a number of rides at Leopardstown on the day and would be free to ride Salmon if required. The booking was made.

Beef or Salmon started at 4/1 favourite. Norton rode him in the middle of the field but found himself blocked in, coming into the straight.

The horses on his outside were slowing down but there were too many in the way and he couldn't get out in time. When a gap was eventually found they finished fastest of all the horses but could not haul in the two leaders, Bubble N Squeak and Queens Wharf, who got a short head verdict ahead of Salmon for second place.

Both of the horses that finished in front of him were 20/1 shots. It was scant consolation later that the winner was disqualified and Salmon was promoted to second place and the owners collected an extra IR£3,000 in prizemoney.

Hourigan had watched the race on one of the racing channels at home and received a report by phone.

"The jockey said he was the best horse in the race," the owners told him.

"Well if he was the best horse in the race why didn't he fucking win it?" snapped a disgruntled trainer.

A run over hurdles at Punchestown was scheduled to prepare Salmon for his chasing debut. That meeting had to be called off as the weather took a turn for the worse and the course was waterlogged, so the novice would start in the big time after just two runs on the flat that season.

The gallops at home were battered by the rain but Salmon was showing good form. He was fit and happy and the schooling was fun. The soft ground didn't seem to worry the horse and there was a buzz of anticipation around the yard. Salmon and Doran's Pride worked together, and that was a sight everyone enjoyed watching.

Riding arrangements for Clonmel still had to be finalised. Hourigan had been patient as he waited for the final declarations for the race.

As expected, the field was small and the inclement weather had not enticed some who might otherwise have chased the big prize. It was a quality field, however, and would be a huge challenge for the novice.

Frances Crowley had entered the winner from 2001, Moscow Express, as well as the very talented, Sackville, which had, at one time, been favourite for the 2002 Gold Cup, only to fall in that race. However, he had some impressive chase wins already on his form, including the Charlie Hall Chase at Weatherby in England a year before.

Cregg House, trained by the veteran Paddy Mullins, and Alcapone from the yard of Michael 'Mouse' Morris, had both been competing in graded company and completed the field of five. A small field was ideal. They were all good jumpers and that all fitted into Hourigan's plan for his young horse. Now he had to get his jockey.

As promised, Hourigan rang Chris O'Toole a couple of days before the race.

"Well, Chris, what are the plans for Paul?" he asked.

"I've just spoken to him," said O'Toole. "He'll have a slice of beef if it is still on the menu."

"Coming right up," said Hourigan.

The trainer was delighted. If anyone could nurse a young horse on his chasing debut against decent opposition on testing ground it was Carberry. They had an association over the years with Carberry regularly riding Hourigan's best horses, especially Doran's Pride whom Carberry had piloted to an Ericsson Chase triumph in 1998.

The bad weather had been unrelenting so conditions would be testing. On arrival in Clonmel on November 24 there was no initial concern about the ground. It had rained heavily all day Saturday, the day before the meeting, and the going was officially described as heavy.

Still, the weather did not deter racegoers who flocked into the racecourse. It was Clonmel's biggest attendance in almost a decade and though Beef or Salmon was a source of interest, all the pre-big race talk had centred on Alcapone and Sackville.

Apart from Salmon, Lisaleen sent out a big number of runners on the supporting card. The mare, Its Echoes Sister, ran in the first race at 12.45, and the contest was the first indication to everyone in Clonmel that the track had suffered considerably in the torrential rain of the previous 24 hours.

Rounding the final turn and entering the straight, the mare slipped on the greasy surface and threw Barry Geraghty out of the saddle, serving up a warning to the jockeys.

For his part, Carberry warmed up for the big race by riding Hourigan's Maverick Dancer in the second race and finished third. A mishap-free race was a good omen among the jockeys who weighted up the conditions. It wouldn't be wise to take any chances on the final bend where conditions were particularly poor.

Punters were finding it difficult to make their choices as the minutes ticked by to the 1.45 start of the Morris Oil race. There was some support among bookmakers for Salmon and, at one stage, he was 3/1 before drifting marginally to 7/2. Alcapone was sent off the 2/1 favourite, but there was no decisive move in the ring. The young Lisaleen horse was creating a stir but investors were focused on one statistic – Salmon's four opponents had won 48 races between them, and many of those were of very high quality.

Clonmel, one of Ireland's oldest racecourses, is a demanding track for even the most experienced jumpers. The one-and-a-quarter-mile circuit has severe undulations, a lung-bursting climb followed by a descent, with an uphill finish that can be very testing for tired mounts.

Beef or Salmon had run in a point-to-point race at the venue twenty-one months previously, but, this time around, the horses would be travelling at greater speeds and the fences would be tougher to jump.

From the start Carberry nursed Salmon, staying close but safe behind the other four. Alcapone and Moscow Express led them at a leisurely pace. Sackville looked most comfortable behind them, swapping third place with Cregg House. Carberry stalked them, all the time encouraging Salmon and building his confidence over the fourteen fences.

Jumping well, Salmon began to move through the small field at every fence. By the second-last the race was between the novice and Sackville.

Alcapone fell at that fence, leaving jockey Geraghty in the mud for the second time on the day. Sackville led coming to the last but Carberry was coasting on Salmon.

He led over the last fence with another fluid jump and put three lengths and a little bit more between themselves and Sackville by the finishing post.

A muddied Carberry arrived back in the winner's slot with a big smile on his face. In really tough conditions this youngster had coped very well. It was as good a debut over the bigger obstacles as Carberry had experienced in some time.

"You've got a real good one here," he reported to Hourigan.

Initial reaction was overshadowed by subsequent events at the meeting. After the fifth race of what was scheduled to be a seven-race card, a delegation of jockeys that included Carberry approached the stewards to express concerns about the deteriorating condition of the racecourse.

After an examination of the course, especially down the back straight and the final bend, it was decided that, in the interests of the safety of the horses and jockeys, the card would have to be abandoned.

Carberry explained the problem: "You would only be asking for trouble if we went back out there. The ground is badly churned up on the take-off side of the fences and it's the same going downhill to the straight."

In the *Irish Independent* the following day, Damien McElroy wrote: "In the circumstances the stewards were left with little option but to call a halt and it's a tribute to Michael Hourigan's Beef or Salmon that he made such a successful transition to the larger obstacles to claim the Morris Oil Chase."

Other views on Salmon's display were mixed. Some felt that if a novice could perform so efficiently and jump so well in wretched conditions, such as those experienced at Clonmel, then he would certainly improve with experience and on better ground. That was how the trainer and jockey certainly felt.

There were others, however, who were less favourable. Some pundits seemed more concerned with Sackville's performance than that of the winner. Flaws in the running and jumping of others were highlighted while Salmon's allowance of almost a stone was seen as of greater significance than the smooth manner in which he had completed the course.

It was the first small foretaste of what would come over the next six seasons.

But in the wake of Clonmel, Carberry, Hourigan and the owners of Salmon faced a different dilemma.

The trainer had mapped out a bold and ambitious plan. He had selected the Hilly Way Chase in Cork, a two-mile race, on December 15 as the ideal stepping stone to Salmon's next big challenge, a Group 1 race against the best chasers in Ireland, and possibly from abroad. That would be the Ericsson Chase at the famous Leopardstown Christmas meeting.

The dilemma centred on Carberry's availability to ride. Noel Meade had a number of top chasers in his yard, including the very talented Harbour Pilot, who would be entered in all the bigger chases in Ireland. Despite the jockey's enthusiasm for the horse, and the manner in which he had ridden him in Clonmel, Carberry could not commit to Hourigan and Beef or Salmon.

It was a problem the trainer had anticipated. As much as he admired Carberry, and despite how well the jockey got on with the horse, Hourigan wanted continuity. He needed a commitment so that horse and jockey could develop a relationship that would take them through an entire campaign. It might happen that Carberry would be available but the trainer did not want the uncertainty.

So, Hourigan initiated Plan B.

• • • • •

Timmy Murphy, the young Irish jockey who had just completed a prison term in England, had spent some time that month recovering from his ordeal by staying with the Hourigans at Lisaleen.

In gaining notoriety Murphy had lost none of the talent that Hourigan had first spotted some years before when Murphy was still in his teens. He had watched him riding out in recent weeks and knew that the touch was still there.

He sensed the hunger in Murphy.

Hourigan recognised the young man's need for a break, a chance to get back on life's treadmill and prove himself again.

"Lads," he addressed the owners, "I know and you know that Timmy Murphy is riding as well as ever. We all know what he's gone through but that's in the past. He would love a chance at the big time again. He gets on well with the horse and I think he deserves a chance."

Joe Craig and Dan McLarnon had been worried about the demands of such a big race on their young horse.

But they put their trust in the judgement of the trainer and they knew that the horse needed not just a talented jockey but one with plenty of experience of big races. They agreed with Hourigan's choice.

Timmy Murphy was on the way back to the big time.

CHAPTER 6

Big Arse, Ratty Little Head, and a Tail that Never Grew

The dark sands of San Pedro beach in Marbella were not quite deserted in mid-October 2002 but far less packed than at the height of the season.

The trees along the beach front swayed softly in the gentle breeze, providing an effective barrier to the sounds of the city. Temperatures reached 25 Celsius around noon and the blue waters were calm and inviting, a cooling refuge if the rays of the sun became too hot. Michael and Ann Hourigan relaxed happily in the tranquillity.

Marbella had become their escape from the hustle and bustle of home. With a flight time from Shannon Airport of just over two and a half hours it was the ideal destination for a short break. These little interludes in the sun allowed them to temporarily discard the stresses of running what had become a very large business. It was also a reward for the hard work of nearly thirty years.

Still, Ann knew her husband could not completely switch off. There were times when she wished that he would leave his mobile phone in the apartment, just for a few hours. But Michael insisted on having it with him just in case anything urgent came up back at the yard. The stables were in good hands, Kay was in charge while her father was away. Still, he liked to be updated on what was happening.

Kay usually rang late in the evening when the daily chores had been completed but, on this day, Michael had just emerged from a cooling dip in the sea shortly after noon when his phone rang. Kay's name appeared.

"Is there anything wrong?" he enquired.

"Nothing, don't worry," Kay calmed him. "There's something I wanted to ask."

Michael waited.

"You know Timmy is getting out in a few days," said Kay. "He'd like to come over and spend a bit of time with us. I said it was okay. Is that alright with you and mam?"

"Of course it is, we'll look after him," he replied instantly.

Timmy Murphy was a brilliant young jockey who had spent some of his late teenage years learning his trade in Lisaleen before departing for England where he became one of the most successful riders in National Hunt racing.

But his career had been publicly torn apart in that summer of 2002 when he was jailed for six months after being found guilty for being drunk on board an aeroplane and indecently assaulting a stewardess. Worse, his name was placed on the sex offenders' register for five years, a mistake which the sentencing judge admitted within a week, removing Murphy's name from the register.

Michael, Ann and the family had followed the case earlier that year with a mixture of both despair and worry.

Michael had been worried before the incident. He knew that Timmy was prone to bouts of heavy drinking and had heard stories about problems between Murphy and trainers in England over the jockey's booze habits and subsequent hangovers. That he was now in trouble because of alcohol was not entirely surprising.

They had been surprised, however, at the enormity of the scandal, the scale of the trouble and the media furore about it. The indecent assault angle lent a more sinister tone to the story. Timmy couldn't defend himself because he didn't remember anything that had happened. His friends, including the Hourigans, could believe the stories about the drinking – they had seen evidence with their own eyes in the past – but the other accusation? That wasn't the Timmy they knew.

The previous April they had been shocked when the jockey was arrested by police at Heathrow Airport following a flight from Tokyo to London. Murphy had been part of a sizeable group of jockeys, owners and trainers that had travelled to Japan for the Nakayama Grand Jump. The race, inaugurated in 1999, was one of two Grade 1 steeplechases run in Japan and one of the richest races in the world for National Hunt horses.

Murphy rode Cenkos, trained by Paul Nicholls, which had finished third in the Champion Chase in Cheltenham a month previously. They finished fifth, the highest placed European horse and a satisfactory result in the midst of an alcohol binge that would become notorious.

The jockey had started drinking heavily on the flight to Tokyo but had recovered sufficiently, under strict orders from Nicholls, to ride in the race.

But the drinking restarted almost immediately afterwards and didn't stop. Flying first-class, Murphy consumed huge amounts of vodka and orange. Even without the exaggerated effects cabin pressure tends to have on passengers imbibing alcohol, Murphy was entering a state of oblivion.

Others tried to curb his excesses but the jockey was too far gone. He tried to get access to the cockpit, thinking it was the toilet, finally urinating in his seat and on the fuselage.

Murphy had no recollection of any of this when arrested at Heathrow. The first hint that there might be a problem was when he saw the armed police waiting at the aircraft door.

"What are they doing here?" he asked no one in particular.

"I think they are here for you," someone close replied.

His shame was multiplied when he was told he had grabbed the leg of a stewardess and put his hand up her skirt.

When brought before Judge John Crocker at Isleworth Crown Court on July 23, Murphy pleaded guilty to both charges despite having no recollection of the flight or the incidents. Close friends from racing provided character witness statements on his behalf at the hearing but Judge Crocker was unimpressed. Timmy Murphy was sentenced to six months in prison and certified a category B prisoner under the English judicial system. Officially, category B prisoners are stated to be 'adult male prisoners (over 21) who are a risk to the public but do not need the highest level of security and the aim is to make escape very difficult'.

Without the indecent assault element to the charges he may have qualified as a category D prisoner, low risk and unlikely to escape. As such, he would have qualified to serve his sentence in an open prison, which would have allowed him some freedom of movement, possibly his own cell with his own keys and the opportunity to serve some of his sentence working within the community.

But Murphy would qualify for none of that as a category B offender. Instead he was sent to the infamous Wormwood Scrubs where the inmates had already read about the celebrity jockey who had been convicted and placed on the sex offenders' register.

The young Irishman had heard of the prison, which has featured in TV programmes, both fiction and non-fiction. Originally built as a prison in the late 1800s, some things hadn't changed much since that time, or so it seemed. The Scrubs housed more than 1,000 prisoners. During the worst of the Troubles in Northern Ireland, in the 1970s and 1980s, a section of the prison was reserved for IRA prisoners.

The Scrubs was as bleak, dark and forbidding as could possibly be imagined, and Murphy was traumatised by the sudden and ferocious change in his life.

Even the news, after a short period, that his name had been removed from the register of sexual offenders did not lighten his mood.

The fact he was no longer on the sexual offenders' register did mean he was no longer a target for violent retribution from fellow prisoners, but it didn't qualify him for a move from the Scrubs, and that was all that really mattered.

What did help his mood were the messages of support he received from family and friends in England and Ireland. Post was distributed to the prisoners following dinner and it became the highlight of the day for Murphy. The encouragement he received lifted his spirits and gave him a new sense of belief that he would have a future when he completed his sentence.

Early on in the sentence he received a letter from Ireland. He recognised the handwriting as Kay's.

She hadn't told anyone at home she was writing, she just felt she had to. She knew Timmy as well as anyone, and better than most. They had been very close once; she was Timmy's first girlfriend and she had looked after him during his early days in England when he needed to be looked after. Here she was again, providing an emotional crutch when it was most needed.

They exchanged letters and Murphy began to reminisce on the time he had spent in the Hourigan household just seven years ago. Those had been some of the happiest times of his life. The Hourigan family had made him so welcome and Michael had nurtured him in a way no one else could have. He had enormous respect for Mike, as he called him.

Even so, he and the Hourigan's had lost touch. Murphy was too busy building his career in England. They would meet from time to time when Hourigan had runners in England. The trainer was one of the first to congratulate Murphy when he rode the 20/1 outsider, Terao, to an unlikely victory at the Cheltenham festival in 1997.

By that stage, Murphy already had a reputation as a wild character. He had fallen out with the trainer, Kim Bailey, and the trade newspapers had not been kind. But Murphy's talent kept shining through. It caught the attention of the young trainer, Paul Nicholls, who began to use Murphy as a freelance before offering him a job.

Murphy got the rides he wanted. He rode the likes of Call Equiname, Cornish Rebel, Earthmover and See More Business. He was riding in the big races and winning a decent proportion of them. He was beginning to make good money and he clearly knew how to have a good time.

But it was his partying that led him into his darkest hours.

As he lay on his bunk in the Scrubs, Murphy wondered if he could go back to Limerick on his release. In her last letter Kay had written: "If you need anything when you are released you know where we are."

He knew he would be comfortable in Lisaleen, it would be the ideal place to recover from his ordeal. He felt comfortable with the Hourigan family and would be protected in the yard.

The media frenzy during his trial had been frightening in its intensity. He had never experienced anything like it before and he knew there would be pressure on him if he tried to resurrect his career on being released. Still, the press would not be likely to find him at Lisaleen and, even if they did, they wouldn't be able to get near him.

In a phone call to his agent, Chris Broad, he outlined his hopes and Broad promised to speak to Kay. As expected, she was enthusiastic and true to her word and, when Mike and Ann gave their blessing, all the arrangements were made.

There was some other good news. Murphy's original sixth-month sentence was halved and the jockey walked free from prison, early on October 22, after 84 days behind bars. He spent a few days with his partner, Dawn, and son, Shane, then flew to Shannon where Ann Hourigan greeted him warmly.

"He looks gaunt and grey," she remarked quietly to her husband. "We'll need to get him right."

But the road back to full health would take time.

A routine was built up: Murphy rode out in the mornings and then returned to the lovely house the Hourigans had built at the top of the hill since the last time he had been here. He would sit in his bedroom or the living room at the front of the house that overlooked the stables and sleep for hours.

Ann ensured he remained undisturbed. When he awoke she fed him good, nutritious food, all the time monitoring his weight and pallor. Both improved by the day. Lisaleen and the Hourigans provided warmth and comfort. It was precisely what Timmy Murphy needed.

He felt at home.

It had been home at one time. Murphy had been working on the Curragh in 1993 with the trainer, Michael Halford. It was an enjoyable time for the aspiring young jockey but Halford trained more horses for the flat than for the jumps and opportunities were limited. Halford recognised the budding talent in young Murphy. He also noticed the youngster liked a good time, a habit that would have to be curtailed if he was to make the most of his natural ability. He knew there was one place where both opportunity and discipline would be in plentiful supply. Halford phoned Michael Hourigan and suggested he take on the youngster. The two men worked out a plan and then informed young Murphy of his fate.

The work in Lisaleen was hard, but the boss was harder. There were few comforts, and accommodation was basic. The only thing there was plenty of was work. Murphy later admitted that Hourigan initially scared him but, gradually, he developed a bond with the trainer. Hourigan liked the way Murphy responded to challenges and to how the boy also loved schooling horses.

Still, the new boss didn't dispense favours easily and never seemed to favour one of his workers over the others. Only at home in the privacy of the kitchen would Hourigan comment on the workers, and then when only Ann was listening. She shared his views: This youngster was good. He wasn't a great communicator and that caused difficulties at times. He was a quiet lad and didn't always meet the boss's exacting standards when it came to hard work, but he loved riding and he loved horses.

Murphy had also shown determination already in his young life. He had started out at Rosewell House on the Curragh, now run by Dermot Weld, the same stable where Hourigan himself had begun his career as a 14-year-old with Weld's father, and had come with a good reference from the Halford yard.

Ann was also aware of the growing friendship between the young Murphy and her daughter, Kay. The pair tried to hide their relationship from the boss and his wife but, typically, mothers could spot these things. In fact, the father wasn't fooled either, though he declined to interfere or comment.

Murphy worked hard at schooling horses, which was a priority at Lisaleen, and when he got his chance on the point-to-point circuit Murphy also satisfied the demands of his boss.

On March 20, 1994 at a circuit near Watergrasshill in Cork, Murphy rode his first point-to-point race for his boss. Murphy and his mount, For Kevin, won. He then picked up another ride when his colleague Robbie Byrnes was injured in a fall. Murphy rode Screen Printer and won.

Two rides, two wins. The stuff of dreams for a youngster.

After that, the rides kept coming and so did the winners. Even when Murphy and the new travelling head lad at Lisaleen, David Wachman, had a disagreement and Murphy left the yard, the point-to-point rides from the stable continued to come Murphy's way. He was still an amateur and good amateurs were hard to find.

The more winners Murphy rode for Hourigan and a growing list of other trainers, the more notice the jockey attracted. As Hourigan expected, the lure of England with a greater number of race meetings – meaning more opportunities for young jockeys and better prizemoney at the time – caught up with his latest prodigy and, in 1995, Timmy Murphy, like many others before him, left Lisaleen to carve out a future abroad.

The pair did not speak much in the intervening years. Hourigan did take note of Murphy's progress, especially when he moved to ride for Nicholls, who was beginning to make a name for himself as he set about building up one of the most successful training establishments in Britain.

But, inevitably, their paths would cross at the bigger race meets. In the Cheltenham Gold Cup in 1998, Doran's Pride was the 9/4 favourite while

Murphy rode See More Business for Nicholls. Hourigan enjoyed a third-place finish with his horse but Murphy had suffered the ignominy of being 'carried out' at the seventh fence when some horses in the field veered quite dramatically to the right. He was travelling on the outside and was forced too wide, unable to steer the horse back to jump the fence.

It was a setback from which Murphy recovered and his reputation as one of the best race riders around grew with each passing season.

His reputation as one of the big drinkers on the circuit also became legendary. He wasn't alone but he was the one riding the better horses and that meant that the gossip spread more easily.

Michael Hourigan didn't like gossip. He always believed in giving people a chance, even a second chance. So he decided to give Timmy Murphy a second chance that autumn of 2002.

Murphy needed time to recover emotionally and physically from his ordeal, to deal with what he had done and to continue his recovery from alcohol addiction. He needed protection.

In Lisaleen he got all of that. Despite being tormented by what had happened, Timmy still didn't feel like talking about it. That was difficult but the Hourigans insisted he be given time. The silences were not easy, but the pair were patient.

Each evening, Michael would drive to the nearby Woodlands Hotel, owned by family friends, the Fitzgeralds, for a swim in the hotel pool and a sauna afterwards. It was his way of winding down after a tough day at the stables. Murphy joined him each evening and began to chat. It was slow and hesitant at first but Michael gave him time and space.

At mealtimes back at the house Murphy became more talkative. Ann was a good listener as well. His mind began to heal, so, too, his heart.

And, as that healing process progressed, Murphy became more comfortable expressing his feelings to these friends who were non-judgemental. They showed him trust and he, in turn, began to trust again. There were others providing support as well and Murphy began to believe, once again, he might have a real future in racing.

As Hourigan and Murphy wallowed in the sauna at the Woodlands one evening, Murphy began to talk about racing and what the future might hold.

"What do you want to do with your life?" Hourigan asked bluntly.

"I'm not sure I know the answer to that, Mike," said Murphy, "but I'll tell you what I do not want to do. I don't want to go back to travelling up and down the motorways of England searching for rides on horses that can't win."

"Well, then," said Hourigan. "I think I might have just the horse for you. I'll see if I can get you the ride on Beef or Salmon."

Hourigan had already spoken to the owners, Craig and McLarnon, about the future of the horse and who would ride him when he switched to chasing.

If Paul Carberry had been available all the time the matter might not have arisen. But Carberry was stable jockey to Noel Meade and would have to ride a Meade horse if entered in the same races as Beef or Salmon. Given the quality of horses in Meade's yard that was a distinct possibility.

Timmy Murphy had ridden Beef or Salmon a few times during morning work since arriving back in Ireland and wasn't overly impressed.

In his autobiography, 'Riding the Storm', Murphy provided a graphic illustration of what he felt about the horse at the time.

"He was pretty ugly, to be fair to him. He had a big arse on him, a ratty little head and a tail that never grew, and he was always miserable in his box," said Murphy of Beef or Salmon.

Murphy was, like everyone else, unimpressed by Salmon's breeding. He did not recognise the stallion, Cajetano, despite the fact the pair had a connection. Just two years earlier, Murphy had had a short association with a horse trained by Mark Pitman (another trainer who would later prove to be one of Murphy's best supporters in his post-prison career). That horse was Dark Crusader, the horse bred from Cajetano by James Maguire in Wexford in 1995. Murphy rode the horse in six races and picked up two wins in lowly novice hurdles at Towcester and Folkestone racecourses in November and December 2000. They were also placed at Towcester and Wincanton.

Murphy had clearly forgotten that horse. But, on his long road to redemption, he would not easily forget this next son of Cajetano.

CHAPTER 7

Not for Sale at Any Price

Michael Hourigan was late, but that wasn't entirely unusual.

When you run a stable of ninety racehorses there are a myriad potential distractions that will wreak havoc with the most meticulously compiled timetable.

He sometimes half-joked that the job of training racehorses would be much more efficiently done if the trainer did not have to spend so much time travelling to and from racecourses.

He hoped there were no speed traps on the roads between Adare and Mallow on this late morning of December 15 as he made his way to Cork racecourse.

He avoided the temptation to glance at the speedometer's needle and was glad that he was travelling alone – if Ann had been beside him he would have had to slow down. The plan had been to leave Lisaleen much earlier but he'd had paperwork to complete, entries to consider for many of the horses that would be running over the Christmas period and he had lost track of time.

On the outskirts of the small and pretty town of Buttevant in north Cork he forced himself to slow down. He eased his foot off the accelerator and even touched the brake.

"No point in getting stopped now when I'm nearly there," he muttered to himself as he checked the time again. He would miss the first couple of races but would at least arrive in time for the feature race of the day, at 1.50pm.

Normally he might have considered the historical context of his surroundings. Hourigan loved the history of horse racing, and this was sacred turf. Buttevant had witnessed the first-ever recorded steeplechase, in the 18th century. Hourigan knew the story well and often thought about the lives and times of the pioneers of the sport in which he had made his life.

The term steeplechase had come from this place. In 1752, at the end of a day of fox hunting, two businessmen from North Cork, Edmund Burke (referred to as David in some historical accounts) and Cornelius O'Callaghan, became engaged in a heated discussion over which of them owned the best horse.

To resolve the debate they organised a race between the horses with the steeple at St John's Church in Buttevant as the starting point and the steeple of St Mary's Church in Doneraile, four and a half miles away, as the finishing point.

The steeples were chosen because they were the most prominent landmarks and the riders could see the steeples and steer their horses towards them. They raced cross-country, jumping walls and other obstacles along the way with a cask of wine awaiting the first to reach St Mary's. Some records show that the Burke horse was declared the winner.

Steeplechasing became a pastime, then a popular sport and, subsequently, a major business and this area had produced many champions, both horses and jockeys. If he'd had the time that morning, Hourigan might have allowed himself to think about the possibility of another champion in the making who would be racing very shortly in nearby Mallow, his destination.

His son, Paul, had led the team from Lisaleen much earlier that day for the short thirty-mile trip south. Four horses had travelled and Paul was to ride Carramore Lass in the first race and Dromhale Lady in the second. Joe Casey had the ride on Errors Holm in that second race. Paul would then help prepare Beef or Salmon for his next big target on the racecourse, the Hilly Way Chase, one of the biggest events of the year at Cork racecourse. Timmy Murphy was riding Salmon for the first time in a race and would meet them at the course.

Murphy had been dividing his time between Ireland and England and was aware of the programme that had been laid out for Salmon.

He'd been delighted to get the call a week earlier confirming what Michael had promised in the sauna at the Woodland's Hotel.

The reports from the yard following the race in Clonmel were very positive. Salmon was buzzing, fresh and ready for his next race. Murphy was, however, a little puzzled about the choice of race since the Cork race was to be run over just two miles, a little short for a horse heading for Group 1 races that would take place over three miles. Knowing Hourigan as he did, he knew there had to be a purpose.

The return to Cork was an emotional one for the jockey. Though he'd been born in Kildare, his father and mother were both natives of north Cork. His father, Jimmy, grew up in Watergrasshill and his mother, Helen, came from Canteen Cross, outside the village of Shanballymore, near Doneraile. Many of those who attended the December 15 meeting were acquainted with the family. Murphy received a rousing welcome when he arrived at the track, another reminder that the racing family was on his side.

Apart from Salmon, Timmy had a number of other rides that day. The meeting did not start auspiciously for him. Satcoslam fell in the second race, but his fortunes quickly improved when he rode a winner, Satco Express, in the third race. It was then time for his first racecourse experience on Beef or Salmon.

He met a slightly flustered trainer just outside the jockey's room.

"I thought I wasn't going to make it," said a breathless Hourigan.

The other horses from the yard had not featured in the opening races. Carramore Lass had finished second last, while Dromhale Lady was an inauspicious fifth in a race Errors Holm failed to finish.

The focus was now solely on Salmon. They talked through the race and the possibilities.

"He's jumping for fun, he's got plenty of pace, mind him," was as much as the trainer would say.

Eight horses lined up for the race in which Beef or Salmon went off at odds of 2/1, second favourite. Fadoudal du Cochet, trained by Arthur Moore and ridden by Conor O'Dwyer, was the 15/8 favourite. He'd won the Grand Annual Chase at Cheltenham in March and was having his second outing of the season. Mick Fitzgerald was back in Ireland to ride Copernicus for Pat Hughes.

Murphy kept Salmon to the rear of the field in a race that was largely uneventful until they approached the final three fences.

Rathbawn Prince fell at the third last but did not distract Salmon. Murphy decided to see just what this horse possessed and looked for a big effort. Salmon not only jumped well but he gave Murphy a pleasant surprise with the speed he displayed as he took the lead at the last fence.

He didn't land absolutely right but the horse picked up instantly and strode away from the outsider River Clodagh and the favourite Fadoudal du Cochet.

"Mike, this guy is even better than you said," a delighted Murphy told the trainer. "His jumping was as good as you said but I didn't realise he had such speed. He's really good."

It was a sentiment expressed by the least sentimental people in racing – the bookmakers. Their reaction was a major contribution to the hype about to unfold. Within days Beef or Salmon appeared in preliminary betting for the 2003 Cheltenham Gold Cup with odds of 25/1.

"Daft," scoffed the sceptics. "A novice can't win the Gold Cup."

Back at home Hourigan had lots to ponder as the coming Christmas period provided many options. There were a number of big races at the Leopardstown festival or he could choose to take a less strenuous route into the New Year.

That would be a careful option but it might not tell him everything he wanted to know about the horse. It might also deprive the owners of substantial prizemoney. And it might deprive the horse of the chance to show that he was as good as Hourigan believed him to be on the biggest stage.

The local Limerick track provided the main alternative to Leopardstown during the festive period and Hourigan always had a lot of entries there.

The Guinness Novice Chase on December 26, St Stephen's Day, was a possibility for Salmon. It was a Grade 2 event with a winning purse of almost IR£20,000. He also studied the novice chase at Leopardstown on the same day, The Denny's Gold Medal. With a purse worth almost IR£40,000 it was an attractive race. All the really good novices would be entered, including some from England.

But foremost in his mind was the Grade 1 option, the big Ericsson Chase, on December 28. He had won this race before with Deep Bramble and Doran's Pride, though both had considerably more experience than Salmon when they raced in it. It was the race that attracted the best chasers from England and Ireland. It was asking a lot of a novice to run in the race but Hourigan was convinced the horse was ready.

He chatted to the owners and they had some surprising news.

"We've had an offer for the horse," Hourigan heard.

"How much?" he wondered.

"Six figures, sterling." The precise figure would later be confirmed as Stg£400,000.

This was one of those occasions when a trainer did not interfere. There was too much at stake for the owners. They had already invested heavily in the horse and they were good owners, so he wanted them to benefit from their investment. If they did sell he would hope to keep the horse, though if the new owners were English they would more than likely move the horse across the Irish Sea.

"We're not selling," they told Hourigan. "And you can tell anyone else who enquires that Beef or Salmon is not for sale at any price."

The curt refusal of the Northern owners to contemplate selling the horse had an impact on Hourigan. These were owners who deserved success.

The winner's purse for the Ericsson Chase was just under IR£60,000 and Hourigan decided to leave the horse's entry in the other races. He'd wait to see what ground conditions were like and what other entries remained for all three races. But, in his own mind, he was content that the Ericsson was the route to travel.

Weather conditions were a concern for owners and trainers all over Ireland at the end of 2002. As Christmas week began, the manager at Leopardstown, Tom Burke, reported that twelve millimetres of rain had fallen on Saturday, December 21. The forecast was for dry weather on Christmas Day and the next, but with rain following.

The news was greeted with dismay in England. Paul Nicholls decided not to send his strong team to Ireland after all and entries began to fall.

But one big name remained in the Ericsson – First Gold would travel from France. The quality of the race was further assured with the return of two previous winners, Rince Ri and Foxchapel King. As expected, Noel Meade left the very talented Harbour Pilot in the race, with Paul Carberry onboard.

Lisaleen stables were a hive of activity; there was no time for Christmas hangovers with more than a dozen horses racing over the period.

On December 26, all focus was on the local track beside Patrickswell, just a couple of miles up the road. The Hourigan operation celebrated a trio of winners on the day, Oliverjohn, King Carew and Dromhale Lady all coming home in front. The big chase, which Hourigan had decided to bypass in favour for a run at Leopardstown, was won by Le Coudray, owned by wealthy Limerick man, JP McManus, and trained by Christy Roche, the only man to ever partner Salmon's dam, Farinella, on a racecourse.

Two days later, the team was split up. Michael led the smaller team of three horses to Dublin for the Leopardstown meeting on December 28, Beef or Salmon being joined by Hi Cloy and Mr Sneaky Boo.

Six other horses were entered on the Limerick card for the same day and a number of them were well fancied, including Laura's mount in the ladies' race, Maverick Dancer.

The skies were clear, the sun was shining and temperatures were bearable at the Dublin track when Hourigan met Timmy Murphy early in the morning.

Murphy had been riding well in England and finished second in the King George VI Chase two days earlier on Marlborough, trained by Nicky Henderson. He had also ridden for trainers such as Henrietta Knight and his old boss, Paul Nicholls. His comeback, inspired in so many ways by the Hourigan family, was almost complete.

He was booked to ride Hi Cloy in the first race at Leopardstown at 12.25. He won at odds of 12/1, beating Rosenca ridden by Paul Carberry.

It was a good start to the day and Murphy was confident. The ground was soft but shouldn't prove to be a hindrance to Salmon's chances, he decided.

Hourigan's phone rang half an hour later. It was Laura, informing him that Jolly Moonbeam had won the first race in Limerick.

"Let me know how the others do," Michael told her.

He relaxed by watching races in which he was not involved and was happy to see Murphy get a clear round to win on Be My Belle in the second race.

Limestone Lad was running in the Stayers' Hurdle and Hourigan enjoyed watching this extraordinary racehorse win his 29th hurdle race.

Hourigan was content as he headed to the saddling enclosure, through the enormous crowds that packed the area behind the stands and in front of the parade ring, to put the saddle on Salmon. Friends from Adare and Patrickswell had gathered at the enclosure to watch the pre-race proceedings and to wish the team well.

Many were seeing Salmon for the first time. Standing at more than 16 hands (about 5 feet and 7 inches), he was a big, well-muscled horse. He looked strong and powerful. The most knowledgeable pointed to his tail, a straggly thing, not the full skirt that you would expect to find on a good racehorse. It didn't seem to make much difference to Salmon.

Hourigan was greeted by JP McManus, who owned First Gold. The horse had travelled uneventfully from France where he was trained by the former jockey, Francois Doumen, at his stables in Chantilly. Just two years previously they had won the King George VI Chase at Kempton. Results since had not been as impressive but a third place finish just two weeks before in the John Durkan Memorial Chase at Punchestown and the owner's celebrated capacity for gambling meant that First Gold would start as favourite in the Ericsson.

The others runners were Rince Ri, winner of the race in 1999 and 2000, trained by Ted Walsh and ridden by his son, Ruby; Foxchapel King, who won this race for trainer 'Mouse' Morris the year before and would be ridden by David Casey. Harbour Pilot was there too, fresh from a creditable second place at the Hennessy Cognac Gold Cup Chase in Newbury, trained by Noel Meade and ridden by Paul Carberry. The Francis Crowley-trained Sackville, third to Salmon in Clonmel, would be ridden this time by Barry Geraghty while trainer, Dessie Hughes, had secured the services of jockey Norman Williamson for the 20/1 outsider, Colonel Braxton.

They were all older, more experienced horses, who had competed in the highest quality races.

In the parade ring, however, Salmon looked well. His athleticism now was plain for all to see. He had blossomed in the two years at Lisaleen and, while there might have been one or two better looking horses in the ring, Salmon was their equal as a physical specimen.

With a brace of winners already notched up that day the jockey also felt confident. He knew his job, there was a race to be won.

But there was also a lesson the horse needed to learn. The pace would not be scorching because of ground conditions, but he would have to jump well and stay in touch with the rest. By the end of the three miles Murphy wanted to see if his horse had the pace that his run in Cork had suggested.

From the start of the race Murphy kept Salmon at the back of the field. He ran wide, ensuring that the horse had a clear view of the obstacles, not worried that he was adding yards to the distance to be travelled.

Foxchapel King set off in front, with Colonel Braxton close at all times. Harbour Pilot, Sackville and Rince Ri were bunched together. First Gold stayed just ahead of Salmon. Timmy Murphy was enjoying this ride.

Coming to the third last of the seventeen fences he began to make his move and, as he passed both First Gold and Rince Ri, the jockey could see that their challenge was over.

As he jumped fluidly over the second last, Salmon moved smoothly into second place behind Colonel Braxton. Murphy could already hear the roar of the crowd and he knew it had to be his horse that was creating the excitement. Just a few lengths separated the first five but there was no doubt as to which was moving best.

As they neared the final fence Murphy knew that one clear jump would win the race. He let Salmon do his own work. The horse flew through the air, the take-off as precise as the landing.

Despite the distance travelled and the testing ground, Salmon quickened on the run to the finish. Murphy took a quick look around. Some really smart chasers were struggling and his six-year-old was having the time of his life.

Crossing the finishing line, Murphy allowed himself a thoughtful smile: *Mike was right again.*

The excitement in the parade ring as the horses arrived back was palpable, and the demeanour of Beef or Salmon added to the mood.

He had just run three miles on heavy ground, jumped seventeen fences and sprinted the last three furlongs, but he still looked fresh. He'd handled the pre-race routine very well and now seemed unconcerned by the volume of people and noise. For a six-year-old the display in the winners' enclosure was as mature and impressive as his performance on the track.

Murphy did not need to say much to the trainers and the delighted owners. "He was as good as you said he could be," the jockey remarked to Hourigan.

Before commenting publicly the trainer spoke briefly with Craig and McLarnon. He had thought about reverting to a novice chase but this performance had confirmed to him that Salmon was good enough to go for the bigger prizes. The Hennessy Cognac Gold Cup at Leopardstown in early February was the obvious target. It was a highly prestigious race and it would also serve as the ideal preparation for a crack at the Cheltenham Gold Cup.

The owners might previously have had reservations about such a lofty challenge but what they had just seen was convincing. Once again, they would trust the judgement of the trainer.

Racegoers, journalists, owners and trainers all wondered just how good this novice could be. Comparisons with Doran's Pride were inevitable.

"How do they compare?" one journalist asked.

"That's not an easy one to answer," said a delighted Hourigan, "but he's going the right way. They are two tough horses but Doran's Pride could let you down with his jumping. This lad is a brilliant jumper."

Outlining the plan for the remainder of the season, Hourigan was direct: "We'll come back here for the Hennessy and we will definitely have an entry for the Gold Cup."

As soon as he mentioned Cheltenham there was a reaction from a variety of bookmaking firms. The six-year-old novice was now a 12/1 chance for the Gold Cup.

The Lisaleen team were packing for home when news from Limerick filtered through. They had won the Ladies' Race in Limerick but not with the 5/4 favourite Maverick Dancer, ridden by Laura. They had lost out by the narrowest distance to stablemate, Its Echoes Sister, a 16/1 chance.

Salmon travelled home a contented horse. The trainer could not have been happier. The yard was buzzing: the Hourigans had a lot of horses running, plenty of them winning or being placed, and there were many more to race over the coming weeks.

The schedule was hectic and though weather conditions didn't make life easy, the mood was as close to euphoric as you can get in a busy stableyard.

It helped that the old boy was back.

Doran's Pride, the star chaser of the 1990s who had propelled this stable to international prominence, was in training again.

Beef or Salmon was the new star but Doran's Pride was everyone's favourite. He hadn't enjoyed a retirement, which translated into boredom. And, to top it all, he had a new friend, Salmon, with whom he could train and race.

The weeks of the new year of 2003 flew past. The team was back in Leopardstown on January 12, when Hi Cloy won a good hurdle race. Timmy Murphy was flying over and back from England where he was picking up a number of good rides, including Thisthatandtother, which won for Paul Nicholls in Wincanton on January 18.

The following day, Doran's Pride ran for the first time since coming out of retirement, a point-to-point race in Kilfeacle, which he won impressively on soft ground. He followed up with wins in Nenagh and Carrigtwohill and was becoming a possible runner for Cheltenham.

Hourigan began to finalise his team for Leopardstown on February 9. Salmon was thriving at work and in great form for the Hennessy Cognac Gold Cup. Hi Cloy was entered for a Grade One Novice Hurdle, Doran's Pride would run in a Hunter's Chase and Jolly Moonbeam and Minella Leisure would complete the travelling party. Doran's Pride had won the Hennessy when in his prime and it was a race that had produced two Cheltenham Gold Cup winners in the past, Jodami and Imperial Call.

The list of previous winners was a veritable Steeplechasing Hall of Fame that included, Forgive and Forget, Carvill's Hill, Nick The Brief, Danoli and Florida Pearl. Florida Pearl was entered again for the 2003 race where Salmon would once more face Colonel Braxton, Harbour Pilot and Rince Ri. It was a small, but elite field of outstanding chasers.

If the trainer had any doubts about the level of interest being generated in his horse they were quickly dispelled when he picked up his copy of the Racing Post on Saturday morning. The front page was devoted to a photograph of Beef or Salmon jumping the last fence at Leopardstown in December under the headline: "Is he The One?"

Timmy Murphy was booked to ride four of the five Hourigan horses on February 9, the exception being Doran's Pride, who would be ridden by Richie Harding.

The afternoon began satisfactorily when Hi Cloy ran well to finish fourth, behind the talented Solerina, but there were a couple of nasty surprises in store for the jockey when he fell from both Minella Leisure and Jolly Moonbeam in the next two races.

"Let's hope you can stay in the saddle for the next one," said a grim-faced trainer as Murphy arrived back, a little sore but unhurt, at the entrance to the jockeys' room.

The big race was scheduled for 3.40pm. Although only five horses contested, the race had captured the imagination of the public. The media had begun to whip up interest in Ireland's newest chasing sensation and more than 16,000 people packed into Leopardstown to see for themselves what was generating the excitement. They would not be disappointed.

Once again Murphy kept Salmon at the rear of the field, a little wide to give him all the room he needed.

Ruby Walsh adopted similar tactics on Rince Ri, leaving Colonel Braxton, this rime ridden by Normal Williamson, Harbour Pilot and Florida Pearl to share the lead. The pace was good on the yielding-to-soft ground and the crowd began to display their excitement when Salmon began to make his move through the field as they went down the back straight for the second time. He sliced through the field, jumping fluently.

Murphy didn't let him loose, keeping him at a steady pace and biding his time. Florida Pearl weakened quickly before the third last fence and was out of contention while the other three were beginning to show signs of stress.

Salmon was flowing. He seemed to breeze past the field, taking the lead at the last and easily pulling away from Colonel Braxton, again showing the same turn of speed that had been so impressive at Christmas. This time the distance between first and second was just four lengths but the winner was cruising.

There was also a new sound at the racecourse that afternoon which some people referred to as the 'Beef or Salmon roar'.

It was clear now that Irish racing fans had a new hero and that the 'Beef or Salmon roar' would be repeated often at the track in the coming years.

"We must not forget he is only seven years old and is still really only a novice," warned Hourigan amidst the pandemonium that greeted the latest success. "But there is no way we can stay away from Cheltenham now."

The bookmakers again reflected the mood. The novice, with just three chases run in his short career, was now just a 10/1 chance for the Cheltenham Gold Cup.

CHAPTER 8

This Game Would Tame Lions

The office telephone began to ring early on Monday morning, February 10 and, over the next four hours, the calls came incessantly. Everyone, it seemed, wanted to talk about the Hennessy Gold Cup and Beef or Salmon.

The build-up to the race had given some indication of the level of interest being generated within the media about the horse. The family and staff were well accustomed to dealing with journalists from newspapers and television over the years and it was an unwritten rule that they handle all queries with courtesy.

Ann Hourigan would deal with much of the media stuff and young Kay was showing early signs that she was adept at the PR side of the horse-racing business. The interest in Salmon, however, was reaching an unprecedented level.

Horse-racing, like any sport, thrives on the arrival of new stars season after season and the creation of new rivalries. In steeplechasing the rivalry between Irish and English racehorses had a rich history and it was most pronounced at the Cheltenham festival and in the Gold Cup in particular.

The great stars of the sport had all conquered the big fences of the Cotswolds, from Golden Miller in the 1930s and Cottage Rake in the 40s and 50s, to the incomparable Arkle in the 1960s, whose rivalry with Millhouse was the stuff of legend.

The 1970s brought L'Escargot, The Dikler and Captain Christy into racing folklore while the 1980s provided Burrough Hill Lad, Forgive 'n Forget, Desert Orchid and the mare, Dawn Run, who snatched a dramatic victory under Jonjo O'Neill in 1986. Garrison Savannah, Jodami, Cool Ground and Imperial Call were just four who wrote themselves into history during the 1990s when Doran's Pride contributed to the drama and the glamour.

But, as the new millennium dawned, the English had a new hero. Best Mate was trained by the hugely popular Henrietta Knight, who had discovered the horse at a point-to-point meeting in Lismore and purchased him from Tom Costello, the well-known and respected horseman from Newmarket on Fergus and who was a friend of the Hourigan family.

Best Mate had been third favourite for the 2002 Gold Cup and won both the race and the hearts of the racing public when beating Ted Walsh's Commanche Court and See More Business. He had gone on to win the King George VI Chase at Kempton on December 26 and was the short-priced favourite to retain his Gold Cup crown.

But now he had a new challenger, and everyone wanted to know about Beef or Salmon.

The horse that no one wanted just three years previously, and who was rescued from oblivion by Michael Hourigan's hunch, was becoming public property. Requests for interviews flooded into the stable and photographers and TV crews clamoured to make appointments. It was a distraction that had to be managed and, in the meantime, there was the business of horse-racing – Beef or Salmon and all of the other horses had to be prepared for various assignments.

Work continued as normal. The horses began each day with half an hour of exercise on the horse walker before heading out to the sand gallops for some strenuous work. They would return to the walker for another stint before resting. If the horses were in the middle of a racing schedule the trainer would restrict the amount of time spent schooling them over fences.

From time to time Michael liked to break the routine for both the horses and the staff. With so much attention on the yard after the Hennessy success for Salmon, and Doran's Pride return to the racecourse, Hourigan decided it was time for a trip to the seaside. Ballybunion, the resort in the north of Kerry, was famous for its championship golf course but Hourigan regularly sent his horses on the fifty-mile trip from Lisaleen to exercise on the long beach along the Atlantic shore.

One cool, bright February morning Michael Junior drove the lorry to Ballybunion with Kay beside him. Padjo and Salmon were going out for the day. Kay had brought a selection of newspapers to catch up on some reading and, while the *Daily Telegraph* did not have a great readership around Adare and Patrickswell, Kay had managed to get hold of a copy of the previous Saturday's paper. It contained an article by Brough Scott, the former jockey-turned-journalist and businessman, which related his visit to the stables a week previously when he had ridden out Doran's Pride. Scott was an eloquent writer and his opening lines delighted Kay.

"Will you listen to this?" she laughed and began to read Scott's article to Michael.

"At 8.30 in the soft early light of a Limerick Friday morning, the most impressive new sight in racing began to draw away from me at full gallop. It was a sight jockeys will have to get used to, most imminently in this afternoon's Hennessy Gold Cup at Leopardstown. The sight was Beef or Salmon's arse.

Forgive the vernacular, but it is a quite magnificent arse. It is huge and round and powerful, a mass of ginger chestnut muscle, which was propelling the seven-year-old contender clear as if he wanted to run a hole in the wind. Forget the videos and the form books, the way to study a star racehorse is from the saddle."

Scott was clearly impressed and his comments added to the hype. Cheltenham had the kind of showdown the festival did best. Once it was Arkle and Millhouse, now, at the dawn of the 21st century, it was Best Mate against Beef or Salmon. The English champ against the novice sensation from Ireland.

Michael Hourigan didn't have much time for socialising in the weeks leading up to Cheltenham. On the rare occasions he did venture into Adare or Patrickswell, he noticed a difference. It wasn't just his companions who were talking about Cheltenham and asking questions about Beef or Salmon.

Everywhere he went, the newsagents, the grocer, the butcher, or the pub, everyone was talking about the Gold Cup. People were making plans to travel. He knew that a large number of locals had travelled to Leopardstown but the number making arrangements to go to Cheltenham amazed him.

"The only people not travelling are the ones we're leaving here to look after the other horses," he commented to Ann one evening.

The media demands continued. They were more prepared this time than they had been when Doran's Pride was the centre of attention. A press day was organised and everyone was invited. They came in big numbers. Camera crews from Channel 4, the racing channels and RTE arrived; racing writers came from England and Ireland. A large number of photographers also attended, their attention firmly focused on the two stars.

Hourigan was ebullient. He knew that there were sceptics out there, some of them standing in his presence with tape recorders and notebooks in their hands, who thought it was too big a risk to send a novice to the Gold Cup.

They pointed out that the horse had rarely run on good ground and never won on it, that he had run in small fields and could be spooked by racing with fifteen or sixteen other, vastly more experienced horses.

He was also aware of the growing clamour about a match between Salmon and Best Mate. With colourful language he dismissed that notion.

"All I know is that my horse has the potential to win a Gold Cup. But the best horse doesn't always win it. When Cool Dawn won [1998] I knew I had the best horse [Doran's Pride] but I was only third. That happens a lot. Look at Sirrell Griffiths' old horse [Nortons Coin, Gold Cup winner in 1990 at a price of 100/1]. There could easily be another one like him or Cool Dawn out there. See More Business, for instance, isn't out of it at all," he told his visitors, and refused to fudge the issue of inexperience.

"I suppose I might worry about crowding with 15 or 16 runners but, once the first mile is out of the way, Timmy will be able to organise him. They may jump a bit quicker than he is used to but I think he will be the better for that. The Cheltenham fences are a plus because they are so well presented. He could take them in his stride. He's the baby in the race, has a lot to do and needs luck in running. But, if he gets it, he should run a huge race," Hourigan added.

The persistent reminders about Salmon's lack of experience irked the trainer, though he tried to hide it. He knew that a championship race with the very best chasers, including Best Mate, was a different proposition than anything the horse had previously encountered. But it could not be avoided.

Salmon had taken on the best that others were prepared to race against him. Some of them had previously run in the Gold Cup and performed well. He had been told he was making a mistake running the horse in a Grade One chase in December. He had been proved right then and he'd been proven right at Leopardstown in the Hennessy.

Hourigan was no Cheltenham novice himself. He ran Deep Bramble in the Gold Cup in 1994 and 1995, and Doran's Pride contested the race every year between 1997 and 2000. The yard had enjoyed success at the Festival and, while there were pitfalls, that was part of what made Cheltenham so special.

The only doubt he now permitted to creep into his mind was that the horse did not have any experience of the course. He could have run him there in January but chose to stay at home. Deep Bramble had raced there first in 1992 when he unseated Enda Bolger in the amateur riders' chase. Doran's Pride had fallen on his first visit to the course in 1994 but returned to win the Stayers' Hurdle a year later.

Still, he was convinced. "I know I'm doing the right thing here," Hourigan told himself. The trainer put any doubts out of his mind.

Timmy Murphy agreed with him, happy too that the ground would suit Salmon. He had won on soft and heavy ground but Murphy believed he would perform better on good ground.

In pre-race interviews Murphy had been adamant: "He's been running on ground he doesn't really handle. I've always said, from riding work at home, that he's a good-ground horse, so the question is if he can take that form to good ground and improve on it."

The pre-race debates also raised a few doubts about Best Mate. No horse had managed to win consecutive Gold Cups since L'Escargot in 1971, though many great horses had tried – Desert Orchid, Jodami and See More Business amongst them.

Best Mate's Cheltenham form was good, however. He'd won a bumper in his first racecourse appearance at the track in November 1999, and was second to Sausalito Bay on the Supreme Novices' Hurdle in 2000, before graduating to Gold Cup glory in 2002.

Salmon was giving off all the right vibes at work and in his stable. His stablelad, Eoin Lynch, was just 17 years old but already had three years' experience working at the stable part-time. An apprentice carpenter by trade, he was being given the experience of a lifetime in looking after Ireland's leading fancy in steeplechasing's blue riband event. Under Eoin's watchful eye, the horse completed his preparations immaculately. There was no late drama.

Lynch was part of the advance party led by Michael Junior that departed the yard at 4am on the morning of March 10. In the darkness they did not notice the early morning activity on the side of the road. It was only later in daylight that Michael Senior and Ann would discover just what the local community had done for them.

There were placards bearing Beef or Salmon's visage everywhere, home-made posters declaring support for the horse. Banners floated from bridges, lamp-posts were decorated with signs wishing the horse and the Hourigans well.

Flags were flying outside shops and pubs in Patrickswell and Adare and local sports club had erected posters expressing their support. There were times over the years when they had witnessed scenes like these for the local hurling clubs in either town but never before had this happened in support of a racehorse.

Michael Hourigan often came across as stern but he had a lump in his throat as he absorbed and acknowledged his community rallying around him. There were tears in Ann's eyes as she reflected on the journey that had brought them here.

At Shannon Airport it seemed as if the entire community was heading for Cheltenham. Extra flights had been laid on and the couple heard stories of people travelling to Dublin by train because they could not get flights from Shannon. Others were travelling by road and boat. The Hourigans would not be lonely in Cheltenham.

"I hope we don't let them down," Hourigan whispered to his wife.

"You won't, and you haven't. Just look. They're already happy."

The team – Salmon, Doran's Pride, Hi Cloy and Clonmel's Minella – settled well in Prestbury Park, the horse-racing Mecca on the outskirts of Cheltenham. At every turn, in the town or at the racecourse, you encountered the Irish. The numbers in 2003 seemed bigger than ever and the Hourigans found themselves at the centre of attention. They didn't have a runner on the opening day but everyone was busy riding out, keeping the horses busy and happy.

The Irish drew first blood in the festival when the appropriately named Back In Front, trained by Edward O'Grady and ridden by Norman Williamson, won the first race, the Supreme Novices, beating the Tom Taaffe-trained Kicking King. The visitors from over the Irish Sea finished the day with another winner, the JP McManus-owned Youlneverwalkalone.

Team Hourigan had Hi Cloy and Clonmel's Minella in action on day two. Hi Cloy fell at the fifth fence in a race won by Hardy Eustace from the Dessie Hughes' yard. while Clonmel's Minella finished down the field in the amateur riders' race.

The laurels for the Irish were worn by Moscow Flyer, who won the feature race of the day, the Queen Mother Champion Chase for trainer Jessica Harrington and jockey Geraghty. The Arthur Moore-trained Native Upmanship was second. A third Irish winner on the day was Xenophon, trained by Tony Martin to win the Coral Cup.

The mood was generally upbeat as Gold Cup day dawned. Salmon had a run on the course with Doran's Pride and was in great form. He ate and drank well, now it was just a question of getting him through the preliminaries.

"He's 5/1, that's a short price for a novice," Hourigan was informed by one friendly pundit.

"At least he doesn't know that," countered the trainer.

And all the time horse remained unfazed by the razzmatazz that surrounds the Gold Cup. He paraded with the other 14 runners in front of the stands before Eoin Lynch left him in the sole guardianship of the jockey. Lynch took his place in front of the stands with the other stable staff, many of whom he knew from Ireland.

Beef or Salmon cantered to the start in familiar company, Harbour Pilot and Colonel Braxton were amongst the Irish entries in the race. But Best Mate was 13/8 favourite. His jockey, Jim Culloty, shared in some small talk with Murphy at the start but, in general, the jockeys were quieter than usual before this race. Even experienced jockeys suffered nerves in a race as big as this.

Murphy was pleased that the race would be run on good ground. He held on staunchly to his belief that the horse's action would be suited to that ground.

He was optimistic about his chances. He'd had good and bad experiences of the big race before. He should have won it in 1998 when riding See More Business but was instead mortified when they were forced to miss the seventh fence and had to pull up. Sitting on Beef or Salmon as they circled at the start Murphy was as confident as he had ever been that he was riding a horse good enough to win the Gold Cup.

The race began without incident. There was a bit of barging at the start as some of the jockeys fought for position, but that soon sorted itself out. Salmon was at the back, out of trouble and being allowed to settle into the race. They cleared the first two fences comfortably, passed the packed stands and around the bend into the back straight.

The third fence can be intimidating for young horses, big and with a slope beyond it that makes landing a little precarious. Salmon jumped okay, but clipped the top of the fence meaning he was slightly off balance on landing and fell.

A huge groan went up from the Irish crowd packed into the racecourse. Murphy rose quickly and looked for the horse. He got a brief fright; Salmon's tumble meant his feet briefly became entangled with the reins, a mishap with the potential to be very serious. But luck was on the team's side and the reins were shaken loose as Salmon's tumble ended.

Lynch quickly caught the horse and led him back. Although there was disappointment at the fall there was also great relief that the horse appeared sound.

The team was busy and mostly unaware of what else was happening. Best Mate had won the race. Truckers Tavern, a 33/1 chance trained by Noel Chance was second, while Harbour Pilot, having twice trailed home behind Salmon in Leopardstown, was third at 40/1.

There was little time then to think of what might have beens. Doran's Pride was in action and his fall at the second fence, in front of the stands, was a bad one.

The eventual outcome put everything else into perspective. As the veterinary surgeon put the old boy to sleep for the last time Michael Hourigan felt as low as at any time in his 53 years. He tried not to show it. He had a family and other horses to be strong for and to look after.

But the pain was etched across his face.

Later, in Birmingham Airport, he took a phone call. It was Tom Costello, the man who had found Best Mate and so many other great champions, who had called to console his old friend. Costello knew there was little he could say that would console Hourigan but he wanted to lend his support.

"This game would tame lions," he simply said.

Back home Salmon seemed no worse for his experience. Hourigan gave him a little time off work just to ensure that everything was in proper working order and that any undetected problems would have time to heal.

The horse was certainly affected by the absence of his old friend. Naturally laid back, Salmon was fractious at the beginning of each day. He would look for Padjo and was confused when he could not find him. His routine was broken and it took him time to re-join the herd without his regular companion.

But, as time moved on, he was back to his old self, eating more than his share and quickly regaining any weight lost in racing and travelling.

The trainer decided to ease the horse back into action, so it wasn't until

April 6 that Salmon appeared in a flat race at The Curragh with Mick Kinane riding. A heavily backed favourite, he won comfortably, beating Kickham and, afterwards, Kinane was enthusiastic about the horse when reporting to the owners and the trainer.

"This is a serious racer, awesome pace," Kinane told them.

Hourigan was delighted. He wanted to end the season on a positive note. There were big meetings coming up at both Fairyhouse and Punchestown and there would be opportunities for the horse to gain the reward Hourigan felt he deserved.

But fate, in the form of the weather, once again intervened. Mild conditions affected the going for both the Power Gold Cup in Fairyhouse and the Heineken Gold Cup in Punchestown. Hourigan refused to run the horse on ground he considered would be fast.

"I can't risk it, we have too much to lose," he declared. Only three horses contested the big race at Fairyhouse on April 22 and Beef or Salmon was not among them.

Eight days later Hourigan drove to Punchestown to check on ground conditions there. He had asked the Punchestown authorities to water the course but they would not risk that because rain was forecast.

"Even if it does rain it won't get into that ground," Hourigan responded.

Both Timmy Murphy and Richard Johnson had ridden horses for Hourigan on the previous day and both felt the ground needed to be watered. Noel Meade had similar worries about the ground for Harbour Pilot and withdrew him from the race.

Hourigan waited as long as he could. He wanted a positive end to the season. He was confident the horse would win the race but he refused to take any risks. He walked around the course and disagreed with the official declaration that the ground was good to yielding. There was no give in it at all.

Whatever about prestige and prizemoney, he would look after his horse. Salmon's season was over. Out on grass Salmon enjoyed a well-deserved rest. Since he first set foot on a racecourse proper on May 5, 2001, Beef or Salmon had run in eighteen races, winning nine that included two Grade 1s. His prizemoney in that period amounted to IR£209,233, equivalent to around €260,000 in the new currency, introduced the year before.

It wasn't bad for a horse that nobody wanted less than three years before.

CHAPTER 9

Christ, What's Wrong with the Horse?

After a summer holiday munching the lush grass of Lisaleen and becoming accustomed to the absence of his old friend, Padjo, Salmon returned to training for the winter season looking remarkably fresh.

He had gained some weight but he had also physically matured. Paul Hourigan schooled him and reported that the horse seemed well in himself. The only problem for his trainer was the unseasonably clement Irish weather.

Looking at the racing calendar, Hourigan had pencilled in a number of races to restart the season but these fell by the wayside because of continuing dry conditions around the country. Both the Grade 1 James Nicholson Wine Merchants' Chase at Down Royal and the Leopardstown Handicap, on November 8, had been marked as possibilities for a return to the track but the lack of rain was continuing to cause problems for the tracks and for trainers everywhere.

The James Nicholson Chase is the feature event of the year at Down Royal. The course manager, Mike Todd, reported temperatures of 16 degrees at the track in the week leading up to the race and was moved to express his frustration to reporters.

"It has been a freak autumn. Rain has been forecast since last Thursday and we haven't had a drop of it. It is 16 degrees here today, breezy and warm. It's doing my head in. We have been watering constantly but, no matter how much we put on, we can't beat nature. The forecasters are predicting half an inch of rain tonight, which would make a significant difference to the track. But the forecasters haven't been right yet," a worried Todd told reporters.

Conditions were not much more favourable at Leopardstown. Hourigan's seasonal plan for the horse was not much different than the year before. He was aiming for the Ericsson Chase again at Leopardstown, a possible run at Cheltenham and then the Gold Cup again but, if the Ericsson at the end of December was to remain a reasonable target, they had to return to the racecourse sooner rather than later.

The delay couldn't be helped, he couldn't run the horse if the ground was too hard but, having by-passed both Down Royal and Leopardstown, Hourigan was beginning to run out of options.

Salmon continued to thrive at home and in regular trips to nearby racecourses. These were designed to keep him sharp and active as he could get too accustomed to home comforts. A mile-and-a-half run around Limerick racecourse would remind the horse of his duties.

But he needed a return to competition, and Hourigan now turned to the familiar surroundings of Clonmel. The Clonmel Oil Chase, the race in which Salmon had first announced his arrival as a chaser of serious intent and now renamed, was scheduled for November 20. Hourigan had six horses entered for the meeting, five of them to be ridden by Murphy and the sixth by Paul Carberry. Adding spice to the occasion was the entry of Edredon Bleu in the big chase. Owned and trained by the Best Mate connections, Jim Lewis and Henrietta Knight, and ridden by Jim Culloty, the horse had won the Champion Chase in Cheltenham in 2000 and would provide a test for the youngster despite being eleven years old.

Mouse Morris was sending Alcapone for another crack at Salmon, and Noel Meade had entered Arctic Copper, so the field would be eleven runners, the largest entry since the race had first been run.

The weather was becoming more favourable as well, as a persistent drizzle in the days leading up to the race provided the ground most trainers wanted.

The Salmon team and his legion of supporters were in confident form. Despite not having raced since April, and not having jumped fences in competition since March, Salmon started as the odds on favourite at 4/5. Trainer and jockey had a brief chat before the race. There was little need for detailed instructions. They would not deviate from the tactics that had served them so well up to now.

From the stands the evidence seemed flattering. Murphy kept Salmon safe to the rear of the field while Jim Culloty led from the start on Edredon Bleu. Salmon, whose jumping was satisfactory rather than fluid, typically picked up over the last half mile and was eating up ground coming to the last. Amongst those standing at the rail watching Salmon coming to the final obstacle that day was his breeder, John Murphy, with some friends from Wexford.

"Have we ever seen a chaser running as quick as that at the end of a race?" they wondered.

As the final fence loomed Murphy was looking for room. Edredon Bleu hung to the right so Murphy tugged his horse slightly to the left to jump the fence between the leader and the rail. They hit the fence hard and Salmon landed awkwardly and lost his footing. Murphy held on grimly allowing the horse to rebalance himself. Salmon scrambled back upright and they gave chase but the momentum was gone. Edredon Bleu held on gamely to win the race by the narrowest of margins from Arctic Copper, with Salmon just a length behind.

The jockey was disconsolate and quiet as he dismounted. Hourigan exuded a more positive approach. "Listen lads, we're a bit disappointed but I know that if we could have got a race or two in him we could have enjoyed a better outcome," he told all who listened. "We had two good races before this last year and this run will do him a lot of good."

He had a little more to concern him after a full de-brief with the jockey. Timmy Murphy had detected something in the horse that he had not experienced before. He couldn't be sure but there were indications that this natural jumper was showing just a hint of hesitation at the fences. He did not want to set alarm bells ringing but something was not right.

"Is he rusty?" asked Murphy.

"He couldn't be," retorted Hourigan. "How could he be rusty? We've produced him right every other time we brought him to the course so why should he be rusty now. He's schooling as well as ever at home."

"Maybe he needed the run," said Murphy, though he was not entirely convinced.

At home Hourigan stepped up the schooling. As soon as he did he noticed some inconsistency in Salmon's jumping. He might be fluent at one fence, but would be slow at the next. There wasn't a clear pattern, just sufficient little kinks that suggested they needed to keep working with the horse and ensure that he was not idling.

The Grade 1 John Durkan Memorial Chase was the next target at Punchestown on December 7. A talented field of regular opponents had gathered – Rince Ri, Le Coudray, Native Upmanship, Knife Edge and Arctic Copper were all back to renew battle with Salmon. There was an English raider too, the Martin Pipe-trained, Tiutchev, which would be ridden by AP McCoy. This was the kind of challenge that the Salmon team loved. There was a first prize of €50,000 and the bookmakers prepared for another raid on their satchels.

Timmy Murphy had flown from England on Saturday night to take the ride on Salmon and a number of other horses from the yard. These included Smart Design and Black Church Yard in the second and third races on the card. He enjoyed little luck in either race and wasn't a happy person by the time he met his trainer near the weigh room.

"Don't run Salmon," was his surprising advice to the trainer. "Some of that ground is terrible; it won't suit him at all. You should withdraw him."

Taken aback and wishing to give due to respect to his jockey's opinion Hourigan took a few minutes alone. He had walked the track before racing and he knew there were patches were the ground was "hard and rough" near the rail. Further away from the rail, however, the trainer felt that the ground was safer. He spoke to Murphy.

"Timmy, we're going to run but I appreciate what you said. Take him around about three yards from the inside. You make the decisions as you go around."

Taking the suggested route would add to the distance to be run by Salmon and that might have an effect on the outcome of the race.

"If it costs, it costs," said Hourigan. "If we lose the race because we're minding the horse, then so be it. I want him back safe and sound. There are plenty of other big races ahead," he assured the jockey.

They had made other, earlier decisions about their tactics. Until now, Beef or Salmon had always been raced off the pace, at the back of the field and coming late, using his great pace over the last few fences. Questions had been raised about his ability to mix it in the middle of the field or from close to the front.

Did he have the stamina? Would he find the pace at the end if he was ridden near the front? Trainer and jockey did feel some irritation when these questions were raised. They chose their tactics because it gave their horse the best chance to win. Having examined the field for the Durkan they were concerned there might not be sufficient pace from the start. If that turned out to be the case then they would be bolder in their approach with Salmon.

Their assessment proved correct. With Tuitchev and Native Upmanship held up at the back of the seven-horse field, the runners ambled along at a gentle pace. Murphy rode Salmon close to the front but even wider than Hourigan had suggested. As well as giving the horse plenty of room and good sight of the fences, he was avoiding the ground that worried him. On the flat, Salmon was moving fluently but his jumping just was not of the calibre that had so excited Murphy a year ago. He was getting over the fences but there was none of the fluency, the easy nature of his previous action.

McCoy lost patience with the pace and brought Tuitchev to the front ahead of Salmon as they jumped the fourth last fence. Murphy asked for more speed from Salmon and got a response. There was nothing wrong with the horse's courage and willingness to race. They took the lead before the second last fence and won comfortably with Tuitchev second and Rince Ri and Le Coudray following them to the line.

Hourigan brought the horse home bristling at some of the reaction to the race. McCoy had called it "an ordinary race" and that annoyed Hourigan. "Why did they travel so far for such an ordinary race?" he snarled.

Once again Salmon's jumping hadn't been fluent but he had won the race with something to spare. "If his jumping was as good as last year he'd be destroying these horses," the trainer thought.

At home he schooled him almost every day for a week. He was worried that he was being too hard on the horse. Time was against him, he needed another run before going to Leopardstown for the festival. The Hilly Way Chase at Cork over two miles had sharpened the horse up properly a year ago. It would have a small field this year and Hourigan decided to run.

Just three others were left in the race when final declarations were made, Rathgar Beau, Knife Edge and Killultagh Storm. Beef or Salmon was once again an odds-on favourite at 2/5. The confidence in the camp was surging even though the trainer and the jockey harboured small but persisting doubts that they had a problem. Hourigan had the horse checked out weekly but nothing could be found.

The race in Cork went as expected. Salmon tracked Killultagh Storm, which Ruby Walsh had ridden to lead from the start. Salmon was always in control, though a mistake at the second last was a reminder to the jockey and trainer that his jumping problem had not gone away. When he cleared the last Salmon showed his customary speed and won the race easily.

Before Murphy had dismounted, the hype had begun to build. Hours earlier Henrietta Knight had suggested she might run Best Mate in Leopardstown at Christmas rather than at Kempton. It was music to the ears of the authorities in Leopardstown and to the media. A blockbuster match-up between Salmon and Best Mate was in prospect; the original had never really happened because of Salmon's fall at Cheltenham. Would Hourigan be prepared to take on the champion? "Why not?" he snapped, leaving no one in any doubt about his belief in Beef or Salmon.

The hype was unavoidable. The trainer and his staff had a frantic period of activity over the next two weeks. They were preparing a huge string of horses for eight days of racing after Christmas. Salmon might be the superstar but every other horse in the yard needed attention. It didn't matter if they were lowly handicappers or potential champion chasers, all were treated the same. Owners were paying the bills and looking forward to racing. Not every horse could win but they all had to be prepared and presented according to the demanding standards of the boss.

Still, the same boss found himself spending more time talking about Salmon than any other horse he'd ever had, even Doran's Pride. Interest in the race was phenomenal. Best Mate's entry had stirred the English media and they joined their Irish counterparts in seeking every tiny detail of information as they built up this latest clash between the two horses.

Hourigan dealt with every query. It could become repetitive but he recognised the need to feed the interest. It was good for racing and it was good for the yard, even if at times it threatened to be a distraction.

But, all the time, in the back of his mind were the concerns he shared with Murphy that something was not quite right with the horse. Veterinary checks did not reveal any physical damage. Was it in Salmon's mind? Had the fall in Cheltenham dented his confidence? On the flat in the Curragh Mick Kinane said he had been "awesome", great praise indeed from one of the greatest flat jockeys in the world. And he had been an unlucky loser in Clonmel and an emphatic winner in Cork.

At times this game was a mystery. Those were the times when a trainer wished the horse could talk and tell him what the problem was.

Timmy Murphy spent Christmas in Ireland and was in Lisaleen to ride out on the morning of December 26. He would ride for Hourigan in Limerick that day; the yard was sending eight horses to the local track and another five were heading to Dublin. Murphy rode Hi Cloy to win the big chase in Limerick. He also had a spin on Salmon on the gallops. The horse seemed to be happy so Murphy hoped that whatever ailed him in his last two races was now healing or had already healed.

Best Mate had indeed travelled from England and was greeted in Dublin with a fanfare. The Ericsson Chase on December 28 overshadowed every other race, though in Limerick a Novice Hurdle race was named in honour of Doran's Pride, and Lisaleen would be represented by Johnjoe's Express who finished fifth. Hourigan had four other entries at the track, while a team of four travelled to Leopardstown – Beef or Salmon, Hi Cloy having his second race in three days, Socrates and Simon Vaughan.

For Murphy and Salmon there was a familiar feel to their race. Le Coudray, Colonel Braxton, Alcapone and Rince Ri were all opposing again. Willie Mullins had entered Alexander Banquet and Ian Williams had sent over from his base in England a very promising French-bred chaser, Batman Senora, that had won a number of good races in Auteuil. He would be ridden by Paul Moloney who had also been booked to ride for Hourigan in the opening race on the card. All attention, however, was focused on Best Mate and Beef or Salmon.

A crowd of 19,289 thronged into the Leopardstown enclosures. Over €900,000 was bet on the race, a record for Ireland. As the horses entered the parade ring many of those thousands jostled for a view. The scenes were reminiscent of Cheltenham and the air bristled with excitement. The two horses at the centre of attention took it all in their stride. They were unfazed by the preliminaries and Murphy got a good feel from Salmon as they cantered down to the start.

It didn't last.

If Best Mate would look imperious for the entire three miles, Beef or Salmon looked porous. His jumping was ragged and Murphy was at work from the first fence. This just wasn't the same horse that had been so brilliant a year before. By halfway Murphy was waving the whip trying to get a response. He hoped the horse might pick up pace between fences but he was labouring from a long way. Salmon never looked like challenging Best Mate and Murphy knew from a couple of fences from the finish that he was riding for a place. Barry Geraghty set Le Coudray off in chase of the champion in a brave, but fruitless endeavour.

Salmon passed the tiring Colonel Braxton to finish in third place, offering Murphy some consolation. "If he can finish third in a race as good as this running that poorly then what can he do when he is right and runs well," he said in an effort to lift his own spirits.

As Best Mate was hailed in the parade ring by an adoring crowd, the Salmon team was left alone to contemplate what had just happened. Hourigan presented a brave face. He could be bullish before a race about the chances for his horse but he believed in accepting defeat with grace. He had a quick word with Murphy.

"The horse is just not right. He doesn't feel right and his jumping is gone ragged," said a very disappointed Murphy. "There was nothing there."

"Okay, don't worry Timmy. It's my job from here, you've done everything you can," said Hourigan.

He spent some time with Joe Craig and Dan McLarnon. "That's not the real Salmon. There's something not right and I'm going to find out what it is."

"Do whatever it takes. Let us know what is happening," they told him.

The bookmakers reacted predictably. Best Mate's odds for the Gold Cup tumbled to 5/4. Interest in Beef or Salmon in the market nose-dived. Beef or Salmon had been 8/1 with some firms but could now be backed at 16/1. There were no takers.

It was a quiet journey home to Lisaleen that night. Hourigan did not have any runners at Leopardstown for the final day of the festival, which was a relief. He needed time. Just to think. The horse would be scoped by the vets to check if there was some kind of infection troubling him. That was routine. He hoped that they would find the source of the trouble but, deep down, he suspected that it would not be so simple.

Timmy Murphy had heard the horse 'gurgle' during the race – which suggested that he might have an infection – but Murphy was as good a judge as Hourigan knew amongst the jockeys and his instinct was that something else was bothering the horse. He would have to undertake a review of everything that

CHRIST, WHAT'S WRONG WITH THE HORSE? • 99

had happened Salmon, especially that fall at Cheltenham. Hourigan wanted to look at the video of that race and of the mistake in Clonmel. He thought about Michael Kinane's comments at the Curragh. Salmon had been brilliant on the flat.

That would be a starting point.

Later that evening at home, Kay called to the house. She gave the report from Limerick and listened to his worries about Salmon. She promised she would take a look at the horse first thing in the morning and keep an eye on him for a few days.

She was true to her word. Salmon didn't seem any worse for his ordeal the next morning when she checked on him at around 7.30am. He ate up well, a good sign, and she walked him around the yard, checking his legs. There was nothing wrong there.

Kay returned to the cottage for breakfast. *The Racing Post* had arrived. She opened it and was temporarily dumbstruck when she saw a photograph of Salmon. Her voice returned.

"Oh, Jesus Christ," she exclaimed, "what is wrong with that poor horse?"

CHAPTER 10

Happy People, Happy Horses

Kay cleared some space on the kitchen table in the cottage that had once been the family home but was now her own. She placed the newspaper flat on the table and stared hard at the photograph of Beef or Salmon.

The more she looked at the photograph, the more concerned she became: "That horse is in pain and we could have a major problem here."

Pain could not be tolerated, certainly not with the horses. Human pain did not elicit the same levels of concern or sympathy. A sore horse demanded immediate action, and the vet's telephone number was on speed-dial. Every horse in the yard would be seen by the dentist at least twice a year, prompting Kay to joke: "The teeth could be falling out of our mouths but no one would mention a dentist. But the horse gets two visits a year, toothache or not."

For as much of her 27 years as she could remember, Kay Hourigan's life was consumed by horses. She was born in 1976, the second child, while the family still lived in Rathkeale and she was nine years old when they moved to Lisaleen. By then she was already riding ponies and helping out with some of the daily chores in the continually expanding stableyard.

By the age of eleven she had joined her brother, Michael, older by two years, riding out lots of racehorses though, initially, she was given the quieter horses.

Early mornings became routine, whatever the weather, and together they would ride out two lots every morning before heading off to primary school in Adare.

The schedule became more hectic when they moved to secondary school in Rathkeale, about nine miles away.

Some mornings they would ride out one lot before rushing off to catch the school bus, while other mornings the schedule was a little different. Their father still kept a few horses in Rathkeale so Michael and Kay would get a lift to the field, gallop the four or five horses and then race to the bathroom to wash and change into their uniforms. The other kids were still wiping the sleep from their eyes while the Hourigans had already completed a morning's work. Classes were held in pre-fabricated buildings that could be cold and damp, but Kay never felt it. Her body temperature was always warm after the activity of the morning.

It was an unconventional lifestyle but one which Kay and Michael accepted willingly. The Sisters of Mercy, who ran the school at the time, might have had reservations but they were never expressed. Kay wasn't academic, but she was diligent in her own way. If the subject was horses, or anything to do with animals, she certainly showed interest and aptitude.

After school, there were always jobs to be done in the evening. Ross Easom and Brian Moran were the two most experienced and valued workers in the yard. They took the young Hourigans under their wing and taught them the basics – feeding, mucking out, grooming and constantly checking on the horses, especially their legs. Their father also kept cattle and they had to be fed and looked after as well.

Kay assumed more responsibility as she got older, especially after Michael began race-riding. On race days the senior staff and the jockeys would be travelling around the country. That meant that there was more work to be done by those who remained at home. Kay's mother, Ann, would collect her from the school rather than allow her to wait for the bus. It meant she would be home by 4pm, quickly change into her work gear and set off to carry out the various chores and checking on the horses.

When she reached the age of 16 she took out a jockey's licence and rode her first race, a bumper in Tralee. For the vast majority of jockeys that rite of passage is almost sacred, a date never to be forgotten, but Kay remembers thinking only, "this is not for me." She rode eleven times on the racecourse and did not manage a winner.

"Dad," she explained one evening, "I'm not cut out for the races. I'm much happier and get more enjoyment working out in the field, cantering the horses, getting them ready for the race. There's plenty of others around here who can ride them."

It never bothered her that Michael, Paul and her sister, Laura, all rode winners. When the youngest of the family, Mark, began to collect rosettes and trophies for showjumping, Kay would laugh, "I don't even have one of those." Her father and mother could see where her talents lay. She was organised, liked order and they could be sure nothing would go wrong under Kay's watch.

Her value to the yard was never more apparent than when her father brought a new horse to the yard in 1992. Nicknamed, Padjo, he was a lively sort that proved hard to break and, even when broken, Padjo seemed to be keen to break anyone who tried to ride him. He was constantly bucking and kicking and there were not many in the yard who wanted to ride him out.

So, Kay did it.

The horse that would be formally named Doran's Pride became Kay's favourite and, though she continued to work with other horses, she organised her life around Doran's Pride. He wasn't always easy and she suffered a number of injuries from falls off the horse but, every morning before school, she rode the horse and his stable was the first she visited when she got home.

She was reluctantly parted from Padjo during the winter of 1995 when she spent six months working for a then up-and-coming trainer in England named Paul Nicholls. But, in December, she got a desperate phone call from home – Doran's Pride was dying, suffering from colic. He underwent two operations and the Lisaleen family lit candles and prayed. Kay waited by the phone, tears flowing, before finally the good news arrived.

She couldn't wait to get home and, once back at Lisaleen, she began to implement many of the lessons she had learned from Nicholls. It was the first sign that someone other than her father would be allowed to make decisions. Order, strict schedules, rosters that would not be altered all became part of the day-to-day routine. And she introduced a new phrase – "happy people, happy horses".

Not that it was easy to be happy all the time. It was impossible, actually, although Kay's philosophy meant they at least had to try. The yard became busier and busier. As Ireland assumed the façade of a wealthy nation, more and more people wanted to own racehorses. The stable grew, the numbers of horses in training grew, and life grew hectic.

There were days, too, when the air was full of excitement. Kay and her brothers and sister would always wait with anticipation when their father was due back from the sales. They always wanted to get a look at his latest purchases, and always the same question: Would there be another one as good as Doran's Pride in the newest batch? The arrival of a new four-year-old on the evening of June 8, 2000, didn't set their pulses racing. He looked strong but had still to be broken.

However, it didn't take long for Kay and the family to get a sense that Salmon might be a good racehorse. They always trusted Paul's judgement. He had been one of the best young riders in Ireland and England in his teenage years but height, and the weight that came with it, didn't help his career as a race rider as he grew older. Still, he was an adept horseman and an astute judge of racehorses and, from an early stage, Paul felt that they had the makings of a good chaser in Salmon. The horse treated hurdles with disdain, running through them rather than jumping them. But when it came to fences, he flew.

Worryingly, he had not flown at Leopardstown on December 28, 2003, and that was why Kay was examining the *Racing Post* photograph the following morning. The horse seemed almost rigid; his tail stuck out, in a line with his nose. She ran her finger along the photograph: "It's like a straight pole, as if the girth is cutting the stomach off him. What's wrong?"

She consulted with her father and together they planned a strategy that would begin with a full investigation of the problem and then the implementation of a cure.

They spoke to the owners, Craig and McLarnon. "Do whatever has to be done," they were told.

The horse didn't scope right and there was mucus in his lungs after the race, but Hourigan suspected there was something more affecting the horse. He played the video of the Cheltenham fall over and over again. He studied the videos of the races in Clonmel, Cork and Leopardstown. Hourigan thought he had spotted something – Salmon was only jumping properly off one leg, the right. He was snapping up the left hind, almost skipping with it. There was something wrong there. It was only a minute movement that took minute examination, but it was telling.

They booked an x-ray at the veterinary surgery run in the Curragh by Ned Gowings and found the answer to their mystery.

Beef or Salmon was suffering from 'Kissing Spine', a condition where large spines sticking up from the vertebrae in the horse's back rub together causing inflammation and discomfort. In Beef or Salmon's case the condition did not cause any problem when he was being saddled or running on the flat. However, his jumping action was clearly affected and was giving him pain.

Treatment in the form of an injection was immediately carried out but Salmon required further intensive treatment. It would have to be the best and it would have to work quickly if he was to have any chance of being fit for the Gold Cup in Cheltenham on March 18, 2004.

The Gold Cup had been Hourigan's target since Salmon had fallen there nine months before. Now that this problem had been identified the target remained the same. It gave them a focus, a timeline to work with. It would be a battle against time, but they would try.

The Hourigans were already aware of the reputation of the physiotherapist, Liz Kent, by the time they made contact with her. She was based at Burgage Stud in Leighlinbridge, in Carlow and, during 2003, she had been credited by trainer John Oxx for her work in helping the Aga Khan's, Alamshar, to recover from a back injury in time to win the Irish Derby.

"Dad, from what I hear it would be easier getting an audience with the Pope," said Kay. "She's one of the busiest people in Ireland."

But Michael Hourigan was not to be denied and, before long, the physiotherapist arrived at Lisaleen for a preliminary examination.

"This horse has got to run in the Gold Cup," Kay told Kent.

"Not a chance," was the reply.

"Well, tell me what to do."

Kay did not have any formal qualifications but she was interested in horse welfare and veterinary methods. Working with horses meant she had constant contact with vets and was accustomed to their methods and their language. She read extensively about physiotherapy and was a quick learner. Liz Kent would lead the treatment programme and she had a willing assistant who was not afraid of hard work.

The physiotherapist devised the treatment for the injury. It involved a relatively modern massage treatment known as Equissage, which was carried out by machine and hand. Initially, Liz visited Lisaleen twice a week, administering the treatment and showing Kay how it was done. When Liz couldn't be at Lisaleen, she provided Kay with two sheets of instructions for what to do each day, plus the tools to do the work with.

Helping Salmon consumed Kay. Michael had to change things in the yard but the staff responded as he'd hoped, realising that Kay would be looking after just one horse for a while. She'd be around to answer questions and to help at times, but her priority now was to work on Salmon and do whatever she could to get him fit for Cheltenham.

For ten hours a day, seven days a week Kay Hourigan devoted herself to this one horse. Her day began at 6.30am when she braved the dark, cold wet mornings but she was committed. There was a different sense of purpose about what she was doing. She would spend two hours working on the horse, loosening the muscles in his back, massaging him. Then she would ride him out, bring him back and cool him off, before feeding him. Twice a week, on Tuesday and Friday, she would load him onto a trailer at 10am and drive almost 180 kilometres to Leighlinbridge where Liz Kent would treat him. Kay and Salmon would arrive back in Lisaleen at 8pm. It was intensive and draining on both Kay and the horse, although he proved to be a good patient.

Since he'd arrived in the yard over three years earlier, Kay had had little to do with the horse, apart from watching him up close with Doran's Pride. Now, the pair were developing a close bond. Salmon realised that some good was being achieved from her attention. When she was late for him, having been distracted by some other event or demand in the yard, he became agitated. It was a very busy yard so distractions were inevitable, despite the best efforts of everyone to allow Kay to devote as much time as possible to Salmon.

Lisaleen was running lots of horses at lots of venues. A young chestnut gelding, named The Parishioner, was proving a decent money spinner, winning three consecutive races in Limerick, Cork and Thurles in five weeks. Vic Ville had also won at the Cork meeting. Kilbeggan Lad was a winner at Gowran Park at the end of January; Hi Cloy was third in the big Dr PJ Moriarty Novice Chase at Leopardstown on February 8. Timmy Murphy was spending a lot of time in Ireland riding for Hourigan and was also able to keep up with Salmon's progress.

All the time, Kay was learning about the injury and about the horse. He was different to Doran's Pride, more laid back. Doran's had loved attention but this fellow, like all champions, enjoyed attention but would get irritated if it continued too long. He was possessive, too. He liked to have Kay to himself. He knew she was there to help him and if anyone else came into the stable he was liable to nip them. This was his time and he did not want to be disturbed.

He enjoyed Kay's company and, in her presence, was well-behaved. To demonstrate his good form he would kick the wall of his stable but, given his strength, that caused its own problems. Kay arrived one morning to find a huge hole in the wall and her horse suffering a damaged hock. The injury wasn't serious but casting blocks and rubber matting were immediately ordered and Salmon's stable became the only one in the yard to have padding.

The clock was against them but, as time went by, it seemed to Kay that Salmon's mood was getting better and better. After a few weeks Kay began to feel a change in the horse when riding him.

"It's like floating on air," she happily reported to her father.

Salmon's movement was improving all the time and Liz Kent was content. She could see an improvement from week to week but she didn't want to build up hopes and urged caution.

Michael, meanwhile, was considering a return to the track. Leopardstown was looming in early February and the big prize on offer was tempting. But the physiotherapist advised him to hold off and, trusting her judgement he demurred.

But, outside the stable, speculation was mounting. Would Salmon go to Leopardstown for the Hennessy? What were the plans? Would he go straight to Cheltenham?

The pressure became intense. Hourigan would have preferred to avoid all the speculation but he had a horse on his hands that the whole country was beginning to fall in love with. There was a lot of prizemoney at stake and that had to be considered also. But, ultimately, he would do what was right for the horse.

He was fortunate having Joe Craig and Dan McLarnon as owners. The pair resisted putting any pressure on him at all. It was obviously frustrating having to wait, day by day, for news but they placed their faith in the trainer and in Kay. There could be no other way. Sending the horse back to the track too soon could cause even more damage.

Still, it felt strange setting out with five horses for the big Leopardstown meeting on February 8 but missing Beef or Salmon. She'll Be Lucky won a handicap hurdle for the yard, while Hi Cloy and Kilbeggan Lad were both placed. Florida Pearl had won the big race for Willie Mullins.

And Hourigan faced another worry about his injured champion. While Salmon's physical recovery pleased him, the mental scar was still there. Salmon should now be able to jump pain free but the horse didn't know that. When faced with one of the schooling fences Salmon remembered only the pain he had suffered in Leopardstown.

Michael thought back to the days many years ago when he took part in dressage. It was the ultimate discipline where horse and rider had to be in perfect harmony, when the rider gave subtle instructions and the horse obeyed. Would some dressage work for Salmon?

Hourigan rang a friend, Alfie Buller, a former Irish international event rider and Olympian at Atlanta in 1994, who ran the Scarvagh House Stud in County Down.

"Alfie, I have a horse with a problem," he announced down the line, before explaining his idea. Hourigan believed he needed someone with dressage experience, "to ride him properly to make him use his hind quarters again."

"Would you not do it yourself, you know how?" asked Buller.

"No, I have half an idea of how to do it but half isn't good enough and I don't have anyone else here to do it."

Buller said he would think about it and get back to him. A day later Buller's wife, Vina, a successful event rider herself, rang Hourigan.

"Vina, I need someone to come here to ride him. I don't want to send him away. I have all the facilities here, including the indoor school. But I don't know where to start."

"You start here and now," she said. "Here's Sue Shortt's number, she's the person you need."

Sue Shortt was from Kilkenny and was one of Ireland's most respected and successful event riders. She had competed in the Olympic Games in Sydney and had qualified to compete in the Games in Athens, in 2004. Contact was made at the start of February and the situation was explained. Treatment with Liz Kent was continuing but they needed something more. Shortt knew Kent and agreed to ride Salmon at Burgage before deciding on a plan of action.

Shortt was immediately impressed when she rode Salmon for the first time. She told Kay the horse would pass an intermediate dressage class at that point. He was, she agreed, a natural mover and she was anxious to get to work immediately and agreed to visit Lisaleen.

In the beginning she came three times a week, working in the indoor school and Salmon responded well. There was a noticeable improvement after just a few days but, most importantly, they could see that his confidence was returning, that he was beginning to realise he was pain-free.

The work continued. Salmon would visit Liz Kent once a week for intensive work and Kay followed Liz's instructions every other day. She dedicated herself to ensuring that Salmon would recover, hopefully, in time for Cheltenham. Meanwhile, Sue continued her routines in the indoor school, gradually building up the work and restoring the horse's confidence and faith in his ability. The horse hadn't seen a racecourse since he had run in Leopardstown in December so Hourigan arranged to bring him to Thurles on February 19 for a guarded two-mile run. It went well.

A week later, on February 26, Lisaleen had a number of entries in Limerick. Hourigan spoke to the track authorities and they agreed to allow Salmon to work out before racing. This would allow Timmy Murphy to ride him as he was rushing to catch a flight immediately after racing.

The pair jumped five fences and jockey and trainer were pleased. Salmon was moving with greater fluency. The power was still there – Murphy could feel it – and the hesitation was gone. Salmon was getting his confidence back. They didn't want to build up hope or expectation but the treatment was definitely having the desired effect. Murphy rode him again in Cork, on March 4, and felt another improvement.

As Cheltenham inched closer Liz Kent was amazed at how well the horse was responding. "We might just make it," she told Kay.

Lisaleen was dispatching a large number of runners throughout the last week of February and the early weeks of March. The trainer, however, was spending more and more time talking about Beef or Salmon. Florida Pearl, winner of big race in Leopardstown in February, and one of Ireland's great chasers, was withdrawn from the Gold Cup. He would never race again because of an injury. Beef or Salmon was now seen as Ireland's greatest chance of preventing Best Mate from creating history by winning a third consecutive Gold Cup. Mullins had kept Alexander Banquet in the race and Noel Meade was sending Harbour Pilot back for another crack at the race.

The hype was building again. The French were coming double-handed. Francois Doumen was preparing First Gold again for the big race; Jair du Cochet had staked his claim for a place in the big race field by winning the Pillar Property Chase at Cheltenham in January and was now second favourite behind Best Mate.

But there was bad news to come from France on the evening of March 9. Hourigan heard it as he returned to Lisaleen from Thurles. Jair Du Cochet had broken a leg while galloping at trainer Guillaume Macaire's stable under race jockey, Jacques Ricou, and had been put down. It was yet another reminder of how cruel The Fates could be in horse-racing.

Hourigan would not rush a final decision on Salmon. He had brought the horse to Thurles racecourse where jockey Joe Casey schooled him over one and a half miles. They schooled him again in Lisaleen the following day. With just eight days to go to Cheltenham, and the travelling party due to leave on the following Monday, a final decision had to be made. Hourigan spoke to the owners: He was happy with the horse, Liz Kent was happy, Sue Shortt was happy, Kay was happy. The decision was made by Joe Craig and Dan McLarnon – if everyone was happy, so were they.

Once the entry was confirmed the media went into overdrive and, once more, the TV cameras began to arrive. Channel 4 sent John Francome to meet the Hourigans and it proved to be an experience the former champion jockey would not forget easily. He spoke at length to Michael and was then introduced to Kay who was massaging Salmon in his stable. It had been a long day and Kay was tired. Later she would admit the pressure was getting to her a little. She understood the media interest, acknowledged its benefit for racing, but she had had enough.

Francome asked innocently, "Are you worried about his jumping?"

"Why would I be worried about his jumping?" Kay barked, "Sure, he's only fallen once. You'd swear he wasn't able to stand up the way you people are asking about his jumping."

Francome tried to make amends for his slip-up. Kay was using a laser unit on the horse. "What's that piece of equipment?" asked the former champion.

"That's a vibrator," snapped Kay.

Taking the fences one at a time: Beef or Salmon.

Michael Hourigan with Beef or Salmon at Lisaleen Stables.

Beef or Salmon gets his nose in front in the Ericsson Chase at Leopardstown in 2002.

▲ Salmon and Timmy Murphy jump the last to win the 2003 Hennessy Gold Cup from Colonel Braxton.

◄ Northern Exposure: Proud owners, Joe Craig and Dan McLarnon, lead the victorious pair after their Gold Cup win.

◄ Victory: Triumphant trainer, Michael Hourigan, raises the Hennessy Cognac Gold Cup.

Tragedy: Timmy Murphy guides Salmon over the fences at Cheltenham 2003, but they fell later in the race, which was won by Best Mate. In a separate race in Cheltenham that same day, Salmon's great ally, Doran's Pride, fell and had to be put down.

Star Turn: Doran's Pride, with Paul Hourigan aboard, racing at Fairyhouse in December, 2000

Lisaleen Stables, Limerick February 2003: Michael Hourigan is pictured leading out Beef or Salmon in a photo reminiscent of one taken three years earlier (inset) with Doran's Pride. A few weeks after the Salmon photograph, Padjo fell in Cheltenham and died.

No Friend of Mine: Beef or Salmon (Paul Carberry) battles it out with Best Mate (Jim Culloty) to win the 2004 Lexus Steelplechase.

Vindication: An emotional Carberry punches the air in celebration of the win. It was Salmon's first victory over Best Mate in a rivalry that dominated racing from 2003 to 2005.

Timmy Murphy and Salmon celebrate victory in the Heineken Gold Cup during the 2004 Punchestown Festival.

◀ Best Mate, three-time winner of the Cheltenham Gold Cup.

End of an Era: Best Mate and Paul Carberry jump the first fence at Exeter in November, 2005. But, later in the same race, the great horse known as 'Matey' collapsed and died.

Best Mate's jockey, Paul Carberry and owner, Henrietta Knight, walk back to the grandstand after his death on the track.

Salmon with Kay Hourigan: It was Kay's determination, with the aid of the entire Lisaleen staff, and physio Liz Kent, that saved Salmon's racing career when a mystery injury struck in 2003.

Following a win in the 2005 Lexus Steeplechase, Michael Hourigan, Paul Carberry and Joe Craig celebrate in the parade ring with Salmon.

Paul Carberry negotiates the fences in the 2005 Gold Cup at Leopardstown Races.

With Andrew McNamara onboard, Salmon jumps during The Racing Post in Ireland Hurdle at Fairyhouse while, below, Paul Carberry pilots him to victory in the 2006 Hennessy Gold Cup.

Flying high: Salmon's great rival War of Attrition gets a congratulatory kiss from owner, Michael O'Leary, after landing the Punchestown Guinness Gold Cup and, below, with Conor O'Dwyer onboard.

Battle Royal: But War of Attrition loses out to Beef or Salmon in the 2006 James Nicholson Wine Merchant Champion Steeplechase at Down Royal, and this time it's Hourigan jockey, Andrew McNamara, who plants a celebratory kiss on Salmon's cheek.

Michael Hourigan in a lighter moment. Below left, Kay Hourigan and, below right, Timmy Murphy.

Last hurrah: Salmon, with Timmy Murphy onboard, leads out the parade before the 2008 Guinness Gold Cup – his last race.

End of an era: Beef or Salmon takes a final bow with Michael and Kay Hourigan as he retires at Punchestown on April 23, 2008, in the company of former rival, and fellow retiree, Hedgehunter.

Francome withdrew, defeated.

When the piece was aired on Channel 4 during the festival, Ted Walsh joked with Francome: "You'd want to be careful with that one, she's a bit dangerous. You'd better stay away from her."

"Don't worry," said Francome, "I will stay far away."

Meanwhile, Michael Hourigan was a little more restrained in his exchanges with reporters. "It's lovely to be going back again and we're back with a fighting chance," he told them. "I'm not going to put my head on the line and say he will definitely win, but the other horse is trying to equal history and that's a very hard thing to do."

Could they beat Best Mate? "Every horse is beatable. Even Arkle got beat and Best Mate has been beaten already this season. Nobody can go into any race thinking they're certainties. What I want from my horse is for him to get into a position to challenge. If he does everything right, and does challenge, and he gets beat, then I'll accept it. If he gets stuffed in those circumstances, then that will just be what he is and we will know."

The trip to Cheltenham was uneventful. Hourigan had just two runners that week, the other being a nice horse he'd picked up cheaply in Tattersalls during 2003 called Only Vintage. The horse ran for the first time in February and had a busy schedule in the build-up to Cheltenham, running three times altogether and winning on his last outing in Leopardstown on February 29. He had been sold and would remain in training in England after Cheltenham. Timmy Murphy rode him in the Champion Bumper, then the last race on Wednesday, finishing seventh behind the Tom Cooper-trained Total Enjoyment, ridden by Jim Culloty.

As Gold Cup day dawned Kay fussed over her charge. She didn't spoil her horses but she was nervous about the day. The memories of 2003 were too fresh. In fact, they would never leave her. She wasn't thinking about winning the Gold Cup, though once it would have been her greatest motivation and desire. Now all she wanted was for this horse with the straggly tail to come home safe and sound. She didn't care where he finished.

Leaving the pre-parade ring she received shouts of encouragement from other stable staff from Ireland. They knew how she was feeling. They had witnessed her pain twelve months earlier. Some had tried to console her then. Many of them had endured the trauma of losing a racehorse and knew the psychological damage it could cause.

The parade ring itself was packed with owners and their families and friends. There were just ten entries for the Gold Cup but there wasn't a blade of grass to be seen, such was the number of people there.

Best Mate was in the ring, looking well. Salmon, Harbour Pilot and Alexander Banquet represented the Irish challenge to the champion. The other six were Truckers Travern, trained by Ferdy Murphy and ridden by Tony Dobbin; Sir Rembrandt, trained by Robert Alner and ridden by Andrew Thornton; Jonjo O'Neill's Keen Leader, ridden by Barry Geraghty; The French horse, First Gold, ridden by Thierry Doumen; The Real Bandit, which would be ridden by AP McCoy and trained by Martin Pipe, and Trucker's Travern, trained by Nicky Henderson and ridden by Mick Fitzgerald.

Salmon was calm and happy in the parade ring and behaved as well as ever in the parade. Kay was the only one who was nervous.

For Salmon and Murphy the race would prove uneventful. The jockey adopted the usual tactics, keeping the horse at the back of the field and giving him a good look at the fences. Coming to the third Murphy briefly wondered if the horse would remember the events of a year ago but they cleared it comfortably and galloped away. The jockey let out a small sigh of relief.

As the battle at the front intensified Murphy had a good view. Salmon was running well and jumping well. "They've done a hell of a job on this fella," thought Murphy. First Gold continued to lead but, coming round the final bend, Best Mate and Jim Culloty were looking for room. Paul Carberry and Harbour Pilot were not giving any and there was momentary panic for the Best Mate team, but it didn't last. The champion was supreme – space opened up in the straight and Culloty steered Best Mate effortlessly through it.

Murphy looked up to see Best Mate eventually find the room he needed and jump to the lead at the second last. From then Murphy had his head down, driving Salmon on. He knew some of the others were tiring, and thought he might snatch third place at least. They took off at the last fence, hit it hard. Salmon was briefly unbalanced but got his feet together quickly. He passed First Gold and was in fourth place and racing. Sir Rembrandt was in third but he was flying home and snatched second place before the line. Harbour Pilot held on for third and Salmon finished strongly in fourth.

With so much focus naturally on Best Mate very few noticed Salmon as he returned to the unsaddling area, which is situated between the parade ring and the pre-parade ring. Kay had met horse and jockey on the course with a look of relief all over her face. "Great job," said the jockey.

The trainer waited inside. He was happy. Salmon had not jumped as quickly as he could but he hadn't been in a race for almost three months so that was understandable. He had finished the race stronger than any other horse, possibly even more strongly than Best Mate.

Hourigan was pleased. He wanted to get him home now and see how quickly he recovered or if there was any reaction to the exertions. But he was a happy man.

"I think we have our horse back," he said to the owners.

CHAPTER 11

The Long Road Back

In the calm after the storm, Lisaleen returned to normal, or as close to normality as was possible.

Beef or Salmon returned home from Cheltenham in good form and the daily routine of treatment, riding out, and more treatment continued, with Kay still spending most of her day working with the horse. Her father was busy with a yard full of horses, overseeing a business that was getting bigger with every passing season.

The horse-racing industry had gone through a period of dramatic growth over the previous ten years. The number of racehorses in training in Ireland had increased by 11 per cent, between 2001 and 2003, with a total of 5,672 horses stabled in yards throughout the country. Since 1996, the number of races had risen by over 17 per cent, with an extra 45 meetings now added to the racing calendar.

Such expansion placed huge pressure on trainers and everyone else involved in the industry. The introduction of Sunday racing had a commercial impact but it also had a social effect. There was little time off, fewer opportunities to take a breather from the stresses of handling a yard full of horses and staff.

But there were also benefits. Prizemoney had rocketed. National Hunt trainers like Hourigan had competed for a total pot in 1997 that equated to €8.9million. The figure for 2003 showed a massive increase of 175 per cent to €24.5 million. Sponsorship of races had also grown by almost €3million.

Almost 1.4 million people had attended race meetings in 2003, an increase of 27 per cent from the previous decade.

The horse-racing and breeding industry had become a significant contributor to the Irish economy. A major report commissioned by the authorities outlined the income generated; admission income alone to racetracks in Ireland in 2003 was €23million. Non-betting expenditure on the tracks reached €21million while off-course expenditure by those attending race meetings was estimated at a massive €89.2million, in 2002.

One of the most striking figures reported was a 204 per cent growth in betting between 1997 and 2003, with €2.1billion wagered in the final year of the study.

The big festivals – Fairyhouse, Punchestown, Galway, Listowel, Killarney and Leopardstown – had become major events on the national calendar. Those festivals were not all about horse-racing. They were social events, places where the new rich flaunted their success. There was social status to be gained by owning a racehorse so yards became bloated. Everyone was busy. "Busy fools," is how Kay Hourigan described herself and everyone else in the business.

For decades many of the best racehorses bred in Ireland were sold to yards in Britain. There was money across the pond and, during the bleak 1970s and '80s, the economy spluttered in Ireland and the cost of keeping a racehorse in training was beyond the reach of many.

The practise of exporting racehorses continued and was big business but there was a lot more money in Ireland after the 1990s and, in the thriving Celtic Tiger economy, many more good horses were now kept at home. That meant greater competition at every level, but especially at the top, the Grade 1 races where prestige counted almost as much as the money. Almost.

Planning for the big four-day Punchestown festival in 2004 began immediately after Cheltenham. It was the big races at these festivals that motivated staff, especially when a yard had a horse of the quality of Beef or Salmon. And there were plenty of other races and decent prizemoney for Salmon's stablemates. Total prizemoney for the festival in 2004 was €1.7million and many of the stars of Cheltenham would make their return to the racecourse in Punchestown.

Hourigan felt that the Grand National meeting at Aintree on the first weekend of April would be too soon for Salmon to race again. He wanted to take care of the horse now, be selective about the number of races he would run, and he didn't want to subject him to too much travel so soon after the trip to Cheltenham. He stayed at home and watched the Grand National with more than his usual interest. Amberleigh House, which had resided at Lisaleen and won six races before being sold and sent to England in late 2000, won the big race on an emotional day for his trainer Ginger McCain, the man who had prepared the great Red Rum for his three memorable victories in the race.

The Heineken Gold Cup on April 28, the second day of the Punchestown festival, was the race chosen for Salmon's next outing. It had become one of the most prestigious races on the Irish calendar since it was upgraded to a Grade 1 Chase for horses aged five years and older. Winners since the upgrade in 1999 were Imperial Call, Commanche Court, Moscow Express, Florida Pearl and First Gold, and Hourigan wanted the name of Beef or Salmon to be added to that illustrious list. The winning prize of €80,000 was not to be sniffed at either.

Salmon's owners, Craig and McLarnon, had been extremely patient during the horse's rehabilitation and had never questioned his treatment or the cost. From time to time they would ring Kay for an update but they did not interfere. Visiting the yard they would joke with Hourigan: "We're not here to talk to you, we're going to talk to Kay, the real boss and she knows what she's talking about." The trainer hoped to repay that loyalty with a big race win and Salmon was giving all the signs that he was back to his best.

The daily routine changed only slightly for the horse. He was still receiving daily treatment for his injury. The massage therapy would be part of his life for as long as his racing career lasted, and Liz Kent would continue to monitor his progress. Everything was put in place to ensure Salmon was happy and content.

Once massaged, Salmon would lead out the string of horses for their early morning work. He always wanted to be at the front. He was the boss and he liked to show it. Even on the gallops, when Kay tried to restrain him, Salmon wanted to lead every other horse. His competitive streak never left him.

They brought him to Listowel for a racecourse workout. Timmy Murphy rode and was pleased. The horse was well and his jumping had improved again since Cheltenham. He was jumping quickly again and the speed was still there on the flat, that had never been affected by the injury, it was only when jumping the big fences that the horse felt pain. Now the pain was gone and the jumping was easy.

It wasn't just his form that pleased the trainer and his staff. The weather was also in their favour. Nearly 40 millimetres of rain had fallen on Punchestown since early March and that would provide ideal conditions for Salmon, good and safe jumping ground.

Lisaleen had fourteen entries for Punchestown over the four days, ensuring that the entire staff would be busy. Hi Cloy, Horner Rocks and For Orla would run on day one; Leaveitso, Dr Julian and Arteea would join Beef or Salmon on the journey on the second day; King Carew, Vic Ville and Native Performance were entered for day three, while Old Kilminchy, Whowouldyouask and The Screamer would run on the final day, with The Spacer entered for a charity race, the last race of the festival. It would be a demanding, even exhausting, few days but it was what they lived for. If you didn't enjoy this kind of intensity then you didn't belong in the business.

For each of the four days, nearly 20,000 spectators packed into Punchestown, dodging showers of rain and even some hail on the first day. All of the home stars of equine racing were on view, with Brave Inca and Hardy Eustace, recent winners at Cheltenham, returning to action. Moscow Flyer, a winner for Willie Mullins at the Grand National meeting in Aintree, contested the Champion Chase on the opening day and beat talented horses such as Rathgar Beau, Native Upmanship, Killultagh Storm and Alcapone.

Hi Cloy was second for Lisaleen in the novice chase on the first day but, even then, all the attention was on Beef or Salmon. No matter who he encountered on the racecourse that day, Hourigan had to answer questions about the well-being of his star horse. Defeat at Cheltenham had not lessened affection for the horse. In fact, his recovery from injury and the bravery shown on his return to the racecourse appeared to have enhanced Salmon's standing with the Irish public.

He would face some regular opponents in the big race on the second day of racing, including First Gold, who was attempting to win the race for the second consecutive year.

Adding to the sense of occasion was the race to win the Irish trainers' championship. Noel Meade was in pole position and had Harbour Pilot in the big race, while Hourigan and Willie Mullins were battling for second place. Hourigan's horses had won over €1 million in prizemoney already that season, underlining his status as one of the country's top trainers.

Mullins had entered Rule Supreme in the Heineken but the horse had endured a heavy schedule since winning the Royal and Sun Alliance Chase at Cheltenham and it was felt he'd lost his edge. He'd run at Aintree where he unseated David Casey and, the previous Saturday, had finished fifth in the Betfred Gold Cup at Sandown. Casey was onboard again and Ruby Walsh was riding Rince Ri, trained by his father, Ted. Come In Moscow would complete the field of six as a 100/1 outsider.

Hourigan and Meade were both pleased that the predicted overnight showers of rain came. The showers weren't heavy but they ensured that the ground was good. By the time racing began the skies were streaked with blue, the weather was fine and the racecourse was packed to capacity.

Timmy Murphy, who had ridden Hi Cloy on the first day of racing, had a comfortable run around the course on Dr Julian, a new arrival at Lisaleen just a month earlier. He was happy that the conditions would suit Beef or Salmon in the big race and had been very pleased with the improvement he felt in the horse at Cheltenham. Everything he'd seen since suggested the horse was continuing to improve and getting stronger and more confident. He was looking forward to finding out just how much progress had been made.

The arrival of the Doumen clan, from Chantilly in France, created quite a stir around Punchestown. They were popular figures: Francois Doumen was typically suave and Gallic and had made many friends in Ireland over the years. He had also earned a reputation as an outstanding trainer. Amongst the best horses he brought across from France to capture big prizes were Nupsala, winner of the King George VI Chase in Kempton in 1986, and The Fellow, which won the Cheltenham Gold Cup in 1994. He had also trained the great hurdler, Baracouda, owned by JP McManus, who had won the Stayers' Hurdle at Cheltenham in 2002 and 2003 and had finished second to Iris's Gift in 2004.

First Gold, was bought by JP McManus from the Marquesa De Moratalla, one of the most influential owners in the history of French racing, in 2000, and went on to win the King George. But the horse was denied his best chance of capturing the Cheltenham Gold Cup when the meeting in 2001 was cancelled due to the foot and mouth epidemic in England. Ridden by the trainer's son, Thierry, he had continued winning top-class races and a year before had won the Heineken when beating the likes of Rince Ri, Native Upmanship and Florida Pearl.

First Gold was Doumen's only entry in Punchestown that week, which led many punters to believe that expectations were high back in Chantilly that the horse could retain its crown. The horse had finished behind Beef or Salmon in Cheltenham but had followed that up with a second-place finish behind Tiutchev in the Martell Chase in Aintree on April 1. He would start as second favourite at odds of 5/2.

There could only be one favourite since the public had already found a horse to love and support. Beef or Salmon was a steady 5/4 favourite throughout the build-up and, when the starter set them off on the three mile and one furlong race over seventeen fences, he retained the favourite's tag.

Doumen, as expected, led from the start. Paul Carberry kept Harbour Pilot a close second and led briefly before settling again behind First Gold. Ruby Walsh kept Rince Ri in third place and Salmon galloped along easily in fourth. Rule Supreme and Come In Moscow were held up at the back of the small field and would never have an impact on the race.

They had jumped fifteen fences and were racing around the final bend into the straight in front of the stands when the real business began. Salmon was about five lengths off the leader when his jockey shook the reins and gave a slight kick to the belly. Rince Ri was left behind in a couple of strides and, by the straight, Salmon was third.

About ten strides from the last fence Murphy looked around him. First Gold was to his right; Harbour Pilot was beginning to veer left and there was daylight in front of Murphy and Salmon. They landed slightly awkwardly over the second last fence but were balanced after a stride. Murphy shook the reins again and Salmon coasted to the front.

Murphy relaxed as they came to the last and allowed the horse to dictate. Salmon gracefully leaped through the air and landed running. It was like watching an archer release an arrow. The horse never deviated from his line. It was … perfection. Atop the horse, Murphy knew how it felt to be on top of the world.

For a couple of strides Murphy asked his horse for a big effort and the race was immediately over. With 150 yards to go to the winning post Murphy put down his hands. He stole a look over his left shoulder at Harbour Pilot, then over his right at First Gold.

The roar of the crowd swept over horse and jockey as they slowed coming to the line, Murphy pumping his fist in triumph. He had never raised his whip, it had stayed under his right arm for the entire three miles.

It had taken 6 minutes and 10.01 seconds to cover the three miles but Salmon was hardly blowing. Murphy felt as if it had been effortless. This was the real Beef or Salmon. On this form there wasn't a horse capable of beating him. There might be critics out there who would not accept it but Murphy was convinced that it was true.

Under a headline, 'Golden Display by Beef or Salmon', *The Irish Times* Racing Correspondent, Brian O'Connor, heaped praise on the winner. "Beef Or Salmon left it until the end of the season to unleash his best but it was worth the wait as he turned in a brilliant performance to win yesterday's Heineken Gold Cup."

O'Connor went on to ask the question that was on everyone's lips in Punchestown. "Yesterday's injury-free Beef or Salmon had everyone wondering what he might have done in last month's Gold Cup if he had got there in top shape," he wrote.

The *Irish Independent* headlined 'Salmon's Great Leap of Faith' and their Racing Correspondent Damien McElroy wrote: "Beef or Salmon finally delivered a Grade 1 success at Punchestown yesterday when living up to the high expectations of his connections and legion of followers as the Tote did unprecedented business to the tune of well over €1m.

"Francois Doumen's 11-year-old tried valiantly yesterday to land back-to-back Heineken Gold Cups, but both the front-runner and his constant attendant, Harbour Pilot, were sunk as Beef or Salmon sprinted on the run to the final fence to justify sustained market support. Paddy Power reacted to one of the most impressive performances of Beef or Salmon's career by shortening the eight-year-old's odds to 10/1 (from 14/1), second favourite behind Best Mate (2/1) for next March's Gold Cup."

Michael Hourigan lavished praise on his daughter, on Liz Kent and Sue Shortt. But he reserved the most special words for the horse and, in comparing him to Doran's Pride, everyone knew how deeply Hourigan felt.

"Doran's Pride was a wonderful horse but this lad is actually better. He has more gears, he jumps better and he is bigger, so he can carry weight. Doran's Pride was the horse of a lifetime but, thank God, I've found a second one," said an emotional Hourigan.

Timmy Murphy's assessment was typically blunt as he spoke to reporters. "He has no breeding and he isn't the prettiest horse in the yard, but he is a bit of a freak. That's the best feel he's given me since last year."

It had been a very tough season for the horse and those who cared for him, which added to the emotion in the enclosure at Punchestown. There had been days when they wondered if the horse would ever recover to reach the standards that they knew he could meet. There had been so much disappointment and, at times, even a little despair that he might never be right. Watching Salmon round the final bend, and cutting down the leaders in such a commanding style, was one of the most precious sights in the racing career of Michael Hourigan.

Salmon was sent out to pasture for the summer even as plans were laid for his immediate future. There were big prizes to be won before the end of the year but one thing was clear – Salmon would go back to Leopardstown and renew his rivalry with Best Mate.

That prospect had the racing world in a tizzy.

CHAPTER 12

End of an Era?

Timmy Murphy had a problem when he returned to England after the Punchestown festival. Compared to the problems he had experienced in the past it might have been regarded as quite trivial, if not downright nonsensical, and he knew for certain that his current dilemma would not win him any sympathy.

He had just been offered one of the biggest jobs in racing as retained rider to the leading English owner, David Johnson. It was an offer that confirmed his meteoric return to the very top of his industry just two years after his plunge into ignominy on the flight from Tokyo. He should have been celebrating wildly but was, instead, wracked with self-doubt and guilt.

"What am I going to do about Beef or Salmon?" he wondered, "How am I going to tell Mike that I might not be available to ride him any more? I don't want to let him down."

Beef or Salmon had saved Murphy's career. The jockey was convinced of that. For that reason he would forever be grateful to Hourigan and to the owners. He could never forget the faith and the kindness shown to him by Hourigan and his family when others had turned their backs on him. But this offer was so good he could not turn it down.

David Johnson was a very wealthy man. Brought up in the East End of London, his father was a docker who would have quailed at the thought of his hard-earned money being wasted on something like horse-racing and gambling. From an early age, however, his son had discovered the thrill of racing. He had a head for figures, too. After leaving school, Johnson had worked his way through the financial services sector, reinvented the mortgage business in Britain, made one fortune and then another when he sold the business in 2002 to GE Finance for £216million.

By then, Johnson was heavily involved in horse-racing. He kept his horses with Martin Pipe and they had become one of the most formidable partnerships in the business. AP McCoy was stable jockey at Pipe's yard but, in April of 2004, he had accepted an offer from Irish financial guru and gambler, JP McManus, to be his retained rider. The move meant riding the best of the horses owned by McManus and trained by Jonjo O'Neill in England, as well as a selection of horses stabled all over Ireland.

Murphy never expected to be in line for the job with Johnson. He didn't even go looking for it when news of McCoy's departure was announced and was surprised when press speculation linked him to the vacancy at Pipe's yard. That speculation did not prompt him to seek the job either – Murphy just didn't think he would be in the reckoning. But David Johnson had not become successful by waiting around. He'd admired Murphy for some time, had used him when McCoy was unavailable in the past, and he wanted Murphy to ride for him.

It was tempting to Murphy for all sorts of reasons. It would provide some security, a guarantee of plenty of rides in big races on good horses like Our Vic, Therealbandit and Comply or Die. Murphy had told Hourigan in the sauna at the Woodlands Hotel in 2002 that he had no intention to flogging himself around the freelance circuit in England again, but that was exactly what he was doing. This offer was the sort he had dreamed of – an escape from insecurity and a certain amount of drudgery.

"Do you think I might still be allowed to ride Beef or Salmon?" he asked Johnson quite sheepishly when they met to discuss the offer.

"I don't think so, no," was the response. It was the only note of negativity on a day full of positives.

He had spoken to Hourigan before meeting with Johnson. The trainer was delighted with the news – he liked to see 'his' guys do well.

"Just make sure you have a clause in the contract that you are free to ride Salmon," Hourigan told him. Murphy winced on the other end of the phone.

The issue did not arise immediately on Salmon's return to the racecourse in the autumn. The horse had enjoyed his summer at Lisaleen but was happy when Hourigan brought him back from the field and had him schooling and riding out every day. Kay was still working on him daily, and Liz Kent was in regular contact as she kept checking the horse. Salmon loved the attention, and he was a happy horse.

Each day he led the string of horses, his ears pricked, content within himself. He was eating well and Kay had been delighted to discover he was one of the cleanest horses in the yard. His stable was never in a bad condition, so mucking out was easy.

She had noticed one peculiarity. He came back in from the fields at the end of the summer with a full tail but, as soon as the hard work started, the tail began to shrivel. They had never seen anything like it before but it didn't seem to affect his performance on the racecourse.

Such was his status that Salmon was entered in all the big Grade 1 races throughout the season. However, for a seasonal re-introduction to the racecourse, Hourigan was taking a slight drop in status, the Grade A Munster National at their local Limerick track. It was a popular handicap chase in which Salmon would be top weight, giving more than two stone to some of his opponents. Lisaleen was sending thirteen runners to the meeting on October 10.

As the meeting was held on a Sunday, Murphy was available to ride. McCoy was also back in Ireland to ride McManus' Risk Assessor in the race, while Jim Culloty was also at home to ride the fancied Barrow Drive for Tony Mullins, and Paul Carberry was riding Takagi for the Edward O'Grady stable. These were all fit, experienced horses and it would take a big performance from Salmon to carry top weight and win on his first outing.

It proved too difficult. Though he finished the race well to claim fifth place, Salmon had struggled with the weight. The jockey was still happy, for a first run of the season it was good enough. The trainer saw enough to suggest the horse would improve from the run. They would keep working him at home but he was on track for his next assignment, the Grade 1 Nicholson Wine Merchant Champion Chase at Down Royal on November 6.

It was an important race for many reasons, none more so than Down Royal was the home track of the owners. Joe Craig and Dan McLarnon had spent their lives in this part of Northern Ireland and the race was a sort of homecoming. Salmon enjoyed huge support from the racing community in the north of the country and this would be their opportunity to pay homage to the star in their own place.

Down Royal has a proud racing history. Situated just outside Lisburn, the racecourse gained some unwanted attention during the Troubles in Northern Ireland as it was situated just beside the notorious Maze Prison, also known as Long Kesh, which contained a complex of buildings that became known all over the world as the 'H Blocks'. This had been the setting for some of the most controversial events of that period which began with the 'blanket' or 'dirty' protest by IRA prisoners in the 1970s that lead to the Hunger Strikes of 1981 which claimed the lives of ten prisoners.

Following the Good Friday Agreement of April, 1998, the decision was taken to close the prison. The last prisoners were transferred from Long Kesh in September of 2000 and the prison was closed. For racegoers travelling from the south to Down Royal, the prison remained a reminder of the dark days of the past.

The racecourse was an antidote to the trauma of those times, an oasis to which people could escape. The course continued to develop and to improve facilities to make it one of the most welcoming tracks in the country. It was popular with jockeys and trainers because it was a true racing course, hewn from the countryside. It hosted both flat and jumps meetings and was the venue for the Ulster Derby each June.

The James Nicholson Wine Merchant Champion Chase, sponsored by the owner of the business who was also a member of the Down Royal executive, had been established in 1999. The first winner was Florida Pearl and subsequent winners were Looks Like Trouble, Foxchapel King, More Than A Stroll and Glenelly Gale. With over Stg£60,000 going to the winner, it was an extremely attractive prospect for owners and trainers.

A year earlier, Hourigan had bypassed the race because of unsuitable ground. Glenelly Gale was the beneficiary for the Arthur Moore stable that time and he was back to defend his title. Harbour Pilot and Cloudy Bays were also entered. Tom Taaffe had sent Kicking King, a horse that was being aimed at the Gold Cup in Cheltenham and had just won a Grade Two Chase at Gowran Park. Colca Canyon, winner of Salmon's last race in Limerick, was also entered and the field of eight would be completed by two outsiders, Zurs and Byron Lamb.

Timmy Murphy was desperate to ride Salmon. He had commitments to his new owner but decided to speak to him anyway. Johnson relented, he had horses running in England the same day but McCoy was available to ride for him. But he issued a warning: "I think this will be the last time."

There was huge support for Beef or Salmon. He was backed down to evens favourite, Kicking King was next in the betting at 3/1 and Harbour Pilot was supported at 4/1.

The race itself followed a familiar pattern. Murphy and Salmon stalked the field from the back, alongside Kicking King. They followed Cloudy Bays, Harbour Pilot and Colca Canyon for the best part of the race. The leading pair in the betting jumped to the front at the third last fence and the race was between them. Barry Geraghty coaxed Kicking King into the lead at the second last but Murphy was biding his time and nursing his horse. He took the lead at the last and strode to the line a comfortable winner.

Lisaleen, his owners and supporters were ecstatic. This was Salmon's 26th race and his 13th victory. The only slight concern was that the horse had suffered an 'overreach' during the race, an injury where the hind foot strikes the front heel during running. It wasn't serious but it was the type of injury that would need attention. Kay already had a heavy schedule keeping this horse going but now there was another detail to attend to. Life with Salmon was proving to be a roller-coaster of emotions, and there were more ups and downs on the way.

Salmon's cut heel added to the complications of getting the horse ready for his next series of races. Another Grade 1, the John Durkan Memorial Chase at Punchestown, which he had won in 2003, was again on his schedule on December 5, before heading for the big chase at the Leopardstown festival which, with a change of sponsor, would now be known as the Lexus Chase. Hourigan was frustrated that preparations were interrupted again. He had hoped that Salmon would have an injury-free winter but now the horse had to be given two weeks off to allow the cut to heal properly. They simply could not risk an infection in the wound, which would have led to a severe disruption of his programme.

The horse was fit and his jumping in Down Royal had pleased everyone. They could only hope that the lay-off would not set him back too much. For a racecourse gallop at Thurles after racing, on December 2, Salmon was fitted with special overreach shoes to protect his injury. With Keith Hadnett in the saddle they had a run on the flat: Salmon was comfortable, the injury was not affecting him and he showed a nice turn of pace at the end of the run. He was ready for the next assignment in three days, and there was further good news. His regular partner Timmy Murphy had declared himself available, free of commitments in England.

Kicking King was back for another tilt at Salmon. It was an interesting entry. His trainer, Taaffe, had indicated in Down Royal that they would take it easy with their horse, who was still only six years old, and would wait until Leopardstown to race Beef or Salmon again. The change of heart presented another challenge to Salmon.

So, too, did Rathgar Beau, Native Upmanship and Harbour Pilot. John James, trained by Homer Scott and ridden by Ken Whelan, would be the outsider in an otherwise elite field of chasers. Salmon's connections were in buoyant mood before the horses even got to the parade ring. Another horse carrying their colours, a five-year-old named Church Island, had won the first race of his career at a price of 8/1 in the third race of the meeting.

The mood was dented only slightly in the Durkan. Salmon ran an ordinary race by his standards. Murphy had asked him for an effort from the fourth last fence but all he got was a mistake, which cost them momentum. Kicking King was in a commanding lead by then and Barry Geraghty was taking no chances. He would not get involved in a battle for pace with Salmon this time and, as a result, they didn't hunt at the back of the field. Instead, Geraghty took command of the race from an early stage, determined to put distance between himself and Salmon long before the final couple of fences. He need not have worried, Salmon was too far back. Harbour Pilot had already been pulled up, the soft ground clearly not suiting him. John James was never competitive and Salmon just edged Native Upmanship for third place.

Murphy was not unhappy with the run. The horse had not been as good as usual but he attributed that to the break in training. He was confident Salmon would be ready, fully fit, for the next big race at Leopardstown. Hourigan was also upbeat. The two-week break from training clearly had an impact on Salmon's performance and the trainer also had to take into account the distance of two and a half miles. Salmon was clearly a better horse at three miles and more. They had three weeks now to catch up on lost work before the next outing. It would turn out to be one of the defining moments in Salmon's racing career.

But, as he left Punchestown that Sunday evening, Timmy Murphy was actually brooding. He had portrayed a positive image in his dealings with everyone that day, riding four horses for Hourigan, winning on Church Island and picking up place money on Salmon and Kerryhead Windfarm. It counted as a decent day's work. But a thought kept tugging at his mood. After two incredible years in which he had rebuilt his career as a jockey and won five Grade 1 races on an incredible racehorse, he feared that his part in the Beef or Salmon story might just have come to an end.

CHAPTER 13

Thank God We Still Have You

In the comfort of her historic home in West Lockinge, a part of Oxfordshire in which the training of thoroughbred racehorses is almost a religion, Henrietta Knight sought solace from the hardships of horse racing through Christmas television.

Her favourite film from childhood, 'The Wizard of Oz', was being shown and Knight became lost in the adventures of Dorothy, Scarecrow, Tin Man, the Cowardly Lion, Aunt Em and Uncle Henry. Her husband, Terry Biddlecombe, grew tired of the fare and went to bed early.

It was the night of December 26, 2004, the end of a long day. They'd arrived home late that evening from Kempton Racecourse, normally a ninety-minute journey but much longer that day because of traffic. Their horses Impek, Edredon Bleu and Lough Rynn had run well without challenging for the big prizes but they'd come home safe and, for Knight, that was all that really mattered.

Work hadn't ended with their return. They were in time to help with the loading of their stable superstar, Best Mate, to his lorry for the overnight trip that would take him by road to Holyhead and then by ferry to Dublin. Three staff, including Best Mate's lass, Jackie Jenner, were making the trip. Keeping the horse company was the recently retired Red Blazer, but Knight and Biddlecombe would remain at their farm until Tuesday's race day, when Best Mate would bid for a second successive victory in the big chase at Leopardstown, being run for the first time under the Lexus banner.

Knight was a natural worrier, she described the eighty horses in her care as her babies. She was also a woman who could not hide her emotions. It was part of her charm and explained, to a degree, why she was so popular and why people like Michael and Ann Hourigan enjoyed meeting her. Whatever happened when Best Mate raced for the fourth time against Beef or Salmon in two days time would not affect the relationship between the two couples.

Her worries that evening centred solely on Best Mate. The journey to Dublin was a long one, the weather was unpredictable and rough seas might upset the horse. He had travelled well the previous year, so there was no reason why 'Matey', her pet name for him, would not travel as well this time. But, until she got the phone call from Jenner to tell her that they had arrived without incident, she would continue to worry.

As Judy Garland skipped down the Yellow Brick Road, Henrietta Knight finally began to relax and, when the credits rolled, she headed for bed where Biddlecombe was already asleep. The exhaustion of the day fell over her and she, too, slept quickly and soundly. But her sleep was broken just before 1.30am by the telephone. Instinctively, she knew there was a problem.

It was Jackie Jenner. On arrival at the port she had discovered that Best Mate had somehow suffered a facial injury, a two-inch gash under his left eye and she needed instructions about what to do next. Knight consulted with her vet, rousing Roger Betteridge from his own slumber. Jenner was told to use sticky tape to plaster the cut and they would get a vet to look at the horse in Ireland. Sleep was lost. Now Knight really did have something to worry about.

With race meetings in Kempton, Huntingdon and Weatherby abandoned early on the morning of December 27 because of frost, the 'odd couple' as they were fondly referred to in racing, kept themselves busy around their farm all the time, anxiously awaiting another call from Jenner. It came in mid-morning: the sticky tape had worked, staying in place and protecting the cut. Jenner had hidden in the horse box during the ferry journey to mind Matey, defying the rules that stipulate that humans must sail on deck. She refused to leave her horse unattended.

Matey showed no ill-effects from his ordeal on arrival in Ireland, but it wasn't possible to stitch the wound because a local anaesthetic would be required and that would breach doping regulations. It was agreed that four staples would be use to close the wound. The area below the horse's left eye was not a pretty sight but the staples worked and Best Mate was in good spirits.

Unaware of the drama unfolding around Best Mate, Michael Hourigan drove from Lisaleen to Leopardstown early that same morning. The previous day, he had watched the big races from Kempton on the big screen beside the parade ring at Leopardstown and admired the performances of the Irish-trained Harchibald and Kicking King as they won the feature events, the Christmas Hurdle and the King George VI Chase. Ann, Kay and Laura accompanied Hourigan on the journey while the lads looked after the horses at the Limerick meeting. Lisaleen had more than 30 runners during that week and they were too busy to worry about horses from other stables.

From time to time, Hourigan's mind did drift to Best Mate and his meeting with Salmon the following day. Twice in Cheltenham, and a year previously in Leopardstown, they had raced each other, but their rivalry had never gathered more fire than an initial spark because of Salmon's fall in 2003 and his subsequent injury. Hourigan was a huge admirer of Best Mate, but he believed that, at his best, Salmon could beat him. And he might never have a better opportunity than the one ahead.

Best Mate had a background as colourful as that of Beef or Salmon. Born in a field in Trim, County Meath, in January of 1995, the first-time foal to Katday arrived into the world a few days early. In November, 1995, he was presented for sale at Tattersalls and was spotted by Tom Costello, a legendary figure in horse-racing, from Newmarket-on-Fergus in County Clare. It was Costello who had telephoned Hourigan the day Doran's Pride had died, offering support and encouragement, a gesture that had been greatly appreciated. Costello had discovered five winners of the Cheltenham Gold Cup, and horses he had bought at sales, and subsequently sold, went on to win two English Grand Nationals and every other major chasing prize in Ireland and Britain. He paid IR£2,500 for the foal and brought him home to Fenloe House.

Costello had enjoyed some success himself as a trainer, most notably when Tartan Ace won the Irish Grand National in 1973. He and Hourigan had a lot in common – they loved the cut and thrust of the sales ring and had a similar philosophy on horses. Costello was once quoted as saying: "I buy a horse I like

– I mightn't be as particular about the pedigree as other people are. We like the horse first and the pedigree later." The words could have come from Hourigan.

Knight and Biddlecombe had been on a scouting trip to Ireland in March of 1999 and attended a point-to-point meeting in County Waterford. It happened to be the day Best Mate first ran in public. He was raw and inexperienced and was pulled up before the end of the race but Knight immediately fell in love with the horse and later sent a fax to Jim and Valerie Lewis, friends and owners of a number of horses at West Lockinge. "Terry and I have just seen the horse of our dreams," she wrote. "He is the perfect racehorse," she added.

Before the month had ended Knight, Biddlecombe and Lewis, a man who made a fortune in the furniture business in England, were boarding a flight from Heathrow to Shannon. Costello collected them and brought them to his home. His son, Tom, showed them the horse, and Lewis and Tom senior negotiated in private. They reached a deal, the details of which have never been revealed, but Best Mate went to his new home in Oxfordshire and history was made.

Outside the racetrack, Jim Lewis was a fanatical supporter of Aston Villa football club and his racing colours were the claret and blue of the team. He also loved coming to Ireland and had attended the announcement of the new Lexus sponsorship at Leopardstown the previous January. He wasn't hard to convince when Knight decided that she wanted to return to Leopardstown in December, 2004, rather than run at Kempton. It was a decision that delighted the racecourse management. They wanted a rerun between Best Mate and Beef or Salmon because they knew it was box-office material.

Hourigan tried to keep Salmon's preparations low-key. There had been too much hype the previous year and Salmon's defeat, and some of the reaction to it, had irked Hourigan. The quality of his horse had been questioned and that hurt. His horse had been injured, the run was not a true reflection of his ability. Hourigan was determined that the record would be set straight.

He had some drama to contend with before Christmas. A decision on who would ride the horse had to be made. He knew from early December that Timmy Murphy might not be available because of his commitments to his new boss. Adding to the uncertainty was a seven-day suspension imposed on the jockey by the British authorities, on December 13, for "improper riding". Murphy had been riding a horse named Semi Precious when they fell at Plumpton. A frustrated Murphy had thrown his whip after the horse.

On appeal the suspension was reduced to one day but confirmation also came through that Murphy would be required by Johnson to ride his horse, Jurancon II, in the Welsh Grand National in Chepstow, on December 28. Johnson had previously accommodated Murphy in his desire to continue riding Beef of Salmon, but that could not continue.

After racing in Thurles on December 19, a racecourse workout was arranged for Salmon. Ruby Walsh rode the horse that evening and gave a fulsome report to the trainer, which set tongues wagging in racing circles. However, Walsh was committed to riding for Paul Nicholls in Chepstow, his mounts including Silver Birch in the Welsh National, and couldn't be available even if asked.

But, while speculation about a jockey reached fever pitch, Hourigan remained patient and calm. He consulted with the owners and advised them of his plan to wait and see if Paul Carberry might become available. Harbour Pilot was an entry in the Lexus but it seemed likely that he would be withdrawn by Noel Meade, having been pulled up in the Durkan and then reported sick.

Carberry's pedigree was unquestioned. From one of the best-known racing families in Ireland and Britain, he regularly rode for Hourigan when available. He had been the jockey Hourigan turned to when he needed Beef or Salmon schooled during the early part of his career and they had won the Clonmel Oil Chase together in 2002.

Hourigan was not a man to dispense praise too readily but he had described Carberry as "a genius" the previous September when the jockey had steered The Screamer to a valuable hurdle race victory in Listowel. He discussed plans with the owners: "If Noel [Meade] withdraws his horse I think we should book Paul." The pair agreed and, two days before Christmas, it was confirmed that Harbour Pilot wouldn't run. Carberry was booked.

Carberry's commitments meant he would not get a chance to ride the horse before the race. Christmas festivities were put on hold as he flew to England early on December 26 to ride Harchibald in Kempton, and he was also booked to ride Le Roi Miguel for Paul Nicholls. He flew home again that evening and drove to Leopardstown the following day where he rode the Dessie Hughes-trained, Central House, to victory in the big Grade 1 chase.

Frost had forced the abandonment of meetings in England but it was the incessant rain that worried the authorities in Ireland. The going was described as soft in Leopardstown on December 27, and more rain was forecast overnight. It came and the ground was softer again when the early risers arrived at the track on Tuesday morning. Knight, Biddlecombe and their jockey, Jim Culloty, walked the course in the morning. Culloty was unhappy, the ground was very soft and he was worried that Best Mate would not handle it at all. Knight belonged to the school of thought that good horses can run on any ground and wouldn't consider withdrawing the horse. They had travelled and they would run. Run him out wide and avoid the worst of the ground, was her advice.

The arrival of Best Mate, who had been stabled near the racecourse overnight, caused a flurry of excitement. News that he had been hurt began to circulate but it soon became apparent that the injury was not serious and would certainly not prevent him from running. Amongst the early spectators arriving were a number of people wearing the Best Mate colours. Beef or Salmon might have been the 'home' horse but Matey had attracted a fan base in Ireland too and would not be friendless on the day.

Jim and Valerie Lewis mingled with old friends on the course after checking on their horse. Jackie Jenner reassured them that the horse had shown no ill-effects from the incident in the lorry or the ferry crossing. He had been buzzing in the field on Tuesday and she was happy that he was ready to run. Jim Lewis posed for photographs with the Best Mate fans and generally entered the festival spirit.

Leopardstown was, as usual, packed to capacity. The variety of bars on three levels of the main stand were doing a lively business and people were crammed into the Tote hall on the lower level. Long queues formed at the hot beef roll counter. The three restaurants at the upper levels were full and, outside, punters milled around the betting ring. They were well wrapped up to protect themselves from the cold but the skies were bright, with lots of blue streaked with cloud.

Carberry began his day's work riding Beaufort County for his boss, Noel Meade, and finished in a respectable sixth place. Next he rode Vic Ville for Hourigan and, while he was last of the four horses to finish the race, nothing more was really expected. The horse had been a 14/1 chance, the outsider.

Mark The Man was his next assignment and, this time, he was expected to win. The horse, owned by JP McManus, was the 4/7 favourite, so hot the casual racegoers didn't have a bet on him. Such odds meant gambling was for the big boys only but, unfortunately for them, the horse hated the soft ground. He made a mistake at the third last fence and Carberry put a halt to his misery by pulling the horse up before the end of the race. He rode another favourite, Rosaker, in the big hurdle race. Again the horse hated the ground. Carberry pulled him out before the last fence. It was time to put on the yellow silks with the green trim for the ride on Salmon.

Kay and Laura had led Salmon to the pre-parade ring behind the stands from the stables in the centre of the course. A section of the crowd spotted them as they crossed the racetrack and greeted Salmon with a loud cheer as Michael joined them to put the saddle on the horse.

Best Mate was a few doors away. Outside the pre-parade ring the crowd was almost five deep. Everyone wanted a close-up look at the two champions. The atmosphere was mounting. Hourigan felt the weight of expectation but he was confident he had brought the horse to the course in good condition. There would not be any surprises today.

There was furious action in the betting ring. Despite the fears expressed about the ground and Best Mate's cut face, punters would not be put off. He opened in the betting as evens favourite but was shortened to odds of 9/10. Salmon had opened at 2/1 but by the time the horses were at the start his odds had grown marginally to 9/4.

Rule Supreme had been entered in the race by Willie Mullins after a series of runs over hurdles. In fact, he had not contested a race over the bigger fences since finishing fifth to Beef or Salmon at Punchestown in April but, today, Barry Geraghty was riding him and they were 11/2. Salmon's old rival, Pizarro, was priced at 9/1 while Cloudy Bays was 25/1 and Barrow Drive a 100/1 outsider.

As the flag fell, Cloudy Bays took off at a sprint and Carberry chose to stay tucked in behind the field, tracking Culloty on Best Mate. It was the start of what he would later described as, "one of the best rides of my life".

Best Mate hit the first fence hard but recovered, while Salmon was jumping for fun. Carberry had a broad smile on his face for the entire three miles and, with three fences remaining, he and Salmon jumped into the lead. They began to pull away before the second-last fence, leaving Rule Supreme to contest second place with Best Mate, but the Mullins horse fell at the last fence.

Culloty tried to rouse Best Mate but Salmon was already sprinting clear. Close to the line, with the roar or the crowd reaching unprecedented levels in the stands, Carberry looked over his right shoulder, surprised to see Culloty labouring on Best Mate. With his right hand outstretched he beckoned Culloty and Best Mate on – "catch me if you can" he seemed to be saying. The crowd went wild with delight.

In the parade ring there was pandemonium. The noise that greeted Salmon was ear-splitting. Hourigan and the owners were beaming, and Kay had tears of joy in her eyes. Carberry, who was not often expressive when the racing was done, was whooping and hollering. Photographers fell over each other trying to record the celebrations.

Ireland's champion had come good again. Michael Hourigan had been right all along.

Carberry's gesture at the finish line was a talking point, and the stewards called him to account for what was being interpreted as "unsporting behaviour". He duly issued an apology, telling reports, "it was just a bit of fun… I was delighted to see Best Mate come over here and wish the horse and Jim all the best in the Gold Cup."

But beyond the jubilation of the racetrack, further afield there was a mixed reaction to Salmon's triumph.

After past defeats, Salmon's jumping had been questioned by some critics, there were doubts cast about his class and little consideration given to his injury problems. But, even now, in the aftermath of such a key win, many of the same critics continued to question the manner of his victory, blaming the ground, blaming the cut face, blaming everything and anything, for Best Mate's defeat. It was galling.

Hourigan and Knight didn't engage in such folly.

"Best Mate is a super horse and probably didn't show up at his best today," said Hourigan.

"It's great for steeplechasing to have good, young horses coming through and Beef or Salmon deserved to win a big one," said Knight. "I've always thought Beef or Salmon was a very good horse. We're good friends of Michael Hourigan and I'm glad he's won. The horse has had a lot of knocks."

Later that evening, as he prepared to fly out for a holiday in the sun with Ann, Hourigan reflected with quiet satisfaction on the day. His belief in Salmon had been justified. He had never questioned himself or the horse, but he had been stung by some of the criticism and the fact that some critics would not give the horse the credit he deserved.

What more could the horse do? He had won fourteen races in his relatively short career, this was his sixth Grade 1 victory and he had won almost €700,000 in prizemoney. He smiled as he thought of Brendan Behan's attitude to begrudgers – "fuck them".

There was a lingering sense that Carberry's actions at the line had angered the connections of Best Mate, a belief that was only dispelled the following October. Best Mate had not raced in the meantime, missing the Gold Cup in 2005 because of a burst blood vessel and, on his re-appearance at Exeter, the Best Mate team were looking for a jockey following Jim Culloty's decision to retire. They chose Paul Carberry.

Tragically, after Carberry had nursed him around the course and pulled him up two fences from the end, Best Mate collapsed. Henrietta Knight was standing just yards away. She was with her baby when he emitted his final breath.

The Hourigan family were stunned when news of the death of Salmon's great rival filtered through. Messages of support were immediately despatched and, in the stableyard, Michael Hourigan checked on his own charges before ending up at Salmon's stable. Even if they never won another race, Salmon's presence was what really counted.

"Thank God we still have you."

CHAPTER 14

Cheltenham's Not Everything

Early in Beef or Salmon's career, just after his John Durkan victory in December 2002, a prescient article appeared in *The Racing Post*, written by the respected journalist and race commentator, Tony O'Hehir. In the article, O'Hehir analysed both the performance of the horse in the race, the reaction to the victory and the possible implications for the future, with particular emphasis on Cheltenham.

He wrote: "The schedule mapped out for the horse between now and the Cheltenham Festival is obviously geared towards getting this second-season novice as much experience as possible before the big day in March."

"The trip and moderate pace (in the Durkan Chase) made Sunday's race as far removed from a meaningful Gold Cup trial as one could get and this column's view is that it told us relatively little."

And then O'Hehir added a note that would gain significance over time: "But there is a tendency to over-emphasise the Gold Cup, almost to the exclusion of other big events, as the only race that really matters for the top-staying chasers, and all the hype about that one race should not mask the fact that there are many big prizes to be raced for, and won, between now and then. Even if he fails to deliver at Cheltenham it will be a surprise if Beef or Salmon does not add a few big races to last season's haul."

O'Hehir was voicing what many people in horse-racing believed but were slow to say publicly, namely that Cheltenham's history and tradition made it the championship of National Hunt racing but that it had also become a monster.

In some recordings of racing history Cheltenham became not just one measure of success for horse, jockey, trainer and owner – it became the only measure. Great triumphs elsewhere, performances of courage, guile and artistry were obliterated from the collective memory. A career would be remembered with only the line "he never won at Cheltenham".

In his career O'Hehir had commentated on the big races from Cheltenham and written extensively about the festival and its champions. Racing was in his blood, as was commentating: His father, Michael, was the legendary RTE commentator who first gave his voice to the Gold Cup when invited to join the BBC team for the race in 1946, which was won by Tom Dreaper's first great champion, Prince Regent.

It was that commentary that led to O'Hehir being invited to commentate from the Canal Turn at the Aintree Grand National later that same year. From then, until he retired in 1984, O'Hehir's voice became synonymous with the race and his 1967 commentary of the carnage at what became known as the Foinavon fence in the National remains one of the most famous in sports broadcasting history. His voice, and his writing in the *Irish Independent,* brought the festival into Irish homes for the first time. He commentated and reported on Cottage Rake's three consecutive successes for trainer Vincent O'Brien and owner Fred Vickerman between 1948 and 1950.

In 1949, O'Brien also trained Hatton's Grace to win the Champion Hurdle, and O'Hehir described the horse on radio as "the ugly duckling of the parade ring". The following day Castledermot won the National Hunt Chase for O'Brien. Cottage Rake was due to run in the Gold Cup on the Thursday but his preparations had been poor because he was suffering from a virus. Gold Cup day was abandoned because of frost and the race was run a month later – by then Cottage Rake was fully fit and won his third Gold Cup.

What would have happened if Beef or Salmon had had an extra month to recover in 2004?

The Gold Cup history was enriched in the 1960s by the arrival of Tom Dreaper's next superstar, Arkle. Pat Taaffe rode him to three consecutive victories and then rode Fort Leney to win the race in 1968. Taaffe also trained Captain

Christy to win in 1974 and his son, Tom, also added his name to the roll of honour. Tommy Carberry, Paul's father, rode l'Escargot to victory in 1970 and 1971 and another unforgettable Irish success came in 1986 when Paddy Mullins prepared Dawn Run, ridden by Jonjo O'Neill, to become the only horse in history to win both the Champion Hurdle and the Gold Cup at the Festival.

In establishing himself as one of National Hunt's top trainers, Michael Hourigan also immersed himself in the history and traditions of Cheltenham and the festival. His earliest adventure in the Cotswolds came in 1992 when he brought Jim Mernagh's Deep Bramble to the meeting for the first time; Jockey Enda Bolger was thrown from the horse at the third last fence.

Two years later, Deep Bramble was brought back to Cheltenham for the Gold Cup but, ridden by Peter Niven, he finished in the middle of the field of 15 runners in a race won by the Francois Doumen-trained The Fellow. Hourigan's protégé, Adrian Maguire, rode Minnehoma that day for Martin Pipe and the comedian, Freddie Starr.

Accompanying Deep Bramble on that trip were two other residents of Lisaleen: Ultra Flutter unseated his rider in the National Hunt Chase, while a youngster named Doran's Pride, ridden by Shane Broderick, contested the Sun Alliance Novices Hurdle and was contesting second place until he fell at the last fence. The race was won by Danoli, trained by Tom Foley and ridden by Charlie Swan.

On March 16, 1995, Michael Hourigan and Lisaleen Stables saddled their first Cheltenham Festival winner. Doran's Pride returned, this time for the Stayers' Hurdle and, again, Shane Broderick was in the saddle. They were sent off as 11/4 favourites and justified that tag when beating Cyborgo by five lengths.

A visit to Gloucestershire in 1996 exposed Lisaleen to the darker side of the festival. A young Timmy Murphy rode a horse called Lamero in the final race of the week, the Vincent O'Brien County Hurdle. They were fourth when they tumbled at the last fence, the fall proving fatal for the horse.

Hourigan had his second Gold Cup runner in 1997 when Broderick rode Doran's Pride to third place behind Mr Mulligan and Barton Bank. Danoli was a faller that day and, 18 days later, Broderick rode a horse named Another Deadly at Fairyhouse. The horse fell and Broderick suffered horrific injuries, leaving him paralysed from the neck down.

In total, Doran's Pride ran in four Gold Cups between 1997 and 2000, finishing third again in 1998 behind Cool Dawn and Strong Promise.

He was eighth, with Paul Carberry in the saddle, in 1999 and Paul Hourigan rode him into sixth place in 2000.

Lisaleen produced a second festival winner in 1999 when Deejaydee won the National Hunt Chase on St Patrick's Day, ridden by Tony Martin. They had been fourth in the race a year previously.

Hourigan always believed Doran's Pride should have won the Gold Cup, particularly in 1998 when he was third to Cool Dawn. The Stayers' Hurdle victory of 1995 had enhanced his status in the eyes of those who believed a Cheltenham success was an obligatory achievement to be ranked amongst the greats. Hourigan believed, too, that Beef or Salmon was good enough to win the Gold Cup. However, as he was often quoted as saying: "I have the best horse in the race but the best horse does not always win it."

The fourth-place finish in 2004 was described by Timmy Murphy as "a remarkable achievement" because of the extent of Salmon's injury and how little time the team had to work on him. That he won a Grade 1 race 41 days later added to the sense that Salmon might have won the big one if he'd had more time.

As Salmon had added three more Grade 1 successes to his record there was no choice other than have another crack at Cheltenham and the Gold Cup.

It became the stated aim for 2005, another testing trial for the horse and those closely involved with him.

Salmon had recovered well from his courageous effort at Leopardstown and was leading the string every morning after Kay had spent a couple of hours working on his back and shoulders, a routine that remained in place. Michael Hourigan was back home after his holiday in Marbella when Bobby McNally steered Kerryhead Windfarm to success in a hurdle race at Punchestown on January 15, 2005, but, following that, they were forced to wait eight weeks and one day for another winner.

Hourigan had considered a different preparation for the Gold Cup. He had questioned his decision in 2003 not to allow Salmon some experience of Cheltenham before the festival.

Now, in 2005, he faced the same dilemma – The Pillar Property Chase at the end of January was one possibility that would give Salmon experience at Cheltenham, but the Hennessy Cognac Gold Cup at Leopardstown, now obviously Salmon's favourite track, was equally prestigious and had a prize fund of €150,000. It attracted top chasers and would provide a proper test for Salmon as well as preparing him for the festival, so Hourigan again decided to stay at home.

Despite the lack of winners from lots of runners, the trainer was pleased with his star. He schooled over hurdles in Lisaleen two days before the race and appeared in good form. There was much speculation about who would ride the horse but Hourigan and the owners were fairly certain that Murphy would not be available for the Gold Cup, in which David Johnson's Celestial Gold was entered. Their policy was that there should be continuity in the riding arrangements so, if Carberry was available for both races, he would ride in both. Murphy understood the situation and accepted it.

Only seven horses contested the Hennessy on February 6. Rule Supreme, which had run so well in Leopardstown at Christmas before falling at the last fence, would again challenge Salmon, and Cloudy Bays was another regular rival. Noel Chance sent Murphy's Cardinal from England; Pizarro was also lining up, as were the outsiders, Jack High and Hersov. But Salmon's army of supporters backed him down to odds of 8/15 and were full of optimism.

Carberry was comfortable early in the race, adopting the usual tactics. Hourigan hadn't issued any specific instructions before the race, joking: "Paul does his own thing anyway." When the jockey asked for an increased effort at halfway he knew immediately that all was not right. Salmon was jumping okay but he didn't pick up on the flat and that was unusual. He wasn't helped when Pizarro fell and almost brought Salmon down with him. Horse and jockey gathered themselves together and challenged again.

Carberry coaxed the horse to the front as they headed to the second last, alongside Rule Supreme. Carberry looked across at David Casey on Rule Supreme and knew he was in trouble. His suspicions were confirmed when he heard an unusual sound that seemed to come from somewhere within Salmon's throat or chest. Rule Supreme moved ahead, Salmon didn't jump the last well and Carberry nursed him to the line in second place.

Back in his stable it was confirmed that Salmon was sick, suffering from an upper respiratory tract infection. The vets prescribed a course of antibiotics and, with four weeks still remaining before the Gold Cup, they remained optimistic that the horse would recover in time for a proper preparation and run. Meanwhile, other horses in the stable were also showing signs of infection so a procedure known as "scoping" had to be carried out on Salmon and others, which tested the patience of both the horses and their handlers.

"Scoping" is an unpleasant but very necessary veterinary procedure involving an instrument called an endoscope. The long, flexible tube with a small video camera attached to the top is inserted through the nose and gives the vet a clear view of what is happening in the horse's airway. Some horses react particularly badly to the examination while others calmly accept it. For the trainer, however, the wait for a diagnosis can be very wearing; a bad scope can wipe out months of hard work.

But, in the early months of 2005, scoping was being carried out in stableyards all across Ireland and in some parts of England. Many trainers reported an unusually high number of bad scopes and plans for many horses had to be altered. Two weeks before Cheltenham, Kicking King was scoped at Tom Taaffe's yard in Straffan. The vet reported a problem and the trainer told the heartbroken owner, Conor Clarkson, that the horse couldn't run.

Best Mate was ruled out of the big festival when he burst a blood vessel. Salmon however, was returning to work seemingly recovered from his ailment. The problem was that he had shown no signs of distress before Leopardstown and they would have to scope again before a decision could be finalised on his participation in the Gold Cup.

The procedure was carried out early on the morning of March 11 and a tense, impatient, Hourigan was forced to wait for a diagnosis. But the all-clear was given and Hourigan marched off to carry out his chores. Salmon travelled the short distance to Limerick racecourse for a gallop with Arteea, who was entered in a hurdle race at the course on the following Sunday, and Paul Carberry, injured while out hunting weeks previously, returned to action on the horse.

It was regarded as a good omen when Arteea won his race, ending the two-month wait for a winner from Lisaleen. Salmon's price for the Gold Cup was cut to 5/1 by the bookmakers. The madness across the Irish Sea was beginning again and Irish racegoers deserted the country in their droves. The Cheltenham authorities reckoned that 7,000 Irish supporters were travelling to attend and that figure would be further boosted by the diaspora already living in England.

They were right. The Irish arrived by land, sea and air with ships, trains, cars, private jets and helicopters discharging them in the days leading up to the Festival which, for the first time, would be held over four days.

The longer Festival would prove a test of stamina for more than the animals competing. In the opening day official racecard journalist, Jonathan Powell, wrote about the extension: "When Cheltenham took the brave, but some would say inevitable, decision to increase The Festival to four days for the first time this year there was a collective drawing in of breath on both sides of the Irish Sea. In falling into line with other famous racing carnivals, Cheltenham was bound to face some criticism. Hards wondered why change something that didn't need to be fixed. But most of us welcomed the initiative and there is no turning back now."

"To be at this unique race meeting each March is an enriching experience. Yet past evidence suggests that common sense is invariably the first casualty for the legion of punters on their annual pilgrimage to the Cotswolds. The strain on emotions and bank balances is unrelenting. To survive at the conclusion of The Festival is to have overcome the most compelling examination of endurance. Now, somehow, we will have to pace ourselves over four days," surmised Powell.

It had taken 82 years, as Powell pointed out, for the decision to be made. Racecourse members had first voted on extending the Festival to four days in 1923 and rejected the notion. In 2005 they agreed.

And the Irish loved it. There were three Irish winners on the first day – Hardy Eustace won the Champion Hurdle, Spot The Difference was first home in the Cross-Country Chase and Nina Carberry rode Dabiroun to win the Fred Winter Juvenile Novices Hurdle.

Salmon was Hourigan's only entry in the festival. He watched Moscow Flyer win the Champion Chase on Wednesday for Jessica Harrington; Missed That won the Champion Bumper and Carberry rode Oulart to win the Pertemps Hurdle. Another Rum was Ireland's only winner on Thursday.

What would Friday hold for Salmon?

By now, Hourigan was a veteran of the big race. The pressure still got to him a little but he handled it better. The pre-race build-up had been the usual round of interviews, telephone calls, speculation. He was glad that the race had finally arrived.

"If Beef or Salmon could run so well last year off an interrupted preparation, then he really should be able to do a lot better now. I know I have a good horse.

He has done a lot in his short career to date to prove that. But you need luck, and this year you need health. If we get both this could just be his year," he told reporters.

But 2005 also found Hourigan in more philosophical mood: "I've had my ups and downs at Cheltenham, but the important thing is to not fall down when things go wrong. It took me so long to get here that I can take the knocks, and, when it's all over, I'll look forward to going home and preparing my horses for other tests."

Salmon was brought to the track early on the morning of the race. His spirits were good. Just two other Irish runners were in the field of fifteen after Willie Mullins withdrew Rule Supreme. The infection that had threatened Kicking King's participation had cleared up in a week, surprising but delighting his trainer, and Tom Taaffe's charge was installed as the 4/1 favourite. Pizarro was back again and Timmy Murphy's ride, Celestial Gold, was 9/2 with Salmon named third favourite at 5/1. There was little talk of strategy between jockey, trainer and the owners before the race; Salmon would be held up while Carberry judged the race.

By the time they had the second fence jumped Carberry had stopped making judgements about how the race was being run, he was thinking only about Salmon. The horse was out of sorts. He never found a decent stride, hit a couple of fences and was never competitive. Watching through his binoculars Hourigan willed Carberry to bring the horse home safely, he wanted nothing else.

The jockey tried one more rallying call but there was no response. On the hill at the top of the course, where the real action often starts at Cheltenham, Carberry relaxed his gait and their race was over. Kicking King and Barry Geraghty, watched from the stands by Tom Taaffe, enjoyed a glorious run and justified his favourite's tag by winning comfortably.

Few words were spoken in the unsaddling area, Hourigan wanted to get the horse home. "Some days it just doesn't happen. They're not machines. It's just a pity they can't tell us what's wrong," he said ruefully to no one in particular. "Let's get him home. I think it might be time for a rest," he added.

Almost a year later, Tony O'Hehir returned to the Cheltenham theme in another article in *The Racing Post* about Beef or Salmon. The context was Salmon's bid for the 2006 Hennessy Gold Cup and another possible run at Cheltenham.

O'Hehir wrote: "Beef or Salmon disputes top spot in the Cheltenham Gold Cup betting despite there being a university, never mind a school, of thought that Cheltenham is not his track. It could be that a horse who had his share of problems in the past, mainly as a result of the crashing fall he suffered in his first bid for Cheltenham glory in 2003, is now thriving in a season during which many other big names have bowed out with problems of one kind or another. Ignoring the rantings of McCririck [TV Pundit, John], who berated the Beef or Salmon camp for going for the Hennessy instead of the Pillar Chase at Cheltenham, the decision to stay in Ireland was a wise one. The small matter of the value of the Hennessy was ignored by McCririck, who appears completely obsessed by the Cheltenham Festival, virtually to the exclusion of everything else. It has been said before, and it merits repeating – an owner can have a hell of a good season and show a handsome profit without a winner at Cheltenham.

"The chances are that the Beef or Salmon team will be heading to Cheltenham with a six-figure prize in the bag and a successful season already behind them," concluded O'Hehir.

The journalist recognised the temptation, the lure of Cheltenham, for trainers like Hourigan and the owners. Salmon kept on beating the best chasers, including Gold Cup winners, on his home soil but each time Cheltenham came around the Salmon team found it impossible to resist. The horse earned the right every year to run in the big race, even if it was not certain that he actually wanted to go there.

The argument was tossed around again in 2006. The horse always travelled well and had never given an indication that he didn't like going to England. He had never acted up in the three previous trips to Cheltenham when the memory of his fall would have been fresher. By the time the Gold Cup came around he was the pre-race favourite and all the indications were that he was fit and ready. He had beaten all the leading contenders and, with Kicking King missing the race through injury, everything seemed set up for Salmon to finally win the big race.

But the horse had a few surprises in store for everyone, especially Kay. He was well behaved when being saddled and in the parade ring he showed no sign of distress. Then, as Kay led him out to the course, Salmon suddenly became restless, bucking violently, wrenching free of Kay and taking off down the track. Paul Carberry let him go, sitting carefully and giving the horse time to calm down. Such a demonstration had never happened before and was totally out of character. "If that lad bucked you'd be afraid he would fall over," Kay had once said about her charge. Neither jockey nor groom could pinpoint anything that might have spooked the horse. He was just unhappy. Kay had never subscribed to the theory that a racehorse would react to a particular course, that Salmon had not won at Cheltenham because he didn't like the place. He had never given her reason to believe it and there had always been a specific reason as to why he did not perform as well there as elsewhere.

But now Kay began to wonder.

Salmon's mood didn't improve when the race began. It was a chore to a horse whose jockeys always commented in how effortless his runs were. But, in Cheltenham, it was all effort with little return. For the first time ever, Irish horses filled the first three positions; War of Attrition led home Hedgehunter and Forget the Past. Salmon, the pre-race favourite, was not among them.

Reflecting immediately after the race, Hourigan had to admit: "I probably have to believe what people say about this horse and Cheltenham now. He just didn't perform today and I don't really have any excuses. There are plenty of good races for him back in Ireland and he will run in the Heineken Gold Cup at Punchestown and then go to grass. I don't know if we will come back here again."

But a year later, perhaps inevitably, Lisaleen was back again for another crack at Cheltenham. It was the same story, Salmon was running so well they couldn't keep him at home: The results demanded that he run again.

Despite all the disappointments of the past it was still an extraordinary achievement for the horse to contest five consecutive Gold Cups but, this time, Hourigan decided on some new tactics. The horse did not travel until the day before the race, a decision that seemed to work as he was much more settled on the day under new jockey Andrew McNamara. Moreover, the Salmon team adopted bolder tactics, taking on the race from the front. In a move loudly cheered by Salmon's legion of supporters, they vowed that if he was going down, he was going down fighting.

But fortune failed to favour the brave and there was no fairytale ending. New stars were emerging from the shadows and, to the cheers of the English punters, Kauto Star broke the two-year stranglehold the Irish had on the trophy.

Salmon was nursed home and this time there was no fuss. His team bowed to the inevitable: This great chaser, who was able to take on all-comers at home and win the biggest prizes available, would never win the Cheltenham Gold Cup.

To some observers that was a mark against the horse. His trainer and his owners, however, had other prizes to console them and other days to enjoy.

Cheltenham was important. After all, its lure had enticed Hourigan and the star of the Lisaleen Stables across the Irish Sea five times.

But Cheltenham wasn't everything.

CHAPTER 15

You're One Lucky Sod, Hourigan

Once part of the lush green plains that lay beneath the rolling Dublin Mountains, Leopardstown Racecourse is now a grassy oasis amidst a desert of industrial expansion.

Where its greenery was previously complemented by other lush countryside colours, the course is now enveloped by differing shades of grey that include a motorway, an ever-expanding industrial estate, roundabouts of organised confusion, all-too-frequent traffic lights and, of course, housing. Development, not all of it the fault of the so-called Celtic Tiger, has tied a concrete scarf around the shoulders of the old course.

The old stands survive, minus their former majesty but managing at least to avoid the demolition crews whose wrecking balls remained poised until the recession shredded grand plans for a refurbishment. Now the mix of old, and more recent, structures stand testament to the vision of the original designers. The success story of Leopardstown is not all about the staging of big races in front of packed houses year after year. It's just as much about survival.

Dublin, when times were simpler and people were occupied with less material matters, was able to support three racetracks. Baldoyle, on the north of the city, was a product of the 19th century and the lands along the coastal road that linked Sutton and Howth with Portmarnock and Malahide, became the most popular place for the racing of thoroughbreds on the island of Ireland. The unique concrete grandstand built at the outset of the 20th century provided protection from the elements only on its lower level, and those who stood on the terrace above were effectively standing on the roof. In many ways, it was reminiscent of parts of the old Aintree.

But on March 25, 1973, the Louth Hunt held its annual point-to-point meeting in Baldoyle. It was a day of nostalgia: The racecourse where Arkle and Flyingbolt had embarked on their historic odysseys was to close for the final time at the end of the day. Insurance difficulties with the old stand were cited as the reasons for the demise of the old course, but that was a flimsy excuse. Developers were hovering and would cast a shadow over the same lands for decades to come.

Across the capital, the Phoenix Park racecourse in the northern corner of one of Europe's largest city parks was barely managing to survive. It had hosted horse-racing since 1902 and boasted some architecturally delightful stands and a narrow, tight track that turned back on itself and was only suitable for flat racing.

At virtually its dying breath, Phoenix Park was resuscitated in 1980 by the intervention of trainer Vincent O'Brien and his enormously wealthy friends, such as Robert Sangster and John Magnier – the original Coolmore syndicate. They took over the running of the racecourse and summer evenings were transformed, but not even their expertise and wealth could sustain the course and, ten years later, the developers finally got their hands on the grounds they coveted. Concrete was poured and the skyline near Castleknock was forever changed.

The destruction of the Phoenix Park racecourse left only Leopardstown. Six miles, or ten kilometres, south of O'Connell Street, it, too, had been subject to the scrutiny of the developers in the 1960s. The affluence of its setting, adjacent to the wealthy suburb of Foxrock, made it extremely attractive to the money men who, across the city, were clamouring to build more houses and office space than Dublin would ever need.

After a period of worrying uncertainty, Leopardstown was finally taken over by the Irish Racing Board, the predecessor of the current ruling body, Horse Racing Ireland. It was a decent bit of business and the racecourse, first used for the purpose in 1888, began to grow in popularity with the Dublin people. Facilities were regularly upgraded and Leopardstown became an early pioneer of corporate entertainment at sports venues. Private boxes were included, restaurants were provided to complement the bar facilities and a golf course in the centre of the track provided income, as did the leisure facilities attached to a wing of the grandstand.

During the months of December and February the course was home to the biggest and best National Hunt meetings. Champion hurdlers and chasers raced for prestige and prizemoney and the access roads were clogged from early morning on race days. From April to November, the wealthy and the lightweights, the owners, horses and jockeys of the flat racing world had the course to themselves.

The left-handed course was a good galloping mile and a half, with a testing rise towards the finishing line. A quaint feature was the sprint track, which began to the right of the grandstand, the horses running against the natural grain. The first couple of furlongs of that sprint track were part of the nineteen acres the racecourse lost in a compulsory sale to the local authorities, Dun Laoghaire Rathdown County Council, in 2001. But the forced sale had its compensations – the racing body received €18.5 million and years later the M50 motorway was completed, providing access at Junction 15 where the sprint start had once been. The old days of traffic jams on the mountain roads and panicked, last-minute dashes were over.

Michael Hourigan and his fellow Limerick trainers, could leave the county at 9am in the morning and walk through the Dublin course's gates a few minutes after 11am without ever testing the speed cameras.

Many times before the opening of the super highway, Michael Hourigan had made the journey from Lisaleen to Dublin's southside. A torturous undertaking, whose first traffic jams would be encountered before ever leaving Limerick city, drivers could be confident of further hold-ups in Nenagh and Roscrea. Motorists prayed for a free run through Borris-in-Ossory and Mountrath before meeting further blockages in Portlaoise. Uncertainty haunted the traffic in Monasterevin and Kildare but Newbridge was a guaranteed disaster until by-passed in the early 1990s. And all that before they reached Dublin, where gridlock really began.

Drivers experimented with various routes to get them to their destination but towing a horsebox with four fractious animals and quick-tempered stablehands cut down the available options. Experience taught Hourigan that success in reaching Leopardstown was a question of timing, so early morning departures were the rule, darkness covering the land and only the sound of the engine breaking the silence as the Lisaleen team left home.

But, if a trainer had ambition and a horse good enough, he would make whatever sacrifices were necessary to travel to Leopardstown. That was where the best in the business gathered in December, January and February and, if you wanted to test yourself against the best, or compete for the biggest purses, then you had to be there. Sponsorship of races was in its infancy when the Black and White Whiskey Champion Chase was introduced in Leopardstown in 1986. The race later became the Ericsson Chase in 1992 and Lexus took over the title sponsorship in 2004. Maid of Money won the race in 1988 when the winner's prize was worth €30,000 in modern money, while the next best first prize on the card that day was worth the equivalent of just €6,000.

Hourigan was always ambitious and, when he found a horse as good as Deep Bramble, he brought him to Leopardstown, enjoying a couple of runs before the pair struck gold in 1993 in the Ericsson. Doran's Pride won the same race in 1998 and, by the start of the 2005-2006 season, Hourigan was plotting a third victory for Beef or Salmon, who had already won in 2002 and 2004.

Salmon contested the Hennessy Gold Cup in February 2006. Originally run as the Vincent O'Brien Gold Cup, this race had been sponsored by the brandy makers since 1991. Doran's Pride had won it in 1998 and Salmon had added it to his list of victories in 2003.

If Beef or Salmon did not like Cheltenham, he surely loved Leopardstown. Before the end of 2003, he had only failed to place once in five starts – and that was at the outset of his career. Whatever fates might await him on his travels outside Ireland, good fortune always seemed to be his companion in Leopardstown. The only worry his trainer was ever had regarding Leopardstown was getting Salmon there healthy.

In the autumn of 2005 that was proving to be much more complicated than anyone could have envisaged.

•••••

In the wake of his 2005 loss in Cheltenham, Salmon's trainer decided rest was as important as work at this stage of his career, so the star of the Lisaleen Stable was given a well-earned break that lasted 205 days.

By the second week of October, Hourigan was kick-starting Salmon's return with a run over the flat in the Irish Cesarewitch over two miles at the Curragh. Rory Cleary lightened the load on Salmon's back by three pounds and the pair finished in the middle of the seventeen-runner field, running well on the straight to the finish.

Hourigan was pleased. He had promised Craig and McLarnon that they would go back to Down Royal for the Nicholson Chase. No horse had won it twice and it would be fitting if Salmon could do it for two Ulstermen. The Northern Ireland Festival of Racing was scheduled for two days, November 5 – 6, and had attracted a huge number of entries from all over the island, as well as a few from England. The Friday fixture welcomed a large local crowd, which was supplemented by those travelling from further afield on the Saturday.

Horses such as Watson Lake and Adamant Approach were generating interest. Adding to the sense of anticipation was champion and classic-winning Flat jockey, Johnny Murtagh, who was continuing his adventures over hurdles – a practice he had abandoned in the early part of his career – atop a good horse trained by Mick Halford named Golden Cross.

But the main focus remained on the potential clash between Beef or Salmon and the latest star of the chasing scene, War of Attrition. Owned by Michael O'Leary, the controversial and very public face of Ryanair, and trained by Michael 'Mouse' Morris, 'War' had taken the notable scalp of Kicking King a month earlier at Punchestown.

It wasn't a two-horse race; Native Upmanship was competing at Grade One level again, while Mariah Rollins had sound form, in Down Royal especially. There was some tension overnight as the course authorities awaited confirmation that War of Attrition would run. Rain was a concern for a horse racing over three miles for the first time but his jockey, Conor O'Dwyer, had ridden on day one and reassured O'Leary and Morris that the chase course was in good condition and safe for the horse to run on.

Two races had already taken place on the second day of the festival when course manager Mike Todd was contacted by police. A coded warning had been telephoned to the Samaritans claiming that four bombs had been placed on the course. Pre-race security clearance had been received but the police couldn't take any chances so Todd informed his Executive and a 'Code Yellow' was issued. A police helicopter hovered over the course and the call to evacuate was announced over the public tannoy. Throughout the thirty years, and more, of the Troubles in Northern Ireland, Down Royal had operated without a break, even when other events were regularly affected. There hadn't been a bomb threat at an Irish racecourse since the Irish Derby had been disrupted temporarily by a hoax in 1987. And, while the Aintree Grand National had been abandoned and the course evacuated in 1997 as a result of a bomb threat, the bomb alert at Down Royal was a savage blow after decades of hard work to rise above the conflict.

It wasn't possible to re-schedule the meeting and worse was to follow. The course was again targeted less than two months later, when another threat was made during the December 26 fixture. Again the course had to be evacuated.

Beef or Salmon was amongst the first of the horses to be loaded into his box and driven away from the racecourse. Hourigan had made an entry the next day in the Leopardstown November Handicap, and booked facilities at the track for an overnight stay as the racecourse had just completed a major refurbishment of its stables. They had built a new overnight yard, modernised the 120 stables already there, and built 20 new stables. A canteen for stable staff was also included in the work and veterinary facilities had been modernised.

Hourigan was disappointed for Salmon's owners and would have preferred a run over Down Royal's fences rather than the flat, but it was important one way or another to get a run to help prepare Salmon for the Christmas Festival.

However, as things transpired, the weekend of drama had only just begun. Salmon had an uneventful overnight stay in Dublin and Kay went to fetch him from the stableyard in the centre of the course to bring him across the saddling area. It was there that she spotted a trickle of blood coming from his nose. The stewards had to be informed and they ordered her father to withdraw the horse.

"Can this weekend get any worse?" wondered Hourigan aloud, an expletive cutting through the air. "Now where do I go with him?"

On the journey back to Limerick, he mulled over the options. The Betfair Chase at Haydock Park on November 19 was a possibility and, while he didn't really want to travel outside Ireland, his alternatives were limited. The race's sponsorship also made it attractive: a Stg£1 million bonus was on offer to any horse that won the Haydock race, the King George at Cheltenham and the Gold Cup. "There's nowhere else to go," decided Hourigan.

A week later he was certain the right choice had been made. Haydock was to be a top-class chase as Kicking King was travelling from Ireland seeking another big prize in England. Keen Leader, Royal Auclair, Take The Stand and Ollie Magern were also taking their chances, while a further familiar name was on the race list. Kingscliff, the horse that had just twenty months previously won the race in which Hourigan lost Doran's Pride, would once again oppose a star from Lisaleen.

Kingscliff was trained by Robert Alner on his family farm in Dorset and owned by a retired engineer named Alfie Sendell, a well-known jumping enthusiast who spent more time at point-to-point meetings than on the racecourses of England. A frequent visitor to Ireland, it was during one such trip to the Puncestown festival in 2002 that Sendell was introduced to, and subsequently bought, Kingscliff.

Bred in County Antrim by farrier Ian Gault, Kingscliff was then five years old. Gault had spent Stg£700 to have his mare, Pixies Glen, covered by Toulon and was presented with a foal in May, 1997. Six months later he picked up IR£2,400 for the foal at the sales in Tattersalls and, three years later, the horse was entered, and later withdrawn, from the sales at Goffs – the same sale where Hourigan purchased Beef or Salmon.

The journey to Haydock was uneventful, Salmon enjoying the company of Almier who ran in one of the early hurdle races and gave his jockey, Jamie Spencer, an uncomfortable experience of National Hunt racing by dumping him onto the frosty ground at the second obstacle.

Paul Carberry was to ride Salmon and Carberry's sister, Nina, was flying to Liverpool that same weekend to have her first experience of the Grand National fences at the Aintree meeting on the Sunday. She rode Forest Gunner and was unseated at the third fence. Paul had a more comfortable ride, though it was cold and wintry at Haydock. Overnight frost had been slow to thaw and, by early afternoon, the stewards were forced to omit four fences on the long back straight. Jim McGrath, the racing commentator writing as Hotspur in the *Daily Telegraph*, described the ground as "just plain horrible". Martin Pipe and David Johnson withdrew Celestial Gold and, suddenly, Timmy Murphy was transformed into the role of spectator.

As the race progressed, Kingscliff's young jockey, Robert Walford, followed instructions when the pace was deemed a little too pedestrian. He moved to the front when they had completed just over two of the three miles to be raced. Carberry, and Barry Geraghty on Kicking King, gave chase and the Gold Cup winner was the first to fold, an excuse being later offered that a nail from the left hind shoe had pierced the horse.

Oblivious to Kicking King's fading, Salmon kept galloping and, at the line, was only a length behind Kingscliff. The bank balance had been satisfactorily enhanced and his trainer was delighted with the effort. For his first race over fences, and only his second race of the season, Haydock was most satisfactory. It was also the second time that Salmon had finished in front of Kicking King in a Grade One chase – those who continued to knock Salmon would have to give him some credit for that. It was, Hourigan thought, the perfect way to prepare for the sequence of Grade One races that would be the programme on their return to Ireland.

• • • • •

But first Hourigan had a dilemma to consider. There was a school of thought that Beef or Salmon should run in the 2005 version of the King George VI Chase, after the race had been switched to Sandown from Kempton, which was undergoing a major refurbishment.

The similarity of the Sandown course to Leopardstown was attractive – it's generally believed that the designs drawn up for the new Leopardstown racecourse in the late 19 century were based on Sandown Park. There are certain similarities in the layout, though there's one considerable difference – in Sandown they run clockwise, while in Leopardstown they run the opposite direction.

Nonetheless, Michael Hourigan thought about another journey across the Irish Sea for the Sandown event. The Kicking King team were bullish about their chances, but Hourigan certainly didn't fear any horse in the race.

Still, he didn't think Salmon had anything to prove. And why travel so far when there was a perfectly good race, the Lexus, to be won at home on a track where the horse, owners and trainer were comfortable and where Salmon's public flocked in huge numbers to support him?

The Hennessy in February at the same track was a major part of that season's plan and, all things considered, Hourigan could not find a reason to change that plan. This year, Salmon would not have another warm-up. That would be the only difference.

Meanwhile, Hi Cloy flew the Lisaleen flag in the John Durkan Chase at Punchestown and had a thrilling victory over Jim, trained by Jim Dreaper, with Forget The Past finishing third. War of Attrition was a disappointing fifth, prompting Mouse Morris to worry. Mouse wanted War to go to Leopardstown to take on Beef or Salmon and prepare for Cheltenham, but his horse wasn't running well. A stomach problem with War was diagnosed and treated.

There were no such problems in Lisaleen. In fact, it was the serenity that was discomfiting, particularly to Kay who had been superstitious since the days of Doran's Pride.

"I would go up the road with my hands over my eyes in case I'd see a lone magpie," she would explain. She stuck to the same routines in the week before a race and, on race day, always wore the same jumper in the Padjo colours of green and red. Having gone through emotional turmoil after his death, Kay had adopted a more relaxed attitude. She didn't worry as much about winning any more. In her mind, the horse would win if the horse was good enough. She simply wanted the horses to come back home safely.

Kay and her father met in the yard a few days before Christmas. All their entries for Limerick and Leopardstown were confirmed and the horses were in good shape. It was early afternoon and the air was still. Just a few staff quietly went about regular chores.

"You're fierce quiet," Michael commented, "is there something the matter?"

"Nothing at all," answered Kay, "and that's what's worrying me. It's awful quiet."

"Christ almighty," her father growled. "You're not happy when there's a problem and you're just as grumpy when there's no problem at all."

They thought about that for a moment, and then father and daughter laughed together. It had been a hard, stressful two years. There had been a lot of really good days, and some terribly bad ones, yet they were thriving and had a great horse on their hands.

"Do you not feel any pressure?" Kay asked.

"Let me tell you a story," her father said. "I was in Fairyhouse one day many years ago with Doran's Pride in a three-runner field [It was the Hatton's Grace Hurdle, run in December 1995]. There was huge expectation and he was 1/5. I was under so much pressure, I was shaking so bad I couldn't hold my binoculars. I had to take them down. My heart was thumping so hard that I would have sworn the fella beside me could hear it. I was so psyched up. I asked myself that day what was wrong with me. I was worrying whether or not I had done enough with the horse. Of course I had. I knew it. So why was I worrying? I was bringing all the pressure on myself. I vowed it would never happen again. And that cured me."

Kay smiled. She knew that her father had done everything he could with Salmon, and she knew she had done everything she could. The horse was in the form of his life. Forcing the doubts from her mind, she couldn't wait to get to Leopardstown.

As usual, Salmon travelled well. He had Church Island and Mystical Breeze for company, both of which were owned by Salmon's connections. In the pristine stableyard at the centre of the racecourse, Salmon had real presence. Just walking from the lorry he exuded power and attracted attention even when surrounded by tons of the best horseflesh bred and reared in Ireland.

Just four opponents would line up alongside him in the Lexus Chase at 2.35pm. The crowd of just over 17,000 was a little smaller than the previous year but, with no Best Mate in the race, all of them were there to see Beef or Salmon.

War of Attrition had recovered to take his place and both owner and trainer were worried only that it was his first time to run over three miles. Hedgehunter, a classy winner of the Aintree Grand National in April, would represent Willie Mullins, and Ruby Walsh had returned from duty in England to ride. Michael O'Brien had entered the tough Forget The Past, with Davy Russell on his back and the quintet was completed by Jack High, trained by Ted Walsh and ridden by Garret Cotter.

Hourigan and Carberry didn't converse much before the race. The usual pleasantries were exchanged with the owners and members of their families. With such a small field there was lots of room in Leopardstown's large parade ring for people to mingle but no one needed to eavesdrop on what, if any, instructions the trainer would give to the jockey of the odds-on favourite.

From the start, Walsh set Hedgehunter off in front. He was a proven stayer, who would try to burn the pace off Salmon. Forget The Past, owned by the property developer, Sean Mulryan, was tucked into second place by Davy Russell, while Conor O'Dwyer steered War of Attrition calmly into third.

Salmon and Carberry stayed a close fourth, just outside Jack High, both horse and jockey enjoying themselves. Carberry worked with the horse through the race, providing encouragement at each fence when required. Examining his competitors' faces, he could see they were having to work harder. If Salmon kept up his work rate, Carberry felt confident they'd have few problems. Coming to the twelfth fence down the back straight Carberry relaxed just a little, something he'd later curse himself for. As he relaxed, so too did Salmon. The fence came quickly, the horse barely ready, and he bustled through it rather than jumped it. Horse and jockey were momentarily shaken and dropped back a couple of lengths. In the stands a moan rose from the crowd and the trainer feared something had gone wrong.

But Carberry rattled the reins. Salmon picked up again and they flew over the next fence. By the fourteenth fence they were cruising towards the front. Hedgehunter began to fade, Forget The Past made an effort but was overhauled in the straight. War of Attrition tried to keep the race alive but, once Salmon jumped the last, the race was over and he eased home four lengths clear of War of Attrition. Forget The Past was a distant fourth, just ahead of Hedgehunter.

"That's his best ever jumping display," declared a beaming Hourigan as Kay led the horse back into the parade ring to huge roars from the crowd.

Carberry was effusive: "He gave me a great feel all the way. When he jumps well you always know that he's going to run well. He sprinted away from them in the end."

The spectre of Cheltenham was raised.

"There's a race to be won here before that," pointed out Hourigan, nodding in the direction of Willie Mullins. Hedgehunter's trainer picked up the remark and the two men exchanged a smile.

The race referred to by Hourigan had a special resonance for the two trainers. Since 1998 the pair had held a vice-like grip on the valuable Hennessy Gold Cup: Hourigan had won it twice, with Doran's Pride in 1998 and Beef or Salmon in 2003, but every other year over that period Mullins had trained the winner. Florida Pearl had won it four times in 1999, 2000, 2001 and 2004, Alexander Banquet won it in 2002 and Rule Supreme had got the better of Beef or Salmon a year before.

Battle was about to re-commence.

• • • • •

Under pleasingly clear skies, the spring air crisp and cool, the Lisaleen team arrived early in Leopardstown on the morning of February 12, 2006. They had six horses racing on the day and, as usual, Kay took charge of Beef or Salmon while keeping an eye on the rest of the runners.

There was plenty of banter with grooms from the other yards. Kay spent some time with Mia Niemela, Hedgehunter's groom. Mia was from Finland but spoke English with an accent that was born of Carlow. They swapped news of their charges and of other horses – Rince Ri would not race against them having been withdrawn and, while they didn't say it, both knew it didn't really matter. The big prize of the day belonged to one or other of their two charges.

Michael and Ann Hourigan travelled separately from the rest of the Lisaleen crew and were meeting the owners of some of the other horses. Amongst the runners was a five-year-old named Mossbank that Hourigan felt had great chase potential. Mossbank was owned by the Gigginstown Stud, the Westmeath breeding enterprise developed by Michael O'Leary in Westmeath, and run by his brother, Eddie. Gigginstown had a number of other runners that day and O'Leary was in Leopardstown to see how his charges were progressing.

O'Leary's schoolmate from their days in Clongowes Wood College, and former Ryanair colleague, Cathal Ryan, son of the Ryanair founder Tony, was also at the races to watch his horse, The Railway Man, run, and the two men talked and joked with each other.

Jim Culloty joined them briefly: Best Mate's former jockey was launching his training career in the Hunter's Chase with the veteran Lord Noelie, who had won many fans during a successful career in England.

But the focus was very much on Beef or Salmon who was endeavouring to win his eighth Grade One race. The level of expectation was enormous and amongst the 16,000 strong crowd that had gathered at the meeting, Hourigan recognised many faces. The favourites were certainly on form, four of the first five races claimed by the favourite, with the sole exception being Ryan's, The Railway Man, who won the Grade One Novice Chase at a price of 16/1.

The punters were emboldened by their good fortune, the betting ring was buzzing and bookmakers were searching the depths of their satchels. Beef or Salmon odds opened at 4/11 but, by the time the horses had left the parade ring and were gathering at the start, the odds were 2/5. Hedgehunter was 100/30 with the rest of the field at 20/1 or more.

"A sure thing," Hourigan heard one punter say, before another, wiser, voice counselled, "In this game there is no such thing as a sure thing".

Before the starter had reached his rostrum at the three-mile mark at the top of the back straight on the right of the grandstand, David Casey had positioned Hedgehunter prominently. He was determined to lead the field and, when the tape went back, he was already a length in front. Carberry almost casually pushed Salmon into the race, just ahead of Jack High at the back of the field.

Prince of Tara, Strong Project, Native Upmanship and Nil Desperandum were strung out in a line behind the leader and Carberry gave Salmon plenty of room and space behind them, dropping to the rear of Jack High from time to time but always looking in charge.

The horses were well spread across the track and Carberry was sitting comfortably. He had time to look at the stand as they passed it for the first time. The pace was sedate and though jockeys would normally have a few words with each other, today they were too far apart.

The field passed the halfway mark, then the starting point, leaving 10 furlongs to run, and headed towards the eleventh fence. Salmon was still second-last but only five lengths from the front and almost directly behind Strong Project, who was running in second place. Using his hands and feet Carberry prompted Salmon for a good jump and they sailed over the fence. But, even as Salmon's front hoofs touched earth, Carberry heard an anguished shout. Strong Project fell in front of him, throwing Johnny Allen over his head.

Salmon reacted quickest. As the jockey shifted his body Salmon took a couple of steps to his right to avoid the fallen horse, then steadied himself and returned to his preferred line in the centre of the course. From the stand Hourigan watched through his binoculars and smiled. The horse had been clever and moved even closer to the front at the next fence.

As they approached the thirteenth fence, Carberry moved Salmon alongside Native Upmansip on his left and Nil Desperandum on his right. Momentarily, Salmon could not be seen from the stands as the horses approached the fence and though Hourigan switched his gaze to the big screen he couldn't see anything there either.

Instead he heard the pitch of course commentator Des Scahill's voice rise an octave, "… and Beef or Salmon hit that one hard… Beef or Salmon lucky to survive an error there…"

Hourigan scanned the course. There. Salmon was running again and was back in the pack. He must have made a mistake, but how had it affected him?

On the horse, Carberry was calm. "What was that about?" he asked his horse after Salmon seemed to change his mind in mid-air and almost fell into the fence.

"Let's get the next one right."

They cleared it comfortably and Salmon was flowing again. They jumped into third place at the next fence and moved easily into second as they started to turn, a length away from Hedgehunter. Casey stayed on the inside as they jumped the second last but Salmon took it in the middle and landed full of running. The two horses were side by side going around the final bend, clear of the rest of the field and concentrating now only on each other.

David Casey was all hands and heels but Carberry only gave Salmon a few pats on the neck. They were careful on the approach to the final fence, veered a little to the right and, as they landed, Carberry hunched low and took a glance to his left.

Hedgehunter was toiling.

Carberry pushed at Salmon.

The horse galloped on and was clear by the time Carberry gave him a congratulatory slap and eased the pressure, before they passed the winning post.

Hourigan looked relieved as Kay led the horse in. Willie Mullins was one of the first to greet him.

"Your lad looked a picture today," Mullins complimented both trainer and groom. "That was a great run."

Mullins then turned to the reporters. "I have no excuses. Our horse jumped well and travelled well. He couldn't have finished an inch closer."

Hourigan gave his reaction: "I was nervous before this even though I tried not to be. He was there to be shot at. But he did it well."

As he dismounted Carberry kept his report short: "This is a serious horse."

• • • • •

Almost twelve weeks later, on the night of April 30, Michael Hourigan looked in on Beef or Salmon before driving up to the house for a rest.

Back in the kitchen he took off his work boots before entering the living room. He sat in his favourite armchair in the corner, the television remote control beside him, but he didn't bother with the TV that night.

He wanted to think.

Four days had passed since Salmon had run at Punchestown, finishing second to War of Attrition in the Guinness Gold Cup in his final race of the season. It wasn't a bad way to finish a season that had seen Salmon again begin the Cheltenham Gold Cup as 4/1 favourite before finally finishing eleventh in a race won by War of Attrition.

Hourigan didn't want to dwell on Cheltenham.

He was happy for Mouse Morris, a man in the game a long time like himself, and happy too for Michael O'Leary. The Ryanair boss was putting a lot of money into National Hunt racing and was a loyal owner. War of Attrition had won the big race well and Beef or Salmon just didn't run his race – he wasn't happy before the race or during it.

It was just a frustration. Cheltenham didn't suit Salmon or Salmon didn't suit Cheltenham. Hourigan didn't know which.

But he did know that, over the course of his career, Salmon had beaten three winners of the Gold Cup. Best Mate had won it three times and Salmon had beaten him. He'd also beaten Kicking King who'd won the Gold Cup in 2005, and finished ahead of War of Attrition on numerous occasions before trailing in behind him in Cheltenham that season.

"Christ, there's not many who can say they've beaten the winners of five Gold Cups," Hourigan told himself.

After Cheltenham, they'd gone to Aintree and were maybe a bit unlucky. Salmon jumped the fifth fence badly and Carberry had got the horse right just in time to bounce off Monkerhostin and be unseated. It wasn't a good weekend for the jockey – he was thrown off Sir Oj in the Grand National and suffered an ankle injury that ended his season.

A run in Fairyhouse over hurdles went fine – Andrew McNamara rode him for the first time in a race, got on well with him and finished third. Timmy

Murphy was free to ride him in the Punchestown Gold Cup, and they ran well, finishing second behind War of Attrition. Lisaleen's Hi Cloy was third.

It wasn't a bad result, really.

A wave of irritation broke across Hourigan. He thought about the references to Cheltenham.

The word failure had been liberally used.

"That's not bloody fair, there's not that many horses good enough to get there four years in a row," he thought. "He's won two more Grade Ones; that's eight now. And he'll win more. I know it. I just don't know if he will ever win in Cheltenham."

"But does it matter?" Hourigan asked himself, the question echoing off the walls of his mind. Salmon was a champion. He had courage and he had talent. Why wasn't he getting the credit he deserved?

Ann joined him, but didn't disturb his thoughts until she sensed his mood darkening. Instinct told her what his thoughts were.

"Let's go out," she suggested.

Over a drink in Adare with friends, Hourigan relaxed and his mood lightened. They talked of politics and local things, of sport and horses.

"Do you know something?" a friend said. "I was just looking at Salmon's career. You mightn't realise it but, in Leopardstown alone, he has won over half a million euro. You're one lucky sod Hourigan."

A smile lit up the trainer's features. Though diminutive in stature, he felt six foot tall. He raised his glass – his friend was right, he was a lucky sod.

●●●●●

Michael Hourigan wasn't the only one raising a toast to Salmon that night.

Far to the east of Adare, along the east coast, John and Marianne Murphy were also relaxing with friends. They had enjoyed their day out at Punchestown the previous Wednesday watching Beef or Salmon and now they raised their glasses.

Ten years ago to the day, the foal that would become Beef or Salmon had been born in the shed behind their home to the first broodmare they had ever owned.

CHAPTER 16

War, Listener and Kauto Star on the Rise

"Maths," said one.

"And computers," reckoned someone else.

"I suppose you could Google how to ride a finish," a third voice added before the room dissolved into laughter.

Andrew McNamara was accustomed to the banter. Not many jockeys were able to include a stint at university on their curriculum vitae so he was a natural target for ribbing from his colleagues and rivals.

But, by the end of the 2005/2006 National Hunt season, McNamara could also include riding winners at Cheltenham and Aintree when he updated that CV. And, when the summer ended, the young man from Croom became the first-choice jockey for all the best rides at Lisaleen Stables, including Beef or Salmon.

Michael Hourigan had known McNamara for most of his life. The jockey's father, also Andrew, was a veterinary surgeon based just eight miles from Lisaleen and was a successful racehorses trainer in his own right. He trained Boreen Prince to win the Arkle Chase in Cheltenham in 1985 and his three children grew up surrounded by horses.

Like his younger brother Robbie, Andrew was tall, standing at six foot by the time he left school. He realised his height would make it difficult for him to pursue a career as a race jockey but he wanted to try. His parents persuaded him to give university a chance, arguing that he would always have horses but his education should continue. He agreed and lasted two years, studying maths and computers. He was academic but his love of horses and racing proved too strong a lure.

Lisaleen was an obvious place to ride out. Hourigan had a yard packed with horses and he was always looking for good riders to work those horses. He had watched the youngster fight the obvious problems that height brought to the sport. It was all to do with weight. To keep weight down the jockey had to be disciplined and McNamara exhibited that discipline.

Andrew had ridden his first winner in 2002 in Wexford on a horse his father had imported from France called La Captive. Each season his tally of winners increased and more trainers began to use him. Hourigan watched his progress and gave him more and more responsibility at Lisaleen. He rode Arteea to win in Galway at the end of October 2005, and Hourigan was impressed with the way he dominated the race. He proved himself to be tactically astute and a shrewd judge of pace and stamina.

McNamara was given the ride on Hi Cloy the following day and they finished second to Jim. "He's a big lad but he has good hands," Hourigan told Seamus McCloy. McNamara held on to the ride for the Fortia Chase at Punchestown, where they finished third behind Central House and Moscow Flyer.

In the John Durkan Memorial in Punchestown in December, McNamara rode his first Grade One winner. War of Attrition, Strong Project, Le Coudray, Native Upmanship and Ned Kelly lined up against him and Jim, with Robbie Power on board, was in the race as well. Robbie Power rode Jim boldly and led over the last but McNamara rode a powerful finish with Hi Cloy, snatching victory on the finishing line.

McNamara went to Cheltenham to ride for Hourigan but picked up a spare ride on Newmill when Robbie Power was injured. He had ridden for Newmill's trainer, John Murphy, before, and knew the horse too. They surprised everyone, with the possible exception of the trainer, by winning the Queen Mother Champion Chase. The entire McNamara family was there to celebrate his triumph.

At Aintree, he rode Hi Cloy to victory in the Melling Chase and, ten days later, on April 17, 2006, he rode Beef or Salmon for the first time on a racecourse. They were third in a hurdle race at Fairyhouse.

Though Timmy Murphy was back on Salmon for the Gold Cup at Punchestown, at the start of the 2006-2007 season Michael Hourigan announced: "Andrew is our first jockey now and the owners are happy for him to ride Beef or Salmon."

● ● ● ● ●

In his office at Down Royal racecourse, Mike Todd perused the entries for the two-day Festival of Racing that would be run on November 3 and 4. Those were the dates that would define the season and preparations were going well. Todd looked out over the course, happy with what he saw. The track looked well. Everything was gleaming in the early winter sunshine.

But Todd was anxious, and everyone involved with Down Royal shared that anxiety. The events of 2005, when bomb threats had forced the abandonment of the second day of the festival and the December 26 meeting, had ruined the season and left a scar. So much hard work had been wasted – they needed a good festival this year to restore spirits and confidence.

The racing family had been supportive and The Ulster Derby meeting in June had been a huge success. All indications were that the November meeting would attract many of the best horses from all over the island. Todd's thoughts turned to the Champion Chase. He flicked through the sheets of paper and found what he hoped he would see.

The list of entries included Beef or Salmon. He continued looking and found more good news – War of Attrition was also entered. It was what he had expected, but to see it confirmed in print was a relief. Now all he could do was hope that the two horses would get to the course safe and sound. A match between the locally owned champion and the winner of the Cheltenham Gold Cup would guarantee a bumper crowd and a successful meeting.

Luckily for his nerves, Mike Todd was unaware of a minor drama taking place in Lisaleen Stables. Kay Hourigan had discovered a nasty cut on one of Salmon's legs when she opened his box one morning. It required five stitches and the horse had to be nursed for ten days. It delayed his return to the racetrack and her father had to adjust his plans and chose a hurdle race at Fairyhouse on

October 21 for Beef or Salmon to commence his season.

Two days before that, Hourigan had travelled to Punchestown. He met Mouse Morris in the stables. The pair swapped news of their horses, had the usual light-hearted banter. War of Attrition was having his first run of the season.

"Are you going to Down Royal with him?" Hourigan asked.

"If everything goes right today that's the plan," said Morris.

"Wouldn't it be great to see himself and Salmon in a battle?" replied Hourigan.

War of Attrition looked well and won in Punchestown by eleven lengths, leaving a horse as talented as Watson Lake in his wake. "Maybe it won't be a battle at all," laughed Hourigan after War's impressive outing. "It could be a slaughter if he improves from that."

Salmon ran well in Fairyhouse. He even gave the hurdles some respect and jumped them rather than running through them. McNamara was pleased. The two-mile trip was not really ideal and suited the winner, Pedrobob, much better but, when McNamara asked for an effort from Salmon, he got a great response and they finished strongly.

Kay led the team to Down Royal early on the morning of November 4 and reported back to her father on arrival: "He's as good as gold … travelled really well."

Andrew McNamara had travelled separately to the Lisaleen crew. His brother, Robert, was also riding that day and he was glad of the company of his younger sibling. Andrew had ridden in big races and was getting more experience all the time but he recognised the burden of responsibility weighing on his shoulders. Salmon was going for his ninth Grade One success and, if he won, there would be opportunities to win a tenth before the end of that season. It was something the young jockey desperately wanted to be a part of.

War of Attrition was obviously the horse to beat but McNamara had respect for the rest of the field. He had ridden Cloudy Bays and won twice on him a year earlier. Paul Carberry had a chance on Justified and Robbie Power was riding Light On The Broom. Willie Mullins had entered Bothar Na and, while Another Rum was the outsider, he also had some very decent form, though not in this calibre of company.

McNamara enjoyed his first ride of the day, winning a hurdle race on a horse named Cluain Arra for Hourigan. That was a good sign. The ground was soft and he was sure Salmon would like it. He had discussed tactics with Hourigan and would try to run in midfield. He expected Cloudy Bays to set the pace, but he'd have to wait and see what Conor O'Dwyer did on War of Attrition.

The race unfolded as he expected.

He ran in third place for two and a half miles, with War of Attrition behind him for most of that distance. But, with two fences to jump, Conor O'Dwyer made his move. War powered into second, behind Justified, before taking the lead. McNamara went with him and Salmon and War jumped the last together.

Salmon was closest to the stands where the crowds packed against the railing, cheering feverishly. This was the race they had come to see and Salmon and War weren't disappointing them. The two horses almost came together, straining muscle and sinew and giving everything as they climbed towards the line. McNamara felt Salmon's efforts. He couldn't look at his opponent. All his energy was focused on his own horse. Yards from the line Salmon got his head in front. It was all that separated them when the judge looked at the photograph. Grade One victory number nine had been achieved.

• • • • •

Walking the course at Haydock Park on the morning of November 18, Kay Hourigan bumped into her old mentor, Paul Nicholls. More than a decade had passed since she'd spent a very enjoyable period of her life with Nicholls and his family at their home, Manor Farm in Ditcheat, Somerset.

"You looked after me so well I put on three stone in weight and spent another year trying to lose it," she chided him.

They talked horses. Her father had mentioned Nicholls' hopes for Kauto Star earlier in the year and now she asked the horse's trainer directly: "How good is he?"

"Kay, I'm always loath to make predictions but I will make an exception in this case," answered Nicholls. "I'm lucky to have a lot of good horses to train but I don't think I have ever had one as good as this. I think he really is something special."

Hours later she understood. Salmon had run well. The French horse L'Ami, Ollie Magern, Iris's Gift and Kingscliff all followed him to the line, but when Andrew McNamara looked up after the last fence all he could see was a horse and jockey (Ruby Walsh) disappearing in the distance. Kauto Star won by eleven lengths.

"I think we have probably seen today the next winner of the Gold Cup," was Michael Hourigan's blunt assessment of the race.

As the search for the tenth Grade 1 success continued, Hourigan warmed up his horse in a hurdle race in Fairyhouse in mid-December. Salmon won with ease and attention began to focus on the next target, the Lexus Chase. L'Ami and War of Attrition would once again provide the opposition, but Robert Alner was also sending The Listener, a relatively young horse with mixed form.

Just over 18,000 attended Leopardstown on the third day of the Christmas Festival. They made Salmon the 13/8 favourite and a coronation was duly expected. Only War of Attrition was regarded as a threat with The Listener at 7/1. When his young jockey Daryl Jacob went to the front from the start and maintained a lead all the way it was expected he would be reeled in. But The Listener kept going. L'Ami stayed with him for most of the race but the effort took a toll.

The alarm bells began ringing three fences from the finish when McNamara sent Salmon in pursuit. He strode away from the other pursuers, including a fading L'Ami, but before the final fence the jockey knew that the cause was lost. Salmon was running well in the heavy conditions but The Listener was eight lengths away and would not be caught.

Hourigan remained chirpy despite the defeat.

"He would have needed to sprout wings from the last but the wings weren't there today," was his reaction. "I'm happy. The winner is an up-and-coming horse. We will be back here in February ready for another go."

CHAPTER 17

Salmon's Never Beaten. He'll Never Stop Trying

The Atlantic breeze whipping in from the west carried an unusually harsh chill for an early February morning. A light dusting of snow across the 90 Lisaleen acres threw off bright reflections from a moon that peered through drifting cloud. A few of the stables' inhabitants shifted uneasily in their boxes as their human minders added an extra rug or two to ensure their warmth.

Michael Hourigan woke early on this particular Friday. The weather forecast had been accurate and he had heard late the previous night that an inspection of Leopardstown racecourse would take place at 8am on Friday morning to determine if racing would go ahead on Saturday. Beef or Salmon was scheduled for another go at winning his tenth Grade 1 chase, this time in the Hennessy Cognac Gold Cup, but the announcement about the late inspection niggled him and left him a little restless during the night.

He drove down the back lane to the stables to check on the horses. Kay was already in with Salmon and, while her schedule was not quite as demanding as it had once been with the horse, there was still some massaging to be done and care to be taken. "I think we'd both miss it now if it stopped," she told her father.

Hourigan acknowledged the different mood in the yard. It was always the same leading up to a big race – you wanted everything to remain the same but there was a heightened sense of expectation. The lads, some from the locale and others from various parts of Eastern Europe, were energised by the big days and they always seemed busier in the build-up.

The sense of occasion had been enhanced by a visit earlier in the week by a team from the television channel, At The Races. The interviewer, Dave Duggan, had spoken to both Michael and Kay and Salmon, for once, had behaved impeccably for the camera. He did try to take a bite of the camera at one stage but otherwise proved more than helpful. He was a wiser horse now, officially eleven years old and his temperament was more mature. Michael helped take the rugs off his back and, once again, admired the musculature and tone of his star. There was no doubt that Salmon was looking well. His skin was glowing and his nature was content.

Back at the house Michael switched on the radio. He generally didn't listen to it a lot – too much bad news – but he wanted to hear the weather forecast and maybe get some word about Leopardstown. All the talk that morning and almost every morning that week was about a rugby match. Ireland were playing France in the Six Nations Championship and, for the first time ever, it would be played in Croke Park, the national stadium of the Gaelic Athletic Association. The seemingly endless debate about whether or not the ground would be made available had finally reached a conclusion. Now, the opening rugby game dominated every other event taking place in Ireland that weekend, so much so that the racing authorities decided to run the Leopardstown meeting on the Saturday instead of the traditional Sunday date, to avoid a clash with the rugby International.

Croke Park had undergone a massive reconstruction. It had all the modern technology to ensure that there was no threat to the rugby game from the weather. Hourigan hoped that natural resources would ensure that Leopardstown would survive. Salmon was in great form. Kay had ridden him on the point-to-point circuit that had been laid out for the meeting the previous Sunday in Askeaton and gave her father an encouraging assessment of the horse: "He almost pulled the arms out of me."

The horse had recovered swiftly from his Christmas defeat to The Listener in Leopardstown, a defeat Hourigan didn't have an explanation for.

"Just one of those days when the other horse ran better," he put it simply, bristling at some of the negativity that followed the run. Salmon was being written off, with one pundit even writing that the horse was "washed up". It was a term that grated on Hourigan and, given the furious reaction from many of those he met at race meetings and point-to-point meetings, he wasn't alone.

But he had more important things on his mind. His horses were running well, but the yard hadn't produced a winner since the previous November. There was nothing wrong – Hi Cloy had run very well in Thurles at the end of January when second to Forget The Past. The winner's performance had prompted his trainer, Michael O'Brien, to enter him in the big race at Leopardstown against Beef or Salmon.

But, despite Hi Cloy's strong showing and a general optimism, Hourigan hated losing streaks and wanted this one to end. He was confident that Salmon would bring the curtain down on it, if he got his chance to run.

The field for the Hennessy was getting smaller by the day. War of Attrition and Hedgehunter had both been withdrawn early in the week and In Compliance, who had beaten War of Attrition in Punchestown in December, was also a non-runner.

As he waited for news of the inspection Hourigan knew that The Listener was back in Ireland for another go at Salmon. His team had travelled on Wednesday, which was good timing from their point of view as horrible weather on Thursday had forced the cancellation of flights and sailings between Britain and Ireland.

Forget The Past would also run, and Michael Cunningham had entered his novice, Patsy Hall. Hourigan was running Hi Cloy, too, ensuring a large contingent of supporters from the north of Ireland would travel to Leopardstown.

The phone rang. Leopardstown was on. Hourigan texted the owners and set about preparing for the weekend.

For the first time on a racecourse Salmon would wear blinkers in the Hennessy. He had worn cheek pieces in his three chases that season, a successful attempt to help him concentrate. Hourigan had thought about the blinkers after the Lexus.

"The older he gets, the cleverer he gets and doesn't want to work as hard as he used to. The blinkers will keep his mind on the job; it will keep the distractions away," reasoned the trainer.

Andrew McNamara had been confirmed as the big race jockey. Although Paul Carberry was once again available to ride, Hourigan and the owners agreed that McNamara deserved his chance. He'd ridden very well in Down Royal and in defeat at Christmas. Carberry would ride Hi Cloy, with Hourigan telling Carberry's agent: "He should get in the money too."

Race day provided a small respite on the weather front. The earlier snow had been replaced by rain on Friday night and, now on Saturday morning, it was dry as they left the stables. The bitter cold failed to deter almost 14,000 racegoers from travelling to the racecourse and the carnival atmosphere prompted Hourigan to suspect the entire population of Limerick had made the journey.

They had lots to celebrate. Eric McNamara's Pearl's A Singer won the second race, while Askeaton's Davy Fitzgerald saw his charge, Mister Top Notch, take the honours in the Grade 1 Novice Chase. All eyes were on Salmon, who would try to make it a treble for Limerick trainers on one of the biggest days of the year.

The people favoured Salmon but the experts insisted The Listener would be too good, and the English visitor was duly odds-on at 5/6. Salmon was 11/4, Forget The Past 9/2, Hi Cloy 14/1 and Patsy Hall 20/1.

Daryl Jacob made his intentions clear from the start: The Listener galloped from the tape and had a foot to spare over the first fence. The horses were spread across the track, Beef or Salmon taking his customary route down the right hand side – "the Foxrock way" according to some of his supporters. Forget The Past trailed The Listener, Patsy Hall chose the inside route and Hi Cloy galloped behind his stablemate.

It was an uneventful race. The Listener continued to lead, five and six lengths ahead of Patsy Hall and Salmon. The ground was sticky but Salmon was comfortable and McNamara, keeping a constant eye on the leader, was enjoying the spin. But as they passed the stands on the right, he could hear the murmur of the crowd. He sensed their tension. He felt it a little himself.

At the first fence on the back straight Salmon was a fraction slow, nothing serious but the jockey needed to rouse his horse just a little. McNamara demanded a little more effort at the next two fences and, running wide, well separated from Forget The Past, Salmon responded to the urging. He jumped sweetly. "That's better," McNamara encouraged his horse.

At the thirteenth fence, Patsy Hall threw Davy Russell off his back. McNamara got a nice jump from Salmon. He looked up. Jacob was working on The Listener, urging him on. The distance between the leader and the rest of the field was lengthening. McNamara decided it was time to go after him. Forget The Past was beginning to struggle. Salmon left him behind but there was still a huge distance between him and The Listener. They went to the second last fence. From the stands the race looked to be over. On landing, Jacob took a look over his right shoulder. He was well clear. He took another look as they went around the final bend. The distance was still considerable. Fifteen lengths, Hourigan heard the course commentator make his estimate. It would take a huge effort from there, he thought, but he didn't give up hope.

Kay Hourigan was pacing around the parade ring, glancing at the big screen. She rolled a rubber band between her fingers, craving a cigarette. She had recently dispensed with the habit and hadn't really missed smoking until today. Paddy Mullins had once told her she was "a bit of a box walker", and she was doing it now, striding over and back while keeping an eye on the screen. Tracey Hennessy, the secretary at Lisaleen, walked with her, and Maggie Fitzgerald, wife of trainer Davy, shouted words of encouragement directed at the screen. "I hope Andy Mc remembers what I told him," intoned Kay.

Andy Mc at that moment was gauging the distance between Salmon and The Listener, oblivious to the fact that the betting exchanges were now offering Salmon at 100/1. They were heading for the last fence and Daryl Jacob now looked back at them over his right shoulder. McNamara gave Salmon a few light smacks of the whip. Salmon renewed his effort. The margin between the horses narrowed a little.

At the last fence McNamara urged Salmon with the reins and they soared through the air. He recalled Kay's words: "You're never beaten on Salmon. He will never stop trying. You'll see him sticking his neck out, all the time trying to get ahead of the other horse. He might not get there but he won't stop trying. He wants to be in front."

McNamara had his whip in his right hand and Salmon drifted towards the rail away from the stands while The Listener gravitated towards the stand. Jacob switched his whip to his left hand and took another look around.

"Is he getting worried?" McNamara wondered, pushing Salmon on. The distance narrowed again but the winning post loomed. McNamara stopped looking ahead, put his head down and urged Salmon on.

The horse, nostrils flaring and sucking in the cold air, responded.

Suddenly McNamara was aware of a new sound. It seemed to rise from the ground, drowning out the familiar racecourse beat of hooves on turf.

A cacophony of voices reached out from the stands to envelop them. Salmon heard it too. He seemed to chase it. McNamara looked up briefly. He could see The Listener's tail. They hadn't been this close since they passed each other in the saddling area.

Horse and jockey became one, speeding over the ground in huge strides. It took just seconds and less than fifty yards. Jacob and The Listener tried to repel the challenge but they were powerless. Salmon sprinted past them yards before the winning post, as fresh at the end of three miles as he had been at the beginning.

In the parade ring Kay was jubilant, jumping on Maggie Fitzgerald's back. "This is better than any Gold Cup," she declared loudly. Tracey gave her a hug. "Go get him," she said and, as Kay ran to find her horse, she could hear the excitement in the noise of the crowd. She heard congratulatory shouts from friends. She wondered where her father was. *He should be so proud*, she thought.

Michael was trying to get to the parade ring but the throng of well-wishers was relentless. People he knew, friends and colleagues, were swamped by people he had never seen before. All wanted to be a part of the occasion, offering words of thanks and adulation.

"Washed up, me arse," was the colourful yelp of one happy punter that made him smile.

He found some respite from the chaos in the chute that leads from the stand to the parade ring. Paul Carberry had already dismounted from Hi Cloy, who had overtaken Forget The Past to claim third place. The two men exchanged a few words before Hourigan was once again swallowed up by hordes of well-wishers. A bellow rose from the thousands who gathered around the parade ring, alerting the trainer to the fact that the horse was being led in. Joe Craig and Dan McLarnon were surrounded by family, children and grandchildren. Hourigan saw Salmon first, then Kay. Father and daughter embraced. Both had tears in their eyes.

Andrew McNamara was breathless.

"Incredible," he told the owners. "He was flat out from a long way out but he never got tired. He kept trying, he gave me everything. What a horse."

Surrounded by journalists grasping notebooks and tape recorders, Hourigan took a moment to compose himself. He hardly heard the questions in the tumult of the parade ring but someone mentioned Cheltenham, prompting him to respond.

"Forget about what's happened in the Gold Cup for the moment and look at what he's done. He's a very good horse and we've never been afraid to run him, never put him aside for one particular race. We dropped him in at the deep end in his first chasing season because we knew what we had and he's done us proud," concluded Hourigan.

The newspapers paid their tribute over the following days. In the *Irish Independent*, Damien McElroy wrote: "Superbly ridden by young Andrew McNamara, this remarkably durable performer, who has drawn a blank on all his sorties to England, appeared to sprout wings in the home straight as he reeled in The Listener, whose supporters must have been counting their money when the English raider doubled his lead heading to the home straight."

Tony O'Hehir put the victory in context in his report for *The Racing Post*. "It was the remarkable 11-year-old's tenth Grade 1 win over fences – and a third Hennessy Gold Cup – and if it was to be achieved then it was entirely fitting that it should happen at Leopardstown, the track at which Beef or Salmon has so often excelled and where he has now gained six of those top-level victories."

In the British broadsheet, *The Independent*, Sue Montgomery outlined the scale of the achievement. "Beef or Salmon's tremendous effort to overhaul The Listener at Leopardstown on Saturday put him in a club so exclusive that there is only one other member. Victory in the Hennessy Cognac Gold Cup was the Michael Hourigan-trained chestnut's 10th at Grade 1 level and, over fences, only Moscow Flyer has won as many. Istabraq heads the all-time leaderboard in terms of top-level wins on 14 – all over hurdles of course – with Moscow Flyer on 13, but the great two-mile chaser's first three came over the smaller obstacles."

It was the crowning moment.

Later that evening, after the horses were quietly stabled and celebratory drinks consumed, Hourigan thought about the future. He knew they would go back to Cheltenham. It was a challenge they couldn't resist but, at the age of eleven, Salmon owed them nothing. There was a new chasing star emerging. Paul Nicholls had told him about Kauto Star a few years previously, and Hourigan had been impressed when he saw him. There would be no weighty expectations resting on Salmon's shoulders in 2007. But to contest five consecutive Gold Cups would be an achievement in itself, and Salmon deserved that. He was entitled to the reverence that such consistency bestowed.

He chatted with Ann about the day. "I think you enjoyed that win better than all the others," she commented when they were alone.

"I did, you know," answered her husband. "They said he was finished, but that showed everything there was about him. He jumped great, he was as brave as a lion and that speed after the last fence was incredible. I don't know of many horses who would have been able to run that quick after three miles on that ground. Maybe now he will get the credit he deserves."

The day's victory meant Beef or Salmon had won nineteen races, ten of which had been of Grade 1 quality. He had earned €1.2million in prize money.

"You know I always dreamed of having one great horse to look after," he said to Ann. "Amn't I a lucky man to have found two?"

CHAPTER 18

Just Bring Him Home

Wednesday, April 28, 2008.
Kay Hourigan slowly walked the few paces from her kitchen to the stableyard. She was a few minutes late and knew her horse would be getting impatient. Some horses were more laid back about their morning routine but this one had a clock in his head. He could tell the time, Kay was convinced of it. He'd be grumpy when she was late and would let her know by being difficult for a few minutes. When the message had been delivered he would quieten and await the care and attention.

Close to 7am on a fresh and bright morning Kay opened the door of Stable 9. Her actions were deliberate, she wanted to savour every moment of this morning because she would not be doing it again. Her emotions were a jumble of relief and heartache, mixed with a measure of apprehension that would not disappear until she led him back into the parade ring sometime around 4.30pm that afternoon.

She had been preparing for this morning for almost four weeks. Her father had called her aside a few days after the Irish Grand National at the end of March and began a consultation with her that lasted a number of weeks. It was about Salmon's future.

Michael mentioned the likelihood that this might be his last season. The talk didn't surprise Kay. Salmon was twelve years old and it wasn't getting any easier for him to compete against younger horses. There had been long discussions with Joe Craig and Dan McLarnon, which continued after the Grand National meeting at Fairyhouse. The final decision would be made between the three men, the trainer and the two owners. Kay would be the first to be told. She deserved that.

Finally, Michael delivered that message: "Kay, we've made the decision. It's unanimous between the three of us. Salmon will be retired after Punchestown," he told her. "I hope you agree with us."

A wave of sadness had swept over Kay. She knew what was coming but, until it was confirmed, she had squeezed the thought from her mind. Now there could be no more pretence.

She looked at her father: "Of course you're right. But it won't ever be the same without him."

Now that the actual day had arrived she was no better prepared for it. She tried to behave normally and waited for the horse to settle, before beginning her work for the final time. When the massaging started, Salmon stood still. "Typical man, loves being pampered but won't admit it," she chided.

The Guinness Gold Cup at Punchestown had been chosen as Salmon's farewell race. The stable's Mossbank was also entered in a field that had attracted another quality entry. There was prestige and big prizemoney on offer but the only topic of conversation was the final showing of Beef or Salmon.

Lisaleen had just one other entry for the day, three horses travelling altogether. Mossbank had a very good chance of winning the big prize while Salmon ... well, he had performed so many miracles over the last six seasons that nothing could be ruled out. Kay's father had expressed confidence to all who enquired that he thought the horse could enjoy the perfect end to his career. Kay wasn't sure he actually believed it, her father was too much of a realist for that.

"I don't care what happens today, as long as I am able to bring you back home safe and sound," she told the horse.

They loaded up, Salmon led up the ramp by Kay. His new pal, Gums, as Mossbank was known in the yard, followed and Spaceman took up the rear. Kay was unusually quiet as they set off. *I really don't know what it is going to be like without him*, she thought, ruefully.

• • • • •

Twelve months had passed since Michael Hourigan first thought about retiring Beef or Salmon. He hadn't expressed his thoughts immediately to anyone but, after Salmon's heroics in Leopardstown in overhauling The Listener and another visit to Cheltenham, the trainer wondered was it time to consider rewarding Salmon for a wonderful career. The horse had exceeded all their expectations. He didn't owe anyone anything.

They had gone to Punchestown after Leopardstown and Cheltenham and the demands of a long season were evident. Salmon was a little weary in the 2007 Guinness Gold Cup and, while they hadn't expected a lot, he still delivered another big-hearted display. On that occasion it just wasn't enough.

Hourigan pushed the thought from his mind over the summer months. He would again campaign Salmon at the highest level. There was nothing to be gained from a drop in class except the hardship of top weight, and Salmon deserved better. The horse would show him what was best.

Salmon's return to the racecourse for the 2007-2008 season had been delayed when ground conditions ruled him out of another run in the Nicholson. They went back to Haydock for the Betfair Chase at the end of November and he finished third to Kauto Star and Exotic Dancer. Temporarily, Hourigan put thoughts of retirement on hold.

"We didn't even get a chance to get a run in him before this and he still ran a blinder," was Hourigan's reaction.

Mossbank and Salmon were both entered in the Lexus Chase where they came up against Denman. The English horse produced a devastating performance to win the race. Mossbank was second, The Listener third and Salmon finished just behind, in fourth. He was four years older than the first two horses and three years older than the third but was still competitive.

Still, as heartening as Salmon's performances were, Hourigan was distracted. For a couple of months he had detected something was amiss with the stable in general, though he couldn't say what exactly. He was running lots of horses and the stable was having some winners but a lot of the horses were off form – it wasn't a dramatic loss of form and certainly did not constitute a crisis, but still... The horses were finishing races but, in many cases, they were just not getting into a position to contest or were unable to fight a finish. They were coming home and showing a little more fatigue than was normal for horses from Lisaleen.

He conversed with the jockeys but they couldn't explain it. He wondered was it something he was doing. Was he pushing them too hard? Was he not pushing them hard enough?

But he had changed nothing. The routines were the same. There was no lessening of intensity in preparation. Schooling always had been a priority and still was.

The mystery endured. Weeks of disappointments would leave him irritated and frustrated and then a couple of horses would win. The Budgee won three in a row in late December and through January. Salmon and Mossbank were running in the best of company and being placed. Hi Cloy won a good race in Thurles in the middle of January. But around the same time, he'd had run a couple of poor races as well. The inconsistency nagged at the trainer. All of the horses were examined but nothing out of the ordinary was found.

The horses seemed happy. But Hourigan wasn't.

"Something's not right. I just wish to Christ I could find out what it is," he said in exasperation.

Outside the stable no one suspected anything. Just days before Salmon ran in the Hennessy Gold Cup at Leopardstown he was given top weight of 11 stone 12 pounds for the Aintree Grand National. The senior handicapper with the British Horseracing authority Phil Smith said Salmon's 'sheer class' entitled him to top weight.

"His record jumps out at you," Smith explained. "Normally it takes me two or three attempts to find a top weight. This time I had one stab at it and came up with Beef or Salmon."

At Leopardstown, however, Salmon laboured. He was at the back of the field as usual but never got anywhere near the leading runners, especially The Listener. Paul Carberry had enjoyed some exhilarating rides on Salmon in Leopardstown but this one was hard work.

Hourigan, Craig and McLarnon consulted. They would have loved to go to Aintree but Salmon just wasn't showing the sort of form that suggested he would be comfortable over the big fences of the Liverpool course. Before the end of the month they announced that Salmon would not go to Aintree. The decision sparked gossip and rumour. "Is this the end for Beef or Salmon?" headlines screamed. The connections remained silent.

The Irish Grand National at Fairyhouse loomed as a likely alternative.

Salmon would carry top weight of 12 stone in that race, but the fences were not as daunting and he would not have to leave the country. Tom Doyle, based in Ireland again after a successful stint in Britain, was booked for the ride and Hourigan was pleased. Doyle was an experienced and dutiful jockey. He would give the horse his chance to win the race but he would not punish a 12-year-old if he felt the challenge was beyond him.

Lisaleen sent out nine runners over the two days of the Fairyhouse meeting. Shanballa was the best of the four on the Sunday while, on Grand National Day – Bank Holiday Monday, March 24 – Hi Cloy, who had reverted to hurdles, gave cause for cheer by finishing second behind Willie Mullins' Shakervilz.

A New Story, ridden by 20-year-old Shane Hassett, finished fourth in the Grand National, behind Hear The Echo, a horse owned by Gigginstown and trained by Mouse Morris.

Salmon had hunted around in the middle of the field after Tom Doyle was told to judge things for himself. If he felt the horse had a chance he would push on – if not there was no point in punishing him. Two fences from the end Doyle decided the horse had had enough and Salmon was one of twelve horses that did not finish the race.

The Hourigan team readied their five horses for the journey home. "We'll talk in a few days," Joe Craig said.

Salmon was fresh and content after his exertions and certainly wasn't giving any indication that he was getting tired of the game. Out on the gallops he was a happy horse. He loved competing against the youngsters and was just as determined to lead them as he was three years previously.

Craig was as good as his word and, over the next ten days, he, Hourigan and McLarnon spoke regularly. Salmon was in good form, but his last victory had been fourteen months before. He was still capable of racing in the big chases, probably picking up a place or two, and there might even be another big win in him. But they had to consider what was good for the horse. Craig had a good home selected for him at his daughter's place, Salmon would be well looked after.

"Let's decide tomorrow," Hourigan told them as April began.

The trainer was troubled. He still had to find the source of whatever was afflicting his horses. The experts could find nothing but he was sure there had to be something. And he was worried about Salmon.

Ann sensed the doubt in her husband's mind. "What's bothering you?" she asked.

"I can't stop thinking about Doran's Pride. I would never forgive myself if that happened again," he concluded.

The owners agreed. They had enjoyed seven incredible years. Sure, there were disappointments along the way but the good days easily outnumbered the bad ones. It was time that Beef or Salmon should be retired.

On April 8, Salmon's entry in the Guinness Gold Cup in Punchestown, to be held twenty days later, was confirmed.

"And that will be that," Hourigan said simply. "We will retire him then."

Later that day, Timmy Murphy answered his phone.

"What are you doing on April 28?" Hourigan asked, without introducing himself.

"I'll have to check with Broady [Chris Broad, his agent]. What's up?"

"We're retiring Salmon. It'll be his last race."

"Give me five minutes. I'll ring you back," said Murphy.

Less than a minute passed before Hourigan's mobile chirped. "I'm free."

• • • • •

The applause began from the moment Kay led Beef or Salmon into the parade ring. His ears pricked up immediately. "Show off," laughed Kay. Mossbank walked behind them and Hi Cloy followed him.

Paul Nicholls stood in the centre of the ring chatting with Ferdy Murphy.

"That's some team," said Nicholls in admiration.

Hourigan was standing nearby, chatting to Willie Mullins. "You'll miss that lad," Murphy said to Hourigan.

"I will Ferdy, and this fella will miss Hedgehunter," Hourigan replied.

Mullins had announced a few days earlier that his own great horse, Hedgehunter, would also be retired. The Punchestown Racecourse Executive asked him to bring the horse to the racecourse that day so that he and Beef or Salmon could be honoured together.

For a moment the three men who had ridden Salmon in his ten Grade 1 triumphs – Murphy, Carberry and McNamara – were captured together in the parade ring. Fittingly, the trio would ride in his final race, Carberry on Mr Top

Notch and McNamara on Sher Beau, trained by Philip Fenton, who had ridden Salmon to his very first victory under National Hunt rules on November 24, 2001. Davy Russell, who had ridden Salmon in his first ever success, that point-to-point victory on February 18, 2001, was riding Mossbank.

Salmon enjoyed all the attention. He sensed there was something happening and knew everyone was looking at him. In the pre-race parade he behaved impeccably.

But, when Kay released him, Timmy Murphy blocked out all sentiment. He wasn't being cold-hearted, there were seventeen fences to be jumped on one of the most demanding racecourses in Ireland. There was a lot of prizemoney at stake, too. Whatever about the sentimental sideshow – and that had its place as well – Murphy knew there was business to be done.

In the end, Neptunes Collognes justified favouritism to win the race for Paul Nicholls and Ruby Walsh. Snowy Morning was second for Mullins and David Casey, while Davy Russell got a lovely run around on Mossbank before the horse tired two fences from the finish and had to be nursed to the line. Mister Top Notch was fourth and New Alco was fifth for Ferdy Murphy and Niall Madden.

Salmon had been ponderous in his final day of jumping. Murphy had to shake him up after the second fence and again in front of the stands. But, at the top of the hill past the stand, Salmon made another mistake and dropped to the back of the field, just ahead of Sher Beau. Murphy was having to work hard to keep Salmon's mind on the job.

"Just bring him home," Kay whispered as she watched her horse labour. The tears began to flow as Salmon crossed the line in sixth place, battling as hard as ever at the finish.

As Kay led him back to the parade ring the crowds began to gather, Salmon's supporters club was out in force. Hedgehunter was brought into the ring as well and a garland of roses placed over his head. Hedgehunter stood quietly, but Salmon had had enough. He shook his head in a very deliberate 'no'. A couple of attempts were made to put the garland on him before Hourigan stepped in. "Give it to me," he said and put the garland over his own shoulders.

Salmon proceeded to eat some leaves from the garland and, serenaded by an orchestra, Beef or Salmon was led from the parade ring for the last time, head high and ears pricked.

• • • • •

After the emotion and sentimentality of Punchestown, Michael Hourigan faced a harsh reality at home. He still had not discovered what it was that was ailing his horses and now turned to science.

Experts arrived and carried out detailed tests all over the yard. Everything the horses ate and drank was tested – water, hay, oats and nuts. Samples were taken from every stable. The men in the lab cots looked everywhere, but found nothing.

"Your horses are looking well. We know they're not getting home but we don't know why. We can't find anything," Hourigan was told.

Late one evening he stood in the yard with Kay. "What are we missing?" he asked.

Kay thought for a moment. "When do you think this started?" she asked.

"I'd have to say it was last August, maybe September," he replied.

"Well, did we do anything different then? Did we change anything? I've been trying to think of something but I can't find an answer," Kay said in frustration.

Her father looked around the yard. He walked a full circle. There was something. What was it? His eyes drifted towards the haybarn across from the stables, including the one that housed Salmon. There, he thought. That's our problem.

"Kay, I haven't had a day's bit of luck since we brought that hay into this place last August."

"But I thought you said everything had been tested," she protested.

"No, we tested what we're feeding them. We haven't started to feed them that hay yet. We need to get it tested."

The results were returned swiftly. The hay contained a fungus called Aspergillus, also found in food such as nuts, which produced a toxin harmful to humans and animals. The hay was removed immediately and stored in a corner of a field far away from the stables, covered in plastic sheeting.

Within weeks there was a marked improvement in the form of the horses. While the contamination did not cause any long-term damage – the effect on the horses' breathing had been minimal – it had been enough to affect their capacity to last to the end of a gruelling race.

Hourigan was relieved but frustrated. As Salmon settled into his new life of retirement in Antrim his devoted trainer reflected on the last nine months of an eight-year career.

"To think he finished up running second and third to the likes of Kauto Star and Denman while breathing in that shit. It just goes to show what a great horse he was."

CHAPTER 19

The Secret of Horse-Racing? You Dream

Life around Lisaleen Stables is not quite so frantic these days. It's still busy but the pace is more sedate. Michael Hourigan trains fifty horses now – some are ordinary, some are good and a few are very good. There are also a few young ones that are promising.

"I don't have another Beef or Salmon at the moment, but you never know what's around the corner," observes Hourigan, with a twinkle in his eye. "I didn't know what I had with him when I first brought him here first, all those years ago."

Nostalgia doesn't pay any bills but he allows time for it now and then, especially when the subject turns to Beef or Salmon. Time is still precious but not quite as elusive as it was in the first decade of the 21st century.

Michael doesn't like to be idle – he now fills in some of his time with his expanded farming interests – but his days are more manageable now, compared to the days that his daughter remembers as "madness, pure madness".

"I don't have as many owners as I used to," says Michael. "But the ones I have now are good owners, they love their racing and their horses."

Salmon has visited.

Michael rode him in the RDS at the Dublin Horse Show where they finished fourth in their class (race horse to riding horse) and he's paraded at Cheltenham and Aintree.

"It's amazing how well he still looks. He still gets everyone's attention," says Michael.

When asked, as he often is, what made him buy a horse that no one else was bothered about, the trainer recalls the first time he saw the horse.

"I couldn't say that there was something special, that I spotted something that others didn't. This is where the dream comes in to owning horses. Every horse you buy you hope that he will be the one, that he will have what it takes to become the champion. That is what you do, no matter who you are when you go out to buy a horse. You dream.

"JP McManus has spent a quarter of a century buying horses that he hoped might win the Gold Cup and this year [2012] he eventually won it with a horse [Synchronised] he bred himself."

Hourigan once believed Beef or Salmon would win the Gold Cup at Cheltenham but his conviction was not born purely from a dream. Instead, that belief unfolded on the gallops in Lisaleen and on racecourses in places like Leopardstown. So convinced was he of his horse, that he entered a novice in the most competitive steeplechase in racing.

"Of course people thought I was mad," he admits. "I think it just confirmed for some people what they always thought of me. He was a novice but [in 2004] he was unbeaten over fences. He had won class races against class horses that all had Gold Cup potential. With another horse you might have had reservations about going to Cheltenham for the Gold Cup but Salmon had done everything you could possibly have asked of him to allow him to qualify for a crack at such a race.

"At the time we would have been mad not to go for it. I wasn't a novice myself, I'd been going to Cheltenham for fifteen years and I had runners in the Gold Cup many times in that period. People said I made mistakes, that I dropped him in at the deep end. But his record spoke for itself. His first three runs over fences were awesome.

"If I made a mistake it was that I didn't give him a race in Cheltenham before the festival, maybe at the January meeting. That would have given him experience."

For her part, Kay Hourigan visibly pales at the mention of Cheltenham.

Lisaleen has had winners there but Kay has always been at home for those. She led up her share of horses at the festival but never had a winner.

"Maybe it was me that was jinxed, not the horse," she ruminates. "I found Cheltenham so draining. I don't know why. It was everything about it, the hype especially. The build-up was always so crazy. We always knew that the hype was part of it, that it was good for racing. But there were days when you really wanted to be left alone to do the job of getting the horse ready for the race."

• • • • •

When asked if, given his time with Salmon over again, there's anything he'd do differently, Hourigan sits back in his armchair and thinks momentarily. A smile forms and his eyes shine with a hint of mischief. It's not what he is going to say; it's his expectation of the reaction to his answer.

"I wouldn't have sent him jumping at all. I would've run him on the flat," he says, insisting it's no joke. "Ascot. Two-mile races, two-and-a-half mile races. I often wonder why I didn't go down that route. I could have done it with Doran's Pride as well. If I had been a flat trainer and Beef or Salmon came into my stable he would never have seen a fence.

"He would have been prepared for races like the Ascot Gold Cup and the other races, the Goodwood Cup, the St Leger. There are races in France that would have suited him. Just look at his record on the flat. He should have won the November Handicap in Leopardstown. Mick Kinane rode him on the Curragh and said he was awesome. Seamie Heffernan had a great ride on him.

"You would have thought someone would have said it to me – 'You fucking clown, why don't you run him on the flat?' – but I suppose they looked on me as a jumps trainer. I can train a flat horse but no one would see me as that. He had the gears, he showed us that all the time. At the end of three miles, and having jumped seventeen fences, he was showing us how quick he was. But I never considered it. He was such a natural jumper and I was a jumps trainer. It never crossed my mind until he had retired.

"If I could put back the clock, that's what I would have done."

• • • • •

Hourigan's enthusiasm never wanes and Kay wonders if her father will ever slow down. In another life he would be preparing to retire but, in Lisaleen, that's not a word to be used when he's close by.

"It's a passion for me to be training racehorses," he tries to explain, "and you always have a dream that you will get the good one.

"I started at the bottom and the dream has come true twice with Salmon and Doran's Pride. Hopefully, we will dream again. With a horse like that you have no bother getting up in the morning. Even if you were sick you would jump out of bed.

"Think about what he did for us. We drove up to Dublin at Christmas and in February and won a big race every year. We just came up to collect the cup – the Hennessy, the Lexus – there was never a feeling we weren't going to win it. That wasn't arrogance or being smart. That's the way it was. It was mapped out every year from the time he came in from the fields in July. Leopardstown was always the aim.

"A good horse, they say, will train himself. That's rubbish. Salmon was easy to deal with once you put everything in place and I had a good team with me. I trained him but I couldn't have trained him unless he was right for me. There was a lot of work to be done with him before he was ready for me.

"He was minded so well. You have no idea the hours of work Kay put into him, she dedicated her life to him for four years. The time people like Liz Kent and Sue Shortt, and everyone else, put into him was incredible. They had to look after him, to fix him after the injury, before I would get a horse that could be trained to go racing.

"He was a real racehorse and the crowd recognised that and loved him for it. I think the catchy name helped a little. He had his critics too – they were never satisfied. Because he didn't win the Gold Cup in Cheltenham, he didn't get the rating he deserved and that wasn't right.

"He tried his heart out a few times in Haydock. He always travelled brilliantly – there wouldn't be a sweat mark on him no matter where you brought him. That fourth place in Cheltenham [2005] was a great performance. He came up that hill quicker than anything else that day. I always said, if the Gold Cup was held at Leopardstown over Christmas or January, Doran's Pride or Beef or

Salmon would have won it.

"He had no quirk, no fault. He was just a Christian. Keeping him right was the problem. You can only wonder about what he might have done if he hadn't got hurt in Cheltenham. And getting him back to the track was hard, it was a constant team effort all the time. He had to be treated so tenderly, you could leave nothing to chance. With another horse you could be happy that you had him right but, with Salmon, you had to be precise: you couldn't work him unless the gallop was freshly done. You would do it for other horses but you might not get the reward. With Salmon we almost always got our reward."

• • • • •

Kay had sworn, after the racecourse death of Doran's Pride, that she would never shed tears for another horse: "I had cried for six months. I thought I hadn't any tears left."

In the parade ring that final day in Punchestown, she discovered another well of tears, though there was only a hint of sadness to her emotions.

"What I felt most was relief. I had spent so many hours with Salmon. The procedure was the same every year just to keep him going. It was hard and it was tough but I loved doing it. And he loved it because he knew it was doing him good."

Not long after Salmon ran his final race, Kay Hourigan found a fresh focus in life. In June, 2009, she married Richard Ryan and the couple's second child was born in 2012. Life is busy but good, and she remains thankful that Salmon had the chance to enjoy a leisurely retirement.

"To see him retire in good health was a blessing and he is having a good life now, too. That's important. He raced at the highest level for a long time – that's difficult and, as the years go by, you are always afraid that something might happen to him. They run out of steam and the horses don't like it when that starts to happen. They are trying but they can't get there any more and they are more frustrated than you are."

"Sometimes, with a horse like him, you would keep him for the point-to-points. We might even have gone hunter chasing with him. But we had been down that route before and we'll never forget what happened Doran's Pride. I know, even though he never told me, that was on my father's mind when they decided to retire Salmon."

Sitting beside her, Michael confirms his daughter's suspicions.

"Yeah, there's no doubt it was at the back of my mind. I remember the way he [Doran's Pride] would look at me when he was out in the paddock. He was pleading with me. I brought him back in and he was killed. I didn't want to let that happen again."

Hourigan pauses briefly.

"We were premature retiring Salmon. We should have waited, we could have had more fun with him. I'm sure of it. The yard wasn't right at the time and we had the fungus problem, but he was still getting placed. But, at the time, we weren't willing to take a chance. And look at him now, he's enjoying himself. Anyone who sees him is amazed at how well he is. He seems to love the shows. I had a great time with him in the RDS."

"We didn't even know dad did dressage," Kay interrupts.

"There's a lot you don't know," her father laughs.

One Beef or Salmon mystery endures.

Since retirement, his tail has grown again.

The scraggly thing, that was the butt of so many jokes, is now a full skirt.

"It would grow during the summer when he was out in the fields," Kay recalls, "but, once the hard work began again in July, it would shrivel. The hard work is over."

● ● ● ● ●

A year after Salmon retired, Down Royal racecourse completed the final stage of a refurbishment and The Beef or Salmon suite was officially opened. Fittingly, it provides perfect views of the finishing straight where the horse twice overtook Gold Cup winners en route to winning the Grade 1 race now known as the Jnwine.com Champion Chase.

● ● ● ● ●

The tea is poured, the freshly made scones are brought to the table. There, in the kitchen of his home near Screen in County Wexford, 120 miles to the east of Adare, John Murphy opens a scrapbook, lovingly maintained by his wife,

Marianne, and chronicling the racing career of Beef or Salmon.

On a shelf in the kitchen stand the trophies: the Weatherbys Ireland Farmers Journal Small Breeder Award 2002, the Irish Thoroughbred Breeders Association South East Regional Award Winner, 2004.

There were other rewards too.

Every time Salmon won a Grade 1 race a cheque for €2,000 arrived in the post, the breeder's reward for his part in the success. Murphy received €20,000 for Salmon's ten Grade 1 successes and another €3,000 for other graded victories.

"Not a bad return," smiles Murphy. "I had great times following him. A group of us travelled everywhere to see him, even Cheltenham. We mightn't go to the races when they're on in Wexford but, if Beef or Salmon was running, we would be off. He gave us a lot of good days."

Those who couldn't travel to Cheltenham would gather in Freddy's Bar in Screen to watch the races. On those afternoons, there was a limited menu available: Beef or Salmon sandwiches.

When Beef or Salmon took his first, faltering steps as a foal in 1996, John Murphy didn't have a stable and the horse's home was a small shed at the edge of the yard. Today, the shed remains, but it's no longer home to any horse.

New foals, when they come along, are now born in one of the three stables Murphy has built since Salmon was here.

"I realised my dream the day Farinella came into the yard," Murphy says. "But I don't think I ever dreamed that I would breed a horse as good as Beef or Salmon. You always hope to be successful at whatever you do but I never thought I would be involved in something like that. That was beyond my dreams."

RACE RECORD

(F) Flat, (H) Hurdles, (C) Chase. Bold type denotes Grade 1 wins.

Point-to-Point

2001

Jan 28th:	Dungarvan, F/13, Damien Murphy.
Feb 18th:	Clonmel, 1/16, Davy Russell.

National Hunt

2001

May 5th:	(F) Fairyhouse, 3/27, Davy Russell.
Nov 25th:	(F) Clonmel, 1/12, Mr Philip Fenton.
Dec 1st:	(F) Fairyhouse, 2/12, Richie Harding.
Dec 26th:	(H) Limerick, F/16, Paul Hourigan.

2002

Jan 5th:	(F) Cork, 1/11, Mr Philip Fenton.
Jan 24th:	(H) Gowran Park, 1/9, Paul Hourigan.
Feb 10th:	(H) Leopardstown, 7/10, Paul Hourigan.
Mar 17th:	(H) Limerick, 5/7, Paul Hourigan.
Apr 7th:	(F) Curragh, 2/17, Seamus Heffernan.
Apr 27th:	(H) Punchestown, 21/22, David Casey.
Oct 28th:	(F) Galway, 1/12, Miss Laura Hourigan.
Nov 10th:	(F) Leopardstown, 2/17, Franny Norton.
Nov 24th:	(C) Clonmel, 1/5, Paul Carberry.
Dec 15th:	(C) Cork, 1/8, Timmy Murphy.
Dec 28th:	**(C) Leopardstown, 1/7, Timmy Murphy.**

2003

Feb 9th:	**(C) Leopardstown, 1/5, Timmy Murphy.**
Mar 13th:	(C) Cheltenham, F/15, Timmy Murphy.

Apr 6th:	(F) Curragh, 1/28, Mick Kinane.
Nov 20th:	(C) Clonmel, 3/10, Timmy Murphy.
Dec 7th:	**(C) Punchestown, 1/7, Timmy Murphy.**
Dec 14th:	(C) Cork, 1/4, Timmy Murphy.
Dec 28th:	(C) Leopardstown, 3/8, Timmy Murphy.
2004	
Mar 18th:	(C) Cheltenham, 4/10, Timmy Murphy.
Apr 28th:	**(C) Punchestown, 1/6, Timmy Murphy.**
Oct 10th:	(C) Limerick, 5/9, Timmy Murphy.
Nov 6th:	**(C) Down Royal, 1/8, Timmy Murphy.**
Dec 5th:	(C) Punchestown, 3/6, Timmy Murphy.
Dec 28th:	**(C) Leopardstown, 1/6, Paul Carberry.**
2005	
Feb 6th:	(C) Leopardstown, 2/7, Paul Caberry.
Mar 18th:	(C) Cheltenham, PU/15, Paul Carberry.
Oct 9th:	(F) Curragh, 9/17, Rory Cleary.
Nov 19th:	(C) Haydock, 2/7, Paul Carberry.
Dec 28th:	**(C) Leopardstown, 1/5, Paul Carberry.**
2006	
Feb 12th:	**(C) Leopardstown 1/7, Paul Carberry.**
Mar 17th:	(C) Cheltenham, 11/22, Paul Carberry.
Apr 6th:	(C) Aintree, U/9, Paul Carberry.
Apr 17th:	(H) Fairyhouse, 3/10, Andrew McNamara.
Apr 26th:	(C) Punchestown, 2/6, Timmy Murphy.
Oct 21th:	(H) Fairyhouse, 2/11, Andrew McNamara.
Nov 4th:	**(C) Down Royal, 1/7, Andrew McNamara.**
Nov 18th:	(C) Haydock, 2/6, Andrew McNamara.

Dec 16th:	(H) Fairyhouse, 1/11, Andrew McNamara.
Dec 28th:	(C) Leopardstown, 2/6, Andrew McNamara.
2007	
Feb 10th:	**(C) Leopardstown, 1/5, Andrew McNamara.**
Mar 16th:	(C) Cheltenham, 13/18, Andrew McNamara.
Apr 25th:	(C) Punchestown, 8/10, Andrew McNamara.
Nov 24th:	(C) Haydock, 3/7, Denis O'Regan.
Dec 28th:	(C) Leopardstown, 4/6, Paul Carberry.
2008	
Feb 10th:	(C) Leopardstown, 5/8, Paul Carberry.
Mar 24th:	(C) Fairyhouse, PU/23, Tom Doyle.
Apr 23th:	(C) Punchestown, 6/9, Timmy Murphy.
Under NH Rules	
51 Races	Won 19, including 10 Grade 1s